THE FORGOTTEN WAR

The Forgotten War

Australia and the Boer War

LAURIE FIELD

MELBOURNE UNIVERSITY PRESS

First published 1979
First paperback edition 1995

Printed in Malaysia by
SRM Production Services Sdn Bhd for
Melbourne University Press, Carlton, Victoria 3053

National Library of Australia Cataloguing-in-Publication data

Field, L. M. (Laurence Melville), 1922–.
  The forgotten war.
  Bibliography.
  Includes index.
  ISBN 0 522 84655 6.
  1. South African War, 1899–1902 — Participation, Australian.
  I. Title.
968.0484

Library of Congress Card number 79-670186

Preface

No wonder it was forgotten after 1918. The 16 378 men who formed Australian contingents to South Africa, the 251 of them who were killed in action or died of wounds, and the 267 who died of disease — these seemed large numbers in 1902; but when next the mail steamers were converted into troopships, the number of men who made no return voyage was nearly four times as great as the total number of enlistments for South Africa.

But the forgetting had begun well before 1914, and one merit of Laurie Field's book is to show how and why.

It was difficult for newspapers to tell readers exactly what their men were doing in South Africa, so unconventional was the fighting, so dispersed were the Australians among imperial units, and so deliberately vague were the British military authorities in their use of the word 'colonial', which might mean men from one or more Australian colony, or New Zealand, or Canada, or South Africa itself. For the last year and a half of the war, Mr Field tells us, Australian newspapers had no correspondents in South Africa. In any case there were few newsworthy feats to report in that time, as the Australians, like other imperial troops, were set to tasks that nobody until now had imagined for soldiers of the queen. The campaigning of 1901-2 was a travesty of what the participants had been brought up to think of as proper warfare, and they were apt to describe it sardonically. In the words of a Tasmanian officer quoted here: 'We cleared the country by burning all farm-houses; and the poultry fell to the victors'. Who wanted to remember that? Finally, not all the properly military engagements of Australian soldiers could be reported at home as triumphs. There were incidents like the one at Slingersfontein in February 1900, in which some West Australians won official praise for having 'entirely frustrated' the enemy; but there was also Wilmansrust, where men from Victoria were caught unprepared in June 1901 and routed.

Mr Field's study is admirably precise. Where did the soldiers come from? How tall were they, and what did they weigh? What did they wear? What were they paid, and why were some of them so angry at not getting more? What songs did they sing? How many separate contingents sailed, and how did the units come to have all those names one reads on the memorials honouring them — no simple A.I.F., as in the greater war, but Victorian Mounted Rifles, Citizens' Bushmen, Imperial Bushmen, Australian Commonwealth Horse . . . Where and when and with whom did they serve in the Cape Colony, Natal, the Orange Free State, and the Transvaal? We now have meticulous answers to our questions, large and small, about these men.

So careful is Mr Field not to exaggerate what the Australians did that his analysis of their importance in the first year of the war is striking. The Boer forces numbered some 87 000, the British about 450 000; but while the defenders were fully mounted, most of the British were foot soldiers ill-suited to fighting against men riding horses on their own home ground. The 83 000 'colonial' soldiers were almost as numerous as the Boers, and unlike the men from the United Kingdom nearly all rode horses. Their contribution to the imperial cause was therefore 'quite out of proportion to their numbers', Mr Field concludes; and of the 30 000 or so soldiers from colonies outside South Africa, Australia supplied more than half. The 3000 in the first two contingents, Mr Field shows, 'took part throughout 1900 in the great sweeping manoeuvres of Lord Roberts which reduced the war to purely guerrilla operations'. If the war had ended in 1900, as was generally expected by informed non-Boer opinion, the deeds of those 3000 might well have been remembered more vividly at home than they were when overlaid by the messier events of the next eighteen months.

Mr Field casts a cool eye on two pathetic episodes which could not easily be accommodated by the patriotic rhetoric of press, pulpit and parliament. The first involved a squadron of the N.S.W. Lancers, 101 strong, who happened to be training in England at their own expense when the war began. They were said to have volunteered for service in South Africa; but at Cape Town only seventy-two of them disembarked from the *Nineveh* and the other twenty-nine steamed on to Australia. R. L. Wallace's recent study *The Australians at the Boer War* muffles the story: 'In some quarters in Sydney their courage had been under question but almost every man returned to Cape Town as soon as his private commitments permitted'. Mr Field shows clearly what those words conceal. His account could be the scenario for a fine Australian film having as hero-victim Corporal Ben Harcus the sharp-shooting postman, recipient of a gold medal in England and white feathers at home, deciding after all to rejoin the regiment in South Africa and dying of enteric fever in hospital at Bloemfontein. The other episode, the execution of Lieutenants Harry Morant and P. J. Handcock for shooting prisoners, is unusual among events of the war in having been not only remembered in this country but mythologized. The life and death of Morant, who as 'the Breaker' had published verse in the *Bulletin*, have been the subject in recent years of a partisan biography, a novel, and a play, fulfilling a *Bulletin* writer's prophecy of 1902 that he would become a hero like Ned Kelly. There is a good unpublished study of the case in a Ph.D. thesis done at the Australian National University by L. D. Atkinson. Mr Wallace has an informative chapter on it. Mr Field's judicious account ends with an arresting question from the *Bulletin*: 'Is it to be the fate of "The Breaker", wearing his blood-smeared halo, to lead Australians back to the Right?' Yes, says the author, he helped to do that; for the court martial and shooting of Morant and Handcock did more than anything else to foster Australian disenchantment with the war.

No previous writer on this subject has studied both politics and public opinion at home and the soldiers' experience in South Africa. Barbara Penny's work has helped Mr Field to tell the Australian part of the story. On events in South Africa he prints less than Mr Wallace of accounts written by soldiers and published at home. Composed as they were, in Mr Field's phrase, by men 'keen to win golden opinions for themselves and their country', these writings are at once precious as self-revelation and dangerous as guides to what actually happened. Working on under-used documents in the library of the Australian War Memorial and on microfilm copies in the National Library of material from the Public Record Office in London, Mr Field has found out much that we did not know about how the last colonial and the first Commonwealth politicians came to deliver those 16 000 men to the imperial cause. Mr Wallace had respectable scholarly warrant for saying that the services of Australian soldiers were 'pressed upon a reluctant Great Britain'. Not so, Mr Field now tells us after pertinacious use of the microfilm reader. On 3 July 1899 Joseph Chamberlain sends secret cables to colonial governments asking if they will send contingents 'in the event of a military demonstration against the Transvaal'. Governors explore the questions with their ministers, and commandants of colonial military forces — imperial officers on loan — stir their part-time soldiers to think of volunteering and encourage politicians to think of offering them. At first it seems that the governments may not give the right answer. Then Queensland responds with an offer which Chamberlain welcomes in a public and fulsome cable. 'Wait and see whether the action of Queensland will change their attitude', says the permanent head of the Colonial Office. It does. As Mr Field tells the story of those cables and memoranda and conversations about Australian participation in the coming war, it makes a revealing case study of how the empire was run.

Here and elsewhere the author expresses no high regard for politicians at either end of the empire, but, unlike many writers about old wars, he does not score off them; and to the soldiers themselves he offers the tributes of curiosity and compassion.

K. S. Inglis
Professor of History in the
Research School of Social Sciences,
Australian National University

Contents

Illustrations

Acknowledgements

A number of people have made significant contributions to this book, which is based on a master's thesis presented at the Australian National University in 1973. I particularly want to thank Barbara Penny, who stimulated my interest in the Boer War and guided and encouraged me in my research and writing. I also acknowledge a considerable debt to Lloyd Robson and Bill Gammage for their detailed criticism of my thesis and their advice that it be prepared for publication, and to Ken Inglis for agreeing to evaluate the book as a contribution to Australian historiography. The staffs of the Australian War Memorial Library, the National Library of Australia, the Mitchell Library, and the Commonwealth Archives, Canberra, all deserve my thanks for providing helpful advice and courteous and efficient service. I also wish to thank the Department of Veterans' Affairs, Canberra, for information on war pensions and benefits, Graham Irwin for preparing a draft of the map of the battle area, my mother for inclining me towards scholarly interests when I was still at her knee, and my wife and family for their understanding and encouragement.

Conversions

1 inch	2.54 centimetres
1 foot	0.30 metre
1 yard	0.91 metre
1 lb	0.45 kilogram
1 stone	6.35 kilograms
1s (shilling)	10 cents
6d (sixpence)	5 cents
1d (penny)	0.83 cent

1 *The Australian Commitment to the South African War*

War began between Britain and the Boer republics on 12 October 1899 over the status of the Uitlander population of the Transvaal. The Uitlanders (foreigners), many of them British subjects, had been flocking to the Witwatersrand goldfields since their discovery in 1886. By 1895 they greatly outnumbered the Boers and were demanding the franchise and other citizenship rights. President Kruger rejected their demands because he realized that giving the vote virtually meant handing over the Transvaal to British domination, which the Boers had resisted for almost a century. The British government, supporting the Uitlanders' demands, feared that Kruger's defiance would fuel the fires of Afrikaner nationalism and consequently pose a threat to British supremacy in South Africa. There could be no compromise on such fundamental issues.

The South African War, more commonly known as the Boer War, was to last for more than two and a half years until ended by the Treaty of Vereeniging on 31 May 1902. It was a war of three distinct phases. During the initial phase of only three months British armies, composed mainly of foot soldiers and led by incompetent generals, were defeated or besieged by Boer commandos of highly mobile mounted infantry. This phase saw the bloodiest fighting and the only real battles of the war. The second phase lasted until September 1900 and involved a British counter-offensive made possible by reinforcements from England and the colonies. Disorganized and outnumbered, the Boer citizen soldiers offered very little resistance to the invasion of their homelands and the Transvaal and the Orange Free State were annexed. The republican armies were not defeated, however, but merely dispersed, and the war entered an unorthodox phase lasting more than eighteen months. In this period of so-called guerrilla warfare, the Boers adopted a strike and retreat strategy and were chased all over South Africa by British mounted columns.

In sheer frustration at being unable to bring a will-o'-the-wisp enemy to bay, Lord Kitchener, who had taken over the British command from Lord Roberts at the end of 1900, turned his attention to the civilian population. To deprive the roaming Boer commandos of their sources of supply the British, with very little discrimination, burned farmhouses and crops, destroyed or confiscated stock, and put the displaced women and children into concentration camps. While not being the hell holes of a later period, these were nonetheless places of disease and neglect which claimed about 20 000 Boer lives and left a legacy of hate which exists to this day.

It was to such a war that the Australian colonies so unwittingly committed themselves and remained officially committed, although public enthusiasm for the adventure waned rapidly as the novelty of troop departures wore off and the true nature of the war became apparent.

There was certainly no lack of enthusiasm in the early months of the conflict, however, as the colonies feted and farewelled the volunteers who were to fight Australia's first war[1] and begin a martial tradition which was to be proudly sustained for seventy years, until it was tarnished by involvement in a war as dubious in merit as the Boer War itself. The intimidatory role in which militia units had been cast by governments during the great strikes of the early nineties had brought discredit on the defence forces, but the exuberant crowds now conveniently forgot the incidents. Even Colonel Tom Price, who had earned the contempt of unionists by an alleged instruction to his troops, when confronting strikers, to 'fire low and lay 'em out', was wildly cheered as he marched through packed Melbourne streets at the head of the second Victorian contingent.

Although the colonists had shown during the Jubilee Celebrations of 1897 that they were devoted to their monarch, the exaggerated imperial sentiments expressed two years later still appear a little unusual when it is recalled that for more than a decade Australians had been cultivating a vigorous nationalism which was strongly opposed to Imperial authority and involvement in Imperial affairs. Imperial Federation had failed because it presumed a dedication to the imperial idea which apparently did not exist; but the response of the colonies in 1899 was such that supporters could again for a brief period promote the idea of a federation of the Empire. Fear of becoming embroiled in Britain's wars had been evident in the colonial debates on the ratification of the 1887 Naval Agreement, as well as in the opposition to the Imperial Federation movement. Yet the colonies now involved themselves without hesitation in a war of conquest in which the deployment and control of Australian troops were handed over entirely to British authority.

Why had Australians overcome their earlier inhibitions and gone so eagerly to war when the cause was questionable and there was no obvious need initially for untried colonial irregular troops? A feeling of insecurity was undoubtedly one factor, for Japan, Germany, France and Russia were all active in the Pacific. The tendency of the last years of the century was clearly towards co-operation with Britain as Australians realized the weakness of their defences. One of the reasons for involvement put forward by supporters of the New South Wales military expedition to the Soudan in 1885 was the need to ensure Imperial military assistance when required by going to Britain's aid when she was at war. The same argument was used widely in 1899 by parliament and press to justify the South African adventure. Also evident in the Soudan commitment was a brash nationalism which demanded that Australia stand beside Britain, 'no longer a mere dependency' but 'her compeer and ally'.[2] This, too, became a rallying cry as the Transvaal crisis deepened. Then there was the widely expressed moral obligation to stand by the motherland when she was in trouble. This was not surprising since the same sentiment was to hold firm fifteen and even forty years later, despite the national growing-up process.

These factors contributed to Australia's entry into the war; but that entry was made inevitable by a series of events extending from May to October of 1899. Involved in the drift to war were the defence forces, the executive branches of the colonial legislatures, the press, the Colonial Office, and finally the legislatures themselves. Such was the sequence of events that most colonial legislatures were called upon merely to give parliamentary sanction to prior executive and military activity.

The initiative to send an Australian contingent should war break out came from the defence forces; and they did much to keep alive the idea of going to war during the months when other Australians were less enthusiastic. In 1899 they showed just the

3

same desire for a foreign adventure as they had shown in 1885, when a contingent of 770 men from New South Wales went to the Soudan, and other colonies tried desperately to have Britain accept their units. New South Wales troopers had also been keen to fight for the Empire in the Afridi campaign of 1897, but the premier, George Reid, had not felt disposed on that occasion to transmit their offer to the Imperial authorities as he thought such an expedition might promote 'a spirit of unrest and military adventure' in the colony.[3] As the Empire faced no significant threat either in the Soudan or on the North-West frontier, the colonial offers could be safely interpreted as rising in part from the desire of men, in a society generally sceptical of military worth, to justify their existence as soldiers and increase their efficiency by engaging in some form of warfare.

The same desire could also be seen in the visits to Britain of Australian military units for the purpose of training with regular troops. In 1893 a detachment of New South Wales Lancers went to Britain at their own expense to compete in the Islington and Dublin tournaments.[4] Such enthusiasm was significant, but equally significant was the success of the detachment. The colonials were able to hold their own with famous British regiments in events such as lemon-cutting, tent-pegging, tilting at the ring and sword exercises. The visit was probably the first important contribution to the building up of self-esteem among Australian militia units.

The feeling would have been enhanced in 1897 when all colonies except Tasmania sent contingents to the Diamond Jubilee celebrations in London, an occasion when Englishmen thrilled to the military potential of the loyal colonies; and the colonies in turn were flattered by the motherland's praise for the physique and bearing of their keen but untried troops who, in addition to marching impressively in that greatest of all displays of Imperial pomp and might, 'again distinguished themselves in the tournament ring'.[5] As in 1893, the troops had met all or the greater part of their expenses themselves.[6]

The keenness of Australian part-time regiments to gain experience with British regulars was shown again in early 1899 when a detachment of 102 New South Wales Lancers visited England for cavalry training at Aldershot. The Home government supplied horses, lodging and rations for the men but other expenses were met by the members of the detachment, the regiment and friends of the regiment. The New South Wales government made no contribution although Reid had supported the idea of troop exchange at the 1897 Colonial Conference. The premier declined to give financial assistance on the grounds that if the Lancers received government support other branches of the service could also demand it.[7]

The praise of a man like Major-General E. T. H. Hutton would have been a factor in boosting the morale of the Australian militiaman to the point where he hankered after war. Hutton, the New South Wales military commandant from 1893 to 1896 and a world authority on the role and training of mounted infantry, proclaimed Australians as 'the finest type on the face of the earth for mounted riflemen'.[8] In a lecture to the Aldershot Military Society, he said of the men of his recent command:

> No man . . . be he a Cromwell or a Napoleon, could drive the Australian troops, but a strong and capable leader, no matter how strict, could lead an Australian army to emulate — aye, and surpass if needs be — the finest and most heroic deeds recorded in the annals of the British army.[9]

Even allowing for the bias of a man who had been responsible for the development of a significant portion of the troops he was now praising, Hutton's estimate, made as it was before an eminent military body, indicated that Australia's infant military forces had established as favourable a reputation as was possible without battle experience.

The need for such experience to preserve the morale of the defence forces became evident as the early months of 1899 rolled by. The colonial legions were almost full, the forces of the six colonies totalling 18 864 men. The figure included a small permanent cadre of artillerymen in most of the colonies, but was principally made up of partially-paid militia. In both New South Wales and Victoria, which together had 70 per cent of the total Australian force, the military strength was 92 per cent of establishment; the discrepancy being more the result of government economy than lack of enthusiasm for the military life. In Queensland the mounted infantry strength was 96 per cent of establishment, although the figure for infantry was only 74 per cent, suggesting the appeal of the more glamorous mounted force and the prejudices of the bushmen who filled its ranks.

Attendance at the annual camps held early in 1899 also indicated a keenness that could not continue to be satisfied by the stereotyped exercises of an Easter encampment. In New South Wales 96 per cent of the mounted infantry were in camp for the full period, and the infantry had a record almost as good. In Queensland the daily average attendance of all permanent and militia units for the eight-day camp in May was 88 per cent. In Victoria militia attendance was also good but an interesting variation was the figure for the attendance of the Victorian Mounted Rifles. Only 44 per cent of all ranks reported to camp.[10] The explanation does not lie simply in the fact that the V.M.R. was a volunteer corps, as distinct from a militia corps, and as such received very little encouragement from the government in the way of equipment and allowances, because other volunteer corps such as the Australian Horse in New South Wales had excellent attendance records. All was obviously not well with the force that Colonel Tom Price had founded and commanded over the years. A lack of *esprit de corps* and poor physical standards became evident when military authorities had to go beyond the 800 members of the V.M.R. and recruit from infantry units to complete a mounted force of 125 for the first Victorian contingent.

New South Wales emerges from the commandants' reports of 1899 as possessing clearly the most efficient military organization in Australia. There existed units of all arms of the service, and as recently as 1898 a volunteer cavalry force of over 500, the Australian Horse, had been recruited with ease. The corps had been raised by Lieut-Colonel K. Mackay of the New South Wales Legislative Council and so great had been the response of bushmen, to whom the call for volunteers was specifically directed, that Mackay submitted a scheme to Earl Beauchamp, the New South Wales governor, for raising 'one or more' regiments of Australian cavalry, to be subsidized by the Imperial government and used for 'the defence of the Empire when and where required'. He was confident of raising 5000 men on an Australia-wide basis.[11]

Because the colonial military situation was so buoyant, it is easy to understand why the existing defence forces became a pressure group aiming at going to war with the Boers.[12] Also of great influence in provoking peace-time soldiers to look to the possibility of more war-like pursuits was a section of public opinion which regarded them as 'feather-bedders' and 'swashbucklers', terms meant to convey contempt for the easy life and vanity of the man in uniform. Radical papers such as the *Bulletin*, the Brisbane *Worker*, and the *Catholic Press* held the military up to ridicule until public opinion deterred them when war came. Even the conservative press found little to praise in the soldier until war commenced and he underwent a metamorphosis to become one of 'our brave boys'. Perhaps most people did see the defence forces as one rough poet saw them:

O they came from Parramatta, an' they came from Inverell,
And they galloped round the Show Ground an' played up like puffick 'ell,
Flashin' swords an' 'oldin ' on their 'ats, all fierce for war's red sport,
While snickerin' town galoots looked on an' cried 'What bloomin' sort?'. . .
Lemon slicin', lemon squashes, decent intervals for booze,
That's the proper sort o' warfare to fit in with modern views. . .[13]

or as Paterson's Driver Smith saw himself: 'A-charging the Randwick Rifle Range and aiming at Surry Hills'.[14] With no Australian military tradition to lean on and with little justification for their existence in terms of manifest threats to Australian security, the defence forces were ready targets for ridicule. Little wonder then that they saw in the worsening Transvaal situation an opportunity to improve their image.

Before the military began to show its hand, however, the civilian sector was given an opportunity to respond to a call to interest itself in the troubles of the Uitlander population of the Transvaal. Early in May the Imperial South African Association in London, a body numbering among its members eighty men of the Imperial parliament, made a request through the press of the principal cities of Australia for moral support for the Uitlanders in their differences with the Transvaal government.[15] In Sydney on 11 May a meeting was convened by the lord mayor and attended by an estimated 250 people who expressed their sympathy for the Uitlanders. A similar meeting was held in Melbourne Town Hall on 16 May, attended by 'a large and evidently sympathetic audience' which supported an Uitlanders' petition to the Queen for redress of grievances. The Melbourne meeting is interesting because it exemplified the nature of the leadership of the civil sector just prior to and during the war. In addition to the mayoral presence Sir Henry Wrixon, M.L.C., was there to move the motion of sympathy, and the president of the Chamber of Commerce was there to second it. Support was forthcoming from other parliamentarians and from the Reverend Dr Bevan, a precursor of the ubiquitous Protestant (usually Anglican) clergyman who was to appear on similar public platforms with never-flagging Imperial zeal in the months ahead.

The meeting also introduced the note of intolerance which was soon to reveal itself throughout the Australian community. When a member of the audience rose to question the validity of anti-Boer attitudes, his voice was drowned in disorder; and when another member who had been in the Transvaal for two years interjected to acknowledge fair treatment at the hands of the Boers, he was advised to 'take some sauerkraut' and to go back to South Africa.[16] Other resolutions supporting the Uitlander cause came from a meeting of an estimated fifty people in Adelaide,[17] and from a meeting in Bendigo of an undisclosed number.[18]

Regarded absolutely, the Uitlander meetings did not demonstrate very much concern on the part of Australians for British subjects in the Transvaal. But even the concern shown loses most of its significance when the support for the Uitlanders is compared with the concern shown by Australians a few months later for Alfred Dreyfus. In Melbourne five hundred citizens petitioned the mayor to hold a meeting to express indignation at the verdict of guilty handed down at the Frenchman's re-trial. The meeting drew 'an unusual attendance of ladies and gentlemen'. The Trades Hall Council passed unanimously a protest motion, and Geelong citizens petitioned their civic leaders to convene a protest meeting.[19] At Bendigo Dr Quick chaired a meeting deploring the verdict; and in Perth 'over 2000' attended a similar meeting in the Town Hall.[20]

Joseph Chamberlain, Secretary of State for the Colonies, seeking support for his hardening attitude towards the Transvaal, was understandably disappointed at the poor support shown in Australia for the Uitlander cause. He had hoped to include details of the meetings in a Blue Book, but comforted himself with the thought that, in any case, the resolutions would not have had any more effect than those of 'a Temperance meeting or Women's

Suffrage Association in this country'.[21] It was not until it was caught up in the hysterical farewells to the first contingent in October that the Australian public discovered its deep concern for oppressed brothers in the Transvaal. It was left to the military to nurture the idea of intervention, aided by the press, which was quick to exploit the gathering storm.

In June 1899 the London cables (sustaining force of the Australian press, which had no correspondents in pre-war South Africa), revealed the gravity of the Transvaal situation. 'The Boer Crisis — British War Preparations — Arms Issued to Burghers', reported the *Age*[22] in a typical headline. Leading articles on the possibility of war had begun to appear in May and continued through June and July. They initially showed some diversity of opinion, which was to disappear by the end of the year when objective reporting and freedom of speech virtually ceased to exist.

The *Age* had declared itself on the morning prior to the Uitlander sympathy meeting in Melbourne. Its leading article revealed a racial arrogance which was to become the burden of much of what was said on the crisis in press and parliament in the ensuing months. The issue was so simple that the *Age* could put it in a 'nutshell'. The trouble was that 'a tyrannous little minority, holding the powers of Government, taxes and impoverishes the majority while denying them the rights of citizens', but unfortunately for peace the British Uitlanders 'had not been schooled to quietly adopt the role of an inferior race'. The paper admitted the existence of Boer grievances, including the fact that 'Great Britain wants the Transvaal, as she wants most of South Africa', but felt that if the Boers 'had the right to take the land from the natives in the interests of a semi-barbarous settlement, Great Britain has the same right to supersede the Boers in the interests of a higher civilization'.[23]

The *Brisbane Courier* was quick to decry the 'haughty tone' of Boer statements, including Commandant Viljoen's belief that God and the Mauser rifle would see the Transvaal through;[24] and cables such as the one quoting Chamberlain's view that the Boer claim to independence was nothing but 'the right to oppress and exploit the Outlanders'[25] became the ready source of opinion for Australians who were predisposed to such interpretations.

The Sydney *Daily Telegraph* saw things more fairly. It regarded Uitlander agitation as having forced Chamberlain's hand, and it implied that the Uitlanders were making very heavy demands on the Transvaal government. It was also honest enough to admit that British prestige was really the issue at stake.[26] After President Kruger's concession of the seven-year residential franchise in mid-July, the *Argus* counselled Uitlander restraint as the Boer was a vanishing quantity. In one sense he was an aboriginal, to be put up with because he was disappearing.[27] The *Bulletin* sympathized with the Boers in their fight for a land they had plucked from the wilderness, but saw little hope for them. They would be doomed if they reformed their electoral system and doomed if they did not, as British arms would be used to back up the grasping Uitlanders.[28]

The first report of activity among the military forces came on 26 June, when the *Daily Telegraph* noted that men of the partially-paid infantry were keen to volunteer for possible Transvaal service. Infantry commanders had for some weeks been contemplating sending a battalion to England for training with Imperial troops at the expense of the regiments concerned. Now with the Transvaal crisis deepening, many of the volunteers for Imperial training suggested that the New South Wales government should offer their services to the War Office as a detachment for the Transvaal. 'Other branches of the forces were equally eager and ready to go anywhere, provided there was a chance of active service'.[29] Major-General G. A. French, the New South Wales military commandant, sanctioned the move (perhaps he initiated it), observing in his usual pontifical manner that a Transvaal contingent was 'a more sensible project than Soudan'.[30] On the same day the *Daily Telegraph* printed a London cable noting a Canadian 'offer' of 2000 picked men for service in the Transvaal in the event of war.[31]

French's activity did not cease with his widely publicized comment favouring a Transvaal contingent. The actions of this ageing Imperial officer in the days and weeks following certainly marked him as a man who saw the South African situation as the 'opportunity of a lifetime'.[32] The *Catholic Press* was soon to regard him as the man responsible for involving New South Wales in the war.[33] Reports of volunteering among New South Wales units during the first two weeks of July suggest the hand of French, because it is unlikely that commanding officers would have called for volunteers without the direction of the commandant. On 8 July it was reported that the officer commanding the Newtown

Company of the Australian Rifles had sought volunteers for possible service in South Africa.[34] From Bathurst came a report that twenty-five men of the Mounted Rifles had volunteered for service in the event of war in response to a 'circular',[35] and in Albury five members of the Volunteer Corps answered a 'call to arms' from 'Headquarters'.[36] As early as 14 July French was claiming 1200–1500 volunteers from the defence force.[37]

Before he could use the enthusiasm of his troops to influence the government, however, the parliamentary executive of New South Wales and Victoria were asked by Chamberlain himself to pledge unequivocal support for Imperial policy in the Transvaal. Facing considerable opposition at home and bitter criticism on the continent over his Transvaal policy, Chamberlain sought a clear declaration of support from certain larger colonies.[38] In a telegram of 3 July he inquired 'whether contingents of the New South Wales Lancers and the Victorian Mounted Rifles would offer to accompany British troops in the event of a military demonstration against the Transvaal'.[39]

The Colonial Office was deeply disappointed at the guarded responses of the governments of the two major Australian colonies. Beauchamp's cable of 5 July was little more than an acknowledgement because Reid was absent from the seat of government, but his assurance that he had sent a special messenger to Reid 'urging prompt action' indicated that in his person the Imperial government had an active agent.[40] The Victorian premier's reply, forwarded through the governor, Lord Brassey, (as was all correspondence with the Imperial government) was evasive: 'Troops already desirous of volunteering. Would the Imperial Government repay cost of preliminary training?'[41] A further cable from Sir George Turner a week later was a similar evasion of decision and an indication that financial considerations were paramount. It read: 'Volunteers offer to serve in South Africa, before the Government takes further action, they desire assurance that Imperial Exchequer bear all expenditure. Could you inform me as to rate of pay. . .'[42] A New South Wales cable was in similar vein, perhaps because the two premiers had been in consultation.[43] Reid promised every facility for voluntary enlistment if volunteers were requested, but 'equipment of troops must involve deficit of revenue, unwilling to incur new taxation or loan'.[44] But this was not the response that

Chamberlain had wanted. On 11 July the Colonial Office replied: 'We do not propose to call for volunteers, but a spontaneous offer of co-operation would be welcomed for reasons previously given'.[45] Three days later Beauchamp telegraphed: 'Premier answers Cabinet do not consider Transvaal affairs constitute crisis justifying spontaneous offer of a detachment of troops . . . At the same time Cabinet believe large number of men would willingly enlist for Transvaal service should the Imperial Government desire it . . .'.[46]

This communication showed clearly the situation as it stood in New South Wales: vigorous military activity directed hopefully towards participation in a looming Transvaal war, and an executive not prepared to commit itself on what would appear to all and sundry to be its own initiative. Expense would have been a big factor in producing ministerial reluctance; Reid's honest appraisal of the Transvaal situation might have been another; and a third factor could have been the attitude of the Labor group whose support kept Reid's ministry in office.

The Colonial Office was clearly disappointed at the results of its request for 'spontaneous' offers of support. 'They do not rise to the occasion', noted Sir Edward Wingfield.[47] A minute from the Colonial Office to the War Office was more caustic. After pointing out that it had been expected that Victoria would volunteer part of its militia force, which would not need the preliminary training mentioned in the Victorian cable of 5 July, the writer suggested 'that Sir George Turner would like to get the cost of the annual training as the price of his loyal offer . . . It is a pity that the troops who are anxious to volunteer could not inspire some of their spirit into their Premier'.[48]

The events of the first weeks of July indicated that the governments of the two largest Australian colonies had no intention of rushing into a military adventure. But ministerial coolness in those colonies was not matched in Queensland, and from the north came the first clear commitment to the Imperial cause in South Africa. The motives behind the offer of Queensland troops were possibly as much opportunist as loyalist, but contemporary historians were ready to credit Queensland with having set an example for other colonies to follow.[49] The offer of troops in the event of war in South Africa was the first gesture by a government in any part of the Empire. It was the only definite offer by an Australian government before the debates of October. Why should Queensland have taken the initiative? And even more pertinent, who in Queensland took the initiative? Only days after the first reports of military volunteering in the mother colony and in Canada there came a move in Queensland, of military origin, to send soldiers to South Africa in the event of war. On 6 July Major-General Howel Gunter, military commandant and an Imperial officer, wrote to the premier, J. R. Dickson, recommending the dispatch of 250 Queensland Mounted Infantry and a machine-gun section in the event of hostilities in the Transvaal.[50] Gunter's letter did not indicate that he was speaking for a number of volunteers, and it is very doubtful whether his approach to the government actually rose out of an upsurge of enthusiasm among Q.M.I. rank and file.

During the October debate an opposition member challenged Dickson to give an 'atom of proof' that a single volunteer had come forward by 10 July, the day the cable was forwarded to the Colonial Office by the governor of Queensland.[51] In fact, criticism of the source of the offer was common throughout the course of the debate and the government made no attempt to reply to it. Thomas Glassey of the Labor opposition was probably near to the truth when he claimed that a few troopers may have expressed a desire for war service, but that the move was really initiated by the military authorities who, he alleged, saw a way of justifying their existence.[52]

When Gunter made his recommendation parliament was in recess, but the commandant found a willing sponsor in the premier. Dickson had only recently assumed leadership of the government, his election being something of a surprise. The favourite, R. Philp, had stood down in Dickson's favour. Coming into the chief executive office as a second choice may have influenced Dickson to look for an opportunity to strengthen his position within the Ministerialist party. The manner in which he later openly revelled in Queensland's distinction at being first to offer troops suggests that he would not have been unmindful in July of the personal honour that might accrue to him in taking the initiative in offering troops.

During the October debate a section of the Labor party constantly accused Dickson of title-hunting, but Dickson claimed as his motive for acting without parliamentary sanction a fear that the chance to help the mother country may have been lost because 'the emergency might have passed away'.[53] The Queensland parliament had risen on 20 June for an adjournment lasting until 2 September. Twenty days after the adjournment Dickson made his offer. In that period had come the New South Wales military activity, the report of a Canadian 'offer' of troops, and Gunter's approach; but no sudden and marked deterioration in the Transvaal situation. It is very likely that Dickson had moved precipitately in anticipation of other colonial offers.

Whatever his motives, on 10 July Dickson cabled the Colonial Office: 'Should hostilities against Transvaal break out Queensland offers services 250 mounted infantry with machine guns'. The Colonial Office replied on 11 July: 'H.M. Government highly appreciate loyal and patriotic offer of Queensland. They hope that the occasion will not arise but if it should arise they will gladly avail themselves of the offer'.[54] From the Queensland government had come, unsolicited, the offer that Chamberlain had sought in vain from New South Wales and Victoria. The Colonial Office, possessing some insight into the forces behind Australian politics, optimistically waited for Dickson's action to affect the attitudes of more thoughtful colonial cabinets.[55]

The Queensland offer undoubtedly had an effect on the already agitated defence forces of New South Wales, and they in turn were to influence the reluctant Reid with their clamouring for action on the Transvaal. Not that the New South Wales premier was prompted to take the tentative action that he did purely by the prodding of the military, for Dickson's move had brought into play the most effective political agent of the period — intercolonial rivalry. Reid was now compelled to change his position, but he was able to do so without committing the government in any definite way. The New South Wales parliament, incidentally, was in session at the time.

Two days after the Queensland offer, together with the approbation of Chamberlain and the *Times*, had been reported in the Australian press, General French went into print with a political statement concerning New South Wales involvement. In an interview widely publicized throughout the Australian colonies, French advocated a self-sustaining federal force of all arms in the event of war in the Transvaal. He was optimistic about the value of Australian troops as part of an Imperial force, seeing them as possessing, among other un-named advantages, a physique superior to British regulars. The cause, he offered, was a good one. The merits of an Australian expedition lay in the fact that 'a large number of Australians' were employed in the Transvaal mines and the dispatch of an Australian force 'would relieve them of the white tyranny exercised over them'. In addition, sending Australian troops would have a favourable moral effect throughout the Empire and would serve to enlighten the world of the unity of Empire. If war did eventuate against the Transvaal there would be no better chance of battle experience because the Boer was a formidable foe. French noted that Canadians had already volunteered and he acclaimed the patriotism of the Queensland offer. Great enthusiasm prevailed, he said, among the New South Wales forces and such enthusiasm would become more manifest with a government offer of troops.[56] The ball had been thrown to Reid.

It could fairly be assumed that Reid took it up rather reluctantly. On the very day of the publication of French's interview, 14 July, Beauchamp had cabled the cabinet's refusal to make a spontaneous offer of troops. But now, only one week later, the governor informed the Colonial Office: 'Premier informs me that some eighteen hundred sixty commissioned officers and men of force in New South Wales have volunteered their services in South Africa if required. I understand however Government is not prepared to bear expenses'.[57]

The offer did not directly involve the government but it could easily be inferred that cabinet had given its sanction to an offer from the defence forces under its control. The official channels through which the offer was passed would also have helped in gaining for the communication something of the status of a government decision. In the October debate on the war Reid argued that he had not involved the government in any way, but Chamberlain, it seems, was no less pleased than if Reid had directly committed the colony. To him the voluntary move by the troops demonstrated the patriotic spirit prevailing in the colony just as well as an offer of troops by the government.[58] Perhaps it was only coincidental, but in a speech to the Commons toward the end of July Chamberlain showed a greater determination to protect British subjects and reassert British suzerainty in the Transvaal. In that speech, amid great cheering, the Secretary of

State for the Colonies 'thankfully recognised' the 'offers' of Canada and Australia.[59] Who knows? French and Dickson may have had a hand in causing the war.

Reid again indicated his distaste for any show of exuberance over the political and military possibilities of the Transvaal situation when, on 26 July, he was once more beset by an external request for a demonstration of Australian support for the British residents of the Transvaal. On this occasion the call came from the Uitlander Council who, in a cable from Natal to Reid (for transmission to the other colonial premiers), sought colonial support for an Uitlander petition to the Queen requesting 'relief from oppression and misgovernment'.[60] The inter-governmental action which followed is well documented, for in addition to official sources there exists a summary of the events of August by the New South Wales attorney-general, Bernhard Wise. During the October debate Wise offered a history of Reid's action and inaction as a retort to a claim by the now ex-premier that William Lyne had lost the leadership of the Australian colonies to Victoria in the short time he had been in office.[61]

Reid had certainly not moved with any show of urgency, for the contents of the Uitlander telegram were not passed on to the other premiers until 1 August. The replies were a lesson on the need for a central government. Queensland would join in any representations of sympathy for the Uitlanders provided they were prudent enough not to embarrass Chamberlain, but Dickson felt that his colony had 'already given proof of practical sympathy by her offer of troops'. Western Australia considered that all that could be done was to express confidence in 'the wisdom and justice of the action being taken by the Imperial Government'. From Victoria Sir George Turner replied that he had already cabled the Colonial Office that popular opinion in Victoria favoured the Uitlanders and that colonial forces were offering their services.[62] South Australia and Tasmania both appealed to New South Wales for a lead, but Reid would not be moved. He ignored the original request from Charles Kingston, the South Australian premier, and a reminder a week later; he rebuffed Kingston's proposal to free the Australian Auxiliary Squadron for service outside its home waters just when the South Australian leader appeared to have the concurrence of the other colonies; and he continued to ignore further urgings from Kingston for leadership in some alternative show of moral support for the Home government. In despair at Reid's silence, Kingston enlisted the aid of Lord Tennyson, the South Australian governor, who addressed Reid through Lord Beauchamp, but to no avail.[63] It would be fair to attribute Reid's reluctance to a considered view of the Transvaal situation, as revealed in a terse memorandum on the interchange of telegrams:

> Put by for the present. I have come to the opinion that the sympathy of the Australian Colonies with the legitimate desires of the British inhabitants of the Transvaal has already been made sufficiently manifest. A difficulty between the British people and the people of the Transvaal scarcely calls for displays of patriotism at this end of the world, the strength of the position being all on the side of Great Britain.[64]

Kingston had to content himself with a local declaration of Imperial loyalty, but when it came to executive action on the part of his own ministry the message that went forth on 4 September was far more non-committal than that of the New South Wales government on 21 July. The communication to the Colonial Office stated that 'from communications made to them' Ministers 'have reason to believe that in the event of any circumstances rendering such action desirable some members of the Defence Forces of South Australia would be found willing to volunteer for service beyond the colony'. Undefined though the offer was, the Home government replied that they would gladly accept it if necessary.[65]

As September advanced, the outlook in South Africa became bleaker. During the previous months there had been periods of optimism, although they must have created some confusion in the minds of Australians, interspersed as they were among gloomier prognostications. London cables, upon which the public relied for information, were not full and factual accounts that anyone disposed towards critical evaluation might ponder over. Invariably they were brief statements of journalistic or political opinion based on very inconclusive negotiations between the contending governments. Small wonder that many members of the colonial legislatures later complained bitterly (or admitted blithely) that they were voting on commitment to a war whose immediate origins they knew little of.

Editorial comment in the Australian press acknowledged the worsening position in the Transvaal. Alleged Boer intransigence brought exasperated outbursts, typical of which was an *Argus* judgement that long-suffering Britain was being forced to strike as she had spared 'an ignorant, obstinate and grasping people' as long as she possibly could.[66] In fact, by September both Briton and Boer were poised to strike. Paul Kruger could no longer contemplate a franchise extension which would spell the eventual end of the South African Republic and now the old patriarch waited for the spring rains to blanket the veldt with forage for the ponies of his commandos. International arbitration was the only alternative to conflict as far as Kruger was concerned, and Britain, asserting her position as suzerain power in the Transvaal, would not accept this. The issue was as clear to the Home government as it was to Kruger, and it went far beyond questionable Uitlander grievances: British hegemony was threatened in South Africa and with it her prestige throughout the world.

On 12 September an ultimatum from Chamberlain was read to the Volksraad demanding a five-year residential franchise, more goldfields members in the legislature, parity of English with Dutch in parliament and law courts, a conference to settle franchise details, and guarantees of concession by the Transvaal. Failing a reasonable response from Kruger Britain would take steps to secure a settlement.[67] Rejection of this ultimatum was featured in the Australian press on 18 September under large headlines such as those in the *Age*: 'Boers for War! — War Considered Inevitable'.[68] During the past four months the Transvaal question had shared prominence with the English tour of Darling's XI, the Dreyfus case, and, occasionally, Australian federation, but now the crisis dominated all other items.

Against this backdrop of heightened tension another colony moved to play its part in the tragi-comedy that was to lead to 'the blooding of the pups'. At this point Victoria assumed leadership of the Australian colonies, for the new government under William Lyne in New South Wales was reluctant to make any decision on troop commitments without reference to parliament, which did not meet until 17 October. The shadow of William Bede Dalley and his unconstitutional action of 1885 hung over the New South Wales ministry.[69]

But in Victoria another military man who considered that his time had come took action. Major-General Sir Charles Holled-Smith, military commandant of Victoria and senior army officer in the Australian colonies, had been in South Africa in 1881 and had experienced at first hand the great humiliation to British arms at Majuba Hill. His personal enthusiasm for a war against the Boers was shown at the end of 1899 when he hastened back to England with the expressed hope that he would soon be on active service in South Africa. But for the present he was intent on getting the Australian colonies more fully involved.

In a press interview reported on 19 September Holled-Smith revealed that 'several weeks ago' he had suggested in a communication to the Victorian minister for defence that a cable be sent to the Imperial authorities inquiring whether Australian assistance was acceptable, and if so, what type of force would be preferred. W. McCulloch had not replied. The commandant favoured a federal force, and he exhorted Australians not to forget their fellow countrymen on the Rand. If Britain were prepared to go to war on behalf of the Uitlanders, surely Australia should do something when so many of her people were involved.[70]

Holled-Smith's statements probably moved the Victorian government to action. On 19 September the minister for defence directed that enrolment of volunteers from all branches of the services begin at Victoria Barracks.[71] This was the first overt act of recruitment for war in South Africa by any colonial government in the Empire. On 20 September Holled-Smith worked out the practical aspects of recruitment with McCulloch. The two men also asked their premier to suggest to other colonial leaders that they send their commandants to Melbourne to confer on a scheme for a united Australian force in the event of colonial troops being required in South Africa.[72] Sir George Turner moved with great haste and telegrams went out on the day that Holled-Smith and McCulloch had conferred.

Other Victorian activity took the form of a cable on 20 September to the Colonial Office which read: 'Many volunteers for South Africa. May we assume that charges will be borne by the Imperial Exchequer?'[73] This cable was another attempt to get a clear statement from Chamberlain on the financing of a possible Australian contingent. Turner was apparently reluctant to expose the rising Imperial loyalty of Victorians to the sobering facts of a budget deficit. More pertinent was Turner's cable of 27 September: 'In event of United Australian force being formed for service in South Africa. What arm or arms should it consist of?'[74] The request was the logical follow-on of Turner's marshalling the commandants into conference, and it would appear that the Colonial Office cable of 3 October, accepting an Australian contingent and dictating its composition, was partly in answer to it, and partly in answer to the earlier communications of New South Wales, Victoria, and South Australia which had told of volunteers coming forward.

While Victoria had been making some headway in its attempt to ensure a federal contingent in case of war, Dickson in Queensland was making moves, overt and otherwise, to retain for his colony the distinction it had won in July. On 19 September he telegraphed Lyne, asking him what New South Wales was going to do. Queensland had made a troop offer but Dickson considered the 'moral effect upon all portions of the Empire would be much greater if the Australian Colonies took concerted action in the matter'.[75] Lyne replied the following day, sympathizing with any move to give moral support to the mother country but declining to take any action that would incur expenditure without parliamentary sanction.[76] According to a press report Dickson next turned to Victoria. On 20 September, the day of Lyne's telegram, he suggested to Turner a meeting of military commandants in Sydney. The telegram was reported to have crossed that of Turner which suggested such a meeting in Melbourne.[77]

Despite his play for a combined effort (with the initiative coming from Queensland), Dickson's next step seemed designed to set Queensland apart from the plans of other colonies. On 22 September, aware of Victoria's initiative regarding the commandants' conference, he sent to the Colonial Office a cable intended to hasten a decision on Queensland's troop offer. It said in part: 'Earliest possible information is desired by my Government whether their offer to send a contingent is likely to be accepted in order to obtain the necessary parliamentary supply'.[78] When the Queensland military commandant presented himself at the Melbourne conference a week later, he brought proceedings to a stalemate by insisting that Queensland's offer of troops, and the provisional acceptance of that offer, placed her apart from any scheme for a federal force. The Victorian minister for defence had to be called in to admonish Gunter, and in the process he drew attention to the contrasting co-operative attitude of the Queensland premier. Perhaps McCulloch only knew the half of it.

The commandants met in Melbourne on 29 September in what McCulloch happily regarded as 'a federal incident of no small importance in the history of Australia'.[79] But the labours of these Imperial officers were anything but federal in spirit. The first day's proceedings showed that while Victoria, South Australia and Western Australia favoured a federal force, New South Wales and Queensland did not. French considered it would take too long for the various colonial governments to sanction a federal force and it would then arrive too late. Gunter thought that as there was no federal authority there could be no federal force. Colonel Stuart of South Australia argued that if the commandants acted in unison the premiers would soon provide a federal authority. And Holled-Smith, the president of the conference, could achieve no agreement on this basic point.[80] On the following day the commandants decided to pass on to the subject of pay and allowances. It was at this stage that McCulloch appeared on the scene and asked leave to address the conference. He had entertained the commandants at a luncheon at Parliament House the previous day and had then left the city. A message from a concerned party (Holled-Smith?) had brought him back to remind the conference of its purpose — to draw up a scheme for a united Australian force for presentation to the colonial governments. McCulloch was particularly severe on Gunter, asking him why he had come to Melbourne at all.[81] The chastened military men returned to their appointed task and by 5 October had drawn up a plan for an Australian contingent of 2053 officers and men (see Appendix A). The conference was of the opinion that if a sufficiently large force representing all arms were to be sent, it could remain intact as an Australian contingent capable of acting alone or in concert with regular troops.[82] So far as the composition of the contingent was concerned, the commandants seemed to have a better appreciation of the needs of a South African campaign than the War Office; and their desire for a unified and self-sustaining Australian force was commendable. The sensitive question of the command and second-in-command was left to the premiers, and the appointment of other officers was left to a projected further meeting of the commandants in Sydney. That meeting never eventuated, nor did the commandants proceed any further with detailed planning after the receipt of

Chamberlain's cable of 3 October, for this prescribed a fragmentation of the Australian military effort (see Appendix B).

The Colonial Office cable which brought an abrupt end to the concept of a federal force was a fascinating document. Considering that the 'offers' of New South Wales, Victoria and South Australia had been so nebulous, the Home government did a pretty fair job of presuming a definiteness that had not existed. The cable acknowledged 'the patriotic spirit exhibited by the people of Australia in offering to serve in South Africa', and furnished 'information to assist organisation of forces offered into units suitable for military requirements'. By prescribing units of 125 men, with two units from each of New South Wales and Victoria and one unit from South Australia, and by stipulating that the units were to be commanded by no one above the rank of major, the War Office was clearly envisaging token forces which could be attached to Imperial regiments.[83]

The stated preference for infantry was also regarded by some as another means of placing the colonial irregulars where they would be least bother. The War Office conditions stated that the units 'may be infantry, mounted infantry, or cavalry. In view of numbers already available, infantry most, cavalry least, serviceable'. The request was rather a strange one considering the vast distances to be covered in South Africa, the small proportionate numbers of British cavalry, and the fact that the Boers would fight mounted to a man. *The Times History* suggested that the amazing dispatch became comprehensible only 'if for "most serviceable" we substitute the more direct phrase "least troublesome".'[84] The same writer also claimed that the War Office was decidedly cool about the colonial offers, feeling that they had enough regulars for the task without calling on colonials who were difficult to manage and of little use. He alleged also that it was only after Colonial Office insistence that the War Office accepted the colonials.[85]

At the Royal Commission on the South African War, Lord Lansdowne, the Secretary of State for War, defended the War Office preferences by claiming that 'cavalry' was not meant to include 'mounted infantry', but he did not say whether 'infantry' included 'mounted infantry'.[86] General Sir Redvers Buller was also a party to the decision and he claimed that he had in mind that all colonials could ride and he would turn them into mounted infantry. What he did not want was a small force of 'irregular cavalry' such as the English Yeomanry.[87] The sincerity of these statements is supported by the fact that the offers of mounted infantry by New Zealand and Queensland were readily accepted. And after all, the commandants' plan was to send 1010 infantry and 935 mounted men. Place these figures against the 580 infantry and 625 mounted men who actually went with the first contingent and we see that the War Office conditions did little to alter the proportional composition of the Australian force.

Many years later there came an echo of the affair when Senator C. F. Cox, former commander of the Aldershot detachment of the New South Wales Lancers, replied in the Senate to a letter to the *Times* of 21 July 1933 from Sir Frederick Robb, a former major-general in the British Army. Robb set out to remove the stigma which he claimed surrounded the name of Lord Wolseley, a former commander-in-chief, because of the infantry-preferred cable. According to Robb, Lord Wolseley thought it an admirable idea to test the quality of colonial troops by exercising the Lancers with regular cavalry upon their arrival at the Cape.[88] This was allegedly done and Sir George White, who was commanding at Cape Town, was supposed to have sent Wolseley an account of 'the almost comic shortcomings of the detachment'.[89] At that time, Robb continued, the War Office was considering the offers of the colonies and Wolseley suggested that because of White's 'adverse' report the colonies should be told to send only dismounted troops. Replying to the criticism, Cox quoted a letter he had written to the *Times* denying that White had ever inspected the Lancers and claiming that even if he had, his criticism was answered by the regiment's meritorious service in South Africa. Robb's allegations, however, could have been refuted by a simple exercise in chronology. The cable accepting Australian troops was dispatched on 3 October. The Lancers were then still in England.[90]

The Australian colonies seemed almost relieved that each could now go ahead with its individual war effort. New South Wales was an exception. Lyne tried desperately to stop the other colonies, particularly Victoria, from making individual and official commitments of troops, for New South Wales was in the frustrating position of being the only colony whose parliament was not in session.[91] In particular, Lyne tried to contain Victorian exuberance by urging that the commandants' report be kept secret until considered by all governments. Turner's reply was that he 'deemed it wise to give publicity to the report'.[92] He did; but for some reason refrained from making public the text of the Colonial Office cable. The Victorian press had to get that information from New South Wales where it had been released by a disgruntled Lyne only because Dickson had already given the Queensland press the text of a similar cable.

Faced with a restive military force, and the certain knowledge that New South Wales was falling quickly to the rear in demonstrations of Imperial loyalty, Lyne was at last moved to circumspect action in order to counter criticism. On 30 September Lord Carrington, honorary colonel of the New South Wales Lancers and a former governor of New South Wales, had cabled the Lancers' headquarters at Parramatta that the Aldershot men had volunteered for service in South Africa. He hoped the government would 'sanction this patriotic offer'.[93] The detachment of Lancers was at that time about to embark for Australia via the Cape, and their commandant at Parramatta sought permission for them to disembark in South Africa. In his memorandum to the chief secretary, Colonel Burns fashioned an argument suited to the situation. Dropping the Lancers at Cape Town would not involve the government in any expense; and here was a body of Imperial-trained cavalry who would do credit to their colony and be the first colonial troops to land in South Africa.[94] Lyne gave tentative approval.

On 6 October the *Argus* was able to announce with confidence: 'It can now be definitely said that Australia will be represented in the war in South Africa'.[95] Thanks to the implications of the commandants' conference and the Colonial Office cable, the active recruiting of volunteers, the chartering of troopships and other martial preparations, the colonies could not doubt that they had reached a point of no return. Yet even as late as the cable of 3 October accepting Australians for war, the will of the people as expressed through their parliaments had still to be made known. Debate now commenced, but under such handicaps that it became a travesty of democratic discussion.

On 5 October Western Australia and South Australia introduced legislation to send contingents. The debate in the Western Australian Assembly was extremely short. A motion was introduced by the premier, Sir John Forrest, which expressed loyalty to the Queen, sympathy for Her Majesty's government, and suggested co-operation with other colonies in dispatching a force if war should be declared.[96] An excellent case against conflict with the Transvaal came from Moran, the member for East Coolgardie. He stressed the ignominy of war with such a diminutive foe; he extolled the sturdy virtues of the Boers, who had created a nation out of the wilderness and were now expected to hand it over to Britain by the franchise device. They were fellow Christians, fellow Europeans and fellow colonists, whose only fault was perhaps ignorance. And having said all that he voted for the motion. Even more disquieting was the response of the premier to a member who asked what was really known in Western Australia about the justice or injustice of the impending war. 'We do not want to know', said Forrest.[97] The motion was carried on the voices.

In South Australia, although a motion to dispatch a contingent of 125 volunteers was introduced in the Assembly on 5 October, two adjournments extended debate to 12 October. The attorney-general, in moving, exploited the earlier Queensland offer, the more recent New Zealand offer,[98] and the motion before the Western Australian parliament. He conceded that Britain did not really need troops, but regarded the offer as an expression of sympathy in 'a period of some Imperial anxiety'; and he quoted the proverb, 'Who gives quickly gives twice',[99] which would have been more truthfully expressed as, 'Who gives quickly gives before the others'.

The influence of press and public opinion on the South Australian debate can be clearly inferred. One member regretted that the subject had not been discussed in committee as a matter involving finance, for anyone 'taking the opposite view to the Premier was liable to be accused of all sorts of want of patriotism and false sentiment'.[100] Another regretted that the press was already attacking 'little Australians', and referred to a letter from a friend who hoped that he would oppose the motion, but suggested he preface his opposition with the singing of 'God Save the Queen' in order that his stand would not be construed as disloyalty.[101] Another, who had referred to the volunteers as 'feather-bed' soldiers, apparently came under such criticism that he spent much time later in the debate praising the soldiers' potential and trying to explain away his comment.[102]

A practice which affected the quality of debate in most colonial parliaments was prominent in the South Australian legislature. A number of speakers withheld their opposition to sending a contingent because they considered that the colony had already been committed by executive action and was therefore honour bound to participate. There was a fair amount of truth in the claim, of course, and quite sincere politicians used it as a substitute for reasoned argument on the morality of the war. Sir John Downer was one who deprecated the action of the government in moving when it did, but he asked members 'not to discount both Britain and the Empire in the eyes of Europe' by rebuffing the initiative taken.[103] One member recited a few lines of doggerel to illustrate Downer's stand, and in so doing described the mental agony of many a confused politician who was confronted with the awesome prospect of involving his colony in international war.

> As for the war, I go agen it,
> I mean to say, I kind of do —
> That is, I mean, that being in it,
> The best thing is to see it through.[104]

It is questionable whether Kingston had acted on any definite indication of the extent of military fervour in the colony when he sent that cautious cable of 4 September. When we recall the imperial ardour that Kingston demonstrated throughout August, as he pestered Reid and other colonial premiers to make a gesture of loyalty to the homeland, we realize that he would have been prepared to act on the most slender evidence; and that is what he appears to have done. Initially, when pressed in debate, Kingston had to admit that he had no idea of the number of volunteers prior to 4 September. 'He was dealing with the House with every candour, but he could not say whether ten persons had volunteered.'[105] Later in the debate he quoted a memorandum from the acting military commandant stating that 100 men had offered verbally in July and August.[106] In his speech-in-reply, however, Kingston defended his action not so much by reference to military initiatives as to the offers of other colonies. Was South Australia to stand out?[107] The motion was carried eighteen to ten with twelve pairs, the premier choosing to ignore the plea of Tom Price, the Labor leader, who wanted Kingston to withdraw the motion and thus go down in posterity for his courage.[108]

Of all the colonial upper houses, the South Australian Legislative Council was the only one to show any semblance of legislative responsibility. In the other colonies motions to send contingents were treated as a mere formality, with members commonly deploring any move to debate the issue. But in South Australia the motion was passed in the Council only on the president's casting vote. Reasons for this atypical opposition were varied. Several speakers either ridiculed the inconsequential size of the proposed force or held that it was not needed; others resented the move by the executive before parliament was consulted; and still others opposed because on the eve of federation small colonial contingents, which would soon lose their identity, were being raised. Support for the contingent was not expressed with any obvious warmth or logic. The mover of the motion put forward as a first reason for going to war the 'great number of Australians in the Transvaal'.[109] He also favoured Australian participation as an answer to those who were disposed 'to sneer not only at Australian troops, but at Australians generally as inferior to the old race'.[110] When he spoke in reply, the chief secretary could only answer the opposition by claiming that South Australia had to follow the example of Queensland, New Zealand, New South Wales and Victoria.[111]

In the meantime, on 10 October, the Tasmanian lower house had approved the dispatch of a contingent. Again a colony had been committed by its parliamentary executive, which on 8 October had cabled to the Colonial Office an offer of assistance. The government had also authorized the enrolment of volunteers. Parliament itself was a little more reluctant and the premier, Sir Edward Braddon, anxious to complete the contingent business before he faced the no-confidence motion that was to bring him down, reduced his request from £7000 and 125 men to £4500 and 80 men to ensure that the motion was passed. An inclination to quibble over the cost of the contingent roused the ire of the *Launceston Examiner*, which expressed devout thanks for oncoming federation, for 'while pettifogging representatives were haggling over the odd halfpence an enemy might be at our gates'.[112]

Also on 10 October, following a one-day debate that was distinguished mainly by the utterance of imperialist platitudes, the Victorian Legislative Assembly approved the dispatch of a contingent. In submitting the motion Turner ran through a gamut of excuses for going to war. He referred to the ill-treatment of

Britons by Boers,[113] to the need to give a practical demonstration of loyalty and Imperial unity; and to the 'very large number' of Australians in the Transvaal. As to the true merits of the case, he could only rely on the British government, which would be fully apprised of the situation. In addition the parliamentary opposition, press and people were behind the Home government so it could fairly be said that the British cause was a just one.[114]

The most virulent attack on the motion came from John Murray of the Labor party; not W. A. Trenwith as one might have expected, for the Labor leader's devotion to Empire apparently counted for more than the prevailing mood of his party. Unfortunately Murray fell into extremes in attacking the motion. He regarded the 'military urge' in Australia as being inspired by the press, the war in general as being inspired by the capitalists, and the likely role of the Australian volunteers as little better than 'wood and water joeys'.[115] It was left to Henry Bournes Higgins to present a reasoned argument, but the ears of parliament, press and people were not then attuned to the sweet music of logic, and for his pains the member for Geelong was discarded by his predominantly middle-class constituents at the next election. Higgins saw the war as one in which Australians had had no voice, and over which they would have no control. Whether the struggle was a just one or not was of paramount importance to him, yet as he saw it the Boer side had not been put by the Australian press, which got its information from a single source, the *Times* correspondent in South Africa, whose reports were bought by a combination to which, Higgins alleged, all Melbourne and Adelaide and some Sydney papers belonged.[116] Among other speakers common themes were the debt of the colonies to 'the old grey mother', support for England as security insurance, and support for England 'right or wrong'. There was a tendency among Labor members to regard the untried Australian soldiers as being destined for undistinguished service in South Africa, and no tendency among supporters of the motion to claim otherwise. The vote was 67 to 13 in favour of the contingent.

Debate in the Queensland Legislative Assembly began on 11 October and went on for four days before the vote was taken on 18 October. When the premier put forward a motion renewing loyalty to the Crown and offering troops in support of long-suffering Transvaal subjects, one might think he would have acted with some trepidation. In the view of A. Dawson, the leader of the Labor opposition, Dickson had virtually declared war on the Transvaal in his infamous offer of July without consulting the representatives of the people;[117] and Dickson might well expect strong opposition from Labor if the virulent attacks of its organ, the Brisbane *Worker*, could be taken as any indication. But he was an astute politician, and if he had taken a long chance on public opinion in July, the odds were now much more in his favour, for, as Dawson painfully observed, there was a 'wave of jingoism . . . passing all over the country'.[118]

Although the premier began the defence of his executive action in July by claiming that a crisis existed at the time, much of his speech was a shrewd appeal to parliament to accept his *fait accompli* on the grounds that great prestige had accrued to the colony through its having led the way. The Queensland offer of troops, he announced, 'has placed Queensland in the foremost rank among the Australian colonies, and it has stimulated her sister colonies to go and do likewise'.[119] Other reasons he gave for promising a contingent were the 'harsh and brutal treatment' of the Transvaal refugees as reported in the press,[120] and the need for actual warfare to train Queensland troops.[121]

Dawson strongly opposed sending a contingent because he did not see the Empire in any danger, and he considered that the money spent 'in sending a mob of swashbucklers to South Africa to show off their uniforms' would be better used for hospitals and libraries. These were inflammatory words to a community which was in the process of readjusting its attitude to soldiers, but Dawson blundered on. He could have no respect for any man volunteering for the Transvaal. Such a person was merely a 'cur', rushing in to take a bite at the 'little poodle' that the 'large mastiff' was attacking.[122] This was the most outspoken attack on the military by any Australian politician, and Dawson was to rue the day. The *Brisbane Courier* labelled him and other Labor members who opposed the contingent as Boer sympathizers, and berated Dawson for his attack on the volunteers.[123] Worse was to follow. The *Worker* alleged that for a week following Dawson's speech 'a gang of bullies' gathered nightly outside his house, frequently while he was absent in parliament, throwing stones on the roof and through windows, and 'insulting his wife and family with vile and low scurrility'.[124] When the debate on the dispatch of the second contingent took place in December Dawson seconded the motion. British defeats had put a different complexion on the war by then, but one wonders what part physical intimidation played in Dawson's change of heart.

Realizing that the Dickson government was most vulnerable on the point of a constitutional aberration, Dawson based his attack on an amendment which retained the loyal expressions of Dickson's motion but registered disapproval of the action of the executive in offering troops in July. There was strong support from both sides of the house on the matter of Dickson's 'impropriety' and the amendment was only lost by 28 to 39. Debate on the motion resumed but, with the constitutional 'red herring' removed, soon petered out without any real attempt to appraise the developing conflict in South Africa. The now guarded, and even conciliatory, references of Labor members to the volunteers indicated a public rebuttal which extended far beyond the editorial comment of the *Brisbane Courier*. At 4.30 a.m. on 19 October the motion was carried on the voices, and was followed by what had become a ritual in colonial debates on the war — three cheers for the Queen![125]

When on 17 October the New South Wales Legislative Assembly began debating the dispatch of troops, all other colonies but Queensland had decided to send contingents, and even in Queensland the debate was well advanced and obviously moving towards commitment. The premier used this situation as a primary *casus belli*. When Lyne moved for the equipment and dispatch of a force for service with the Imperial Army in South Africa, he made no attempt to justify New South Wales participation other than on the grounds of the need to demonstrate Imperial solidarity in the eyes of the world, and the need to emulate the other colonies. It would be 'singular indeed' if the mother colony stood back.[126] The *Bulletin* saw Lyne as 'a dry, elderly politician, who had waited long and patiently . . . before coming into his kingdom'.[127] The mediocrity implied clearly emerged in Lyne's speech, which omitted any reference to the principles or morality involved in going to war. When questioned on this omission, the premier declined to debate the merits of the case. The Imperial government had entered on war and it was the duty of New South Wales to support it.[128]

Lyne's prosaic handling of the issue was not lost on Reid, now leading the opposition parties. He undertook to supply something of the 'high ground of principle' he found lacking in Lyne's appeal to the house. Reid failed, however, to present a principled argument for intervention in South Africa because, as on the federation issue, he found something good on both sides. He praised the 'magnificent courage' of the Boers and conceded that they were 'fighting for the integrity of their own land', but he still upheld that ideal of the Imperial government which sought to protect a Briton wherever he might stray.[12] It was left to others to make profounder observations in a debate which was to extend over three full days.

W. M. Hughes typified a more honest and more discerning approach to the Transvaal crisis. He deplored the lack of any official source of information from which the merits of the case could be learned. Of the Uitlander grievances he suggested that men had to be amenable to the laws of the country to which they went voluntarily. He defended Kruger's stand, for if the Transvaal did not fight it would be 'blotted out of the map of Africa by the slow and insidious process of political reform'. A staunch imperialist, Hughes sought refuge from charges of disloyalty by ranging himself alongside Chatham, Fox, Bright and Gladstone — men who had also stood out against wrong wars.[130]

The speech of W. A. Holman is less interesting in itself than in its consequences. It was in large part a tirade against swindling speculators on the Rand, Cecil Rhodes, British action against inconsequential powers, and soldiers who were going to fight for they knew not what just to improve their musketry. In the midst of it all Edmund Barton introduced into the chamber a little game that members had been diverting themselves with in the lobbies. He asked Holman if he wanted the British or the Boers to win. The member for Grenfell replied that he would support his country in a just cause, but as he believed from the bottom of his heart that this was the most iniquitous, most immoral war ever waged with any race, he hoped the English may be defeated.[131] Holman's answer caused uproar in the House and reverberations in a large section of the city and provincial press, the Labor member serving as a focal point for much of the ill-feeling towards his party which the debate had engendered. So sharp was the criticism that Holman tried to redeem his position by claiming that he had expressed a wish for Boer victory over the Chartered Company and not over England. This mollified his parliamentary colleagues, but sections of the public remained unimpressed.

During a public lecture by Holman in Hobart on 'The Labour Movement and Militarism', the audience got out of hand. A group of sailors burst into 'Sons of the Sea', the gaslights were turned off, Holman was tipped off the platform and assaulted, and as he was escorted away the audience broke into the anthem. The people had come to judgement. Holman's more discerning patriotism was not of the times. [132] Later, as a by-play to the celebration in Grenfell of the relief of Mafeking, Holman was burned in effigy; an experience which would have been no less painful to him than the clouts of the tars. [133]

The remainder of this, the most thoughtful debate among all the colonial parliaments, could be reduced to a number of generalizations. It was widely held that Australian troops would not be of any material assistance, but would merely symbolize Imperial loyalty and solidarity in an antagonistic world. Reid's July 'offer' of troops was put forward to some extent as a pretext for non-debate, but the factor most inhibiting discussion was a widespread acceptance, even by men of the stature of Barton, that the rights or wrongs of the war could not be debated because parliament did not possess the necessary knowledge of the Transvaal situation.

The most honest of all speeches, perhaps, came from one John Dacey. He said, 'I am going to vote for British supremacy in South Africa'. He carried no brief for the 'transient' Uitlanders, but his sympathy with the Boer cause extended only to that point where they wished to become paramount in South Africa. [134] The vote was 78 for and 10 against. All the negatives were Labor members, although seven other Labor men present had voted for the motion. These included James McGowen, the party leader, who had equated loyalty to the cause of Empire with loyalty to the cause of labour: you did not question whether it was right. [135]

And so the last obstacles to Australia's going to war were removed. The legislatures had given their blessing to a movement that had reached a point of no return even before a word was uttered on the subject in any colonial parliament. No individual colony could possibly have stood apart from the eager rush to support the Empire, and few politicians had either the conviction or the courage to oppose involvement in the Transvaal. The only significant opposition came from the Labor parties, which, despite division within their ranks, managed to introduce into the debates some of the deeper issues involved in joining in the war. [136]

During the debates the conservative press had constantly played its hand for commitment, directly by editorial comment, and indirectly by denigration of the Boers and by reports of military enthusiasm and preparations for war. The radical press had constantly over-played its hand against commitment by seeing the war due entirely to the machinations of capitalists and military officers. All too rare were thoughtful leading articles such as the one which appeared in the Broken Hill *Barrier Miner* on 13 October (although it accepted without question the current reports of Boer ill-treatment of women and children). This newspaper questioned the rejection by Britain of the Boer request for arbitration, and drew attention to Australia's role in the crisis. It suggested that Australia's responsibility should have been to encourage its powerful protector to accept arbitration, but instead, 'Have we not rather encouraged her to look to arms?' The lack of knowledge of the issue was also questioned, as were Australia's motives: 'Parliaments have voted money, not because they have inquired and believe England right, but because they want to share England's greatness and England's glory'.[137]

Few individual citizens came forward to question the government decision on the war, for already press and public opinion were intolerant and repressive. G. Arnold Wood, the Professor of History at Sydney University, was one man informed enough and courageous enough to attack the *Daily Telegraph* when it sought to dismiss all opposition to the war as the work of a few 'lime-lighters'. Wood asserted in a letter to the editor that opposition in England was widespread (he made no such claim for Australia), that it mainly had a Christian basis, and that for an empire built on 'principles of righteousness' the war that England was now entering on was an unjust one.[138] A. B. Piddington, later a prominent jurist, wrote to the same paper pointing out that siding with England in a quarrel that was none of Australia's making was a violation of 'the sane and just policy of the Monroe Doctrine for Australia'; and he suggested that if Australia had to have her baptism of blood one day 'let it be blood that will be spilt like that of the Boers, in defence of freedom and fireside, and not in a war of pillage and despotism, which must end without glory, because it begins without right'.[139] But the warnings of these men were lone voices that were lost in the tumult.

Henry Lawson, in one of his rare comments on the war, looked at the situation just as the last of the colonial parliaments endorsed commitment, and tried to work out the mania that gripped the land. Lawson's statement is worth quoting at some length, not only because of his stature, but also because of the truth of much of what he said:

> What does it all amount to? Only this: That, because of the craving for the sensational born of the world's present social system — the mad longing for change, intensified in Australia by the hopeless flat monotony of the country and its history — some of us are willing — wilfully, blindly eager, mad! — to cross the sea and shoot men whom we never saw and whose quarrel we do not and cannot understand. Our cry is 'For England!' or 'Blood is thicker than water!' and so we seek to blind and deceive ourselves as fools who are unanimous in their eagerness to sacrifice right, justice, truth — everything, to satisfy their selfish craving for what they consider a picnic — to have 'some fun' — to have a spree.[140]

Something had certainly gone wrong with Lawson's land of simple democratic virtues, for now enlightened editors closed their eyes to truth, justice and humanity; mild men of God became hysterical advocates of a war of conquest; politicians in the most advanced democracies in the world put aside their liberal principles for the sake of Empire, while those who did not abjectly recanted in December their sins of October; and the people, who by repute gave everyone a 'fair go', engaged in witch-hunts against real or imaginary 'pro-Boers'.

2 Preparations for War

The Colonial Office cable of 3 October 1899, which accepted colonial 'offers' of troops and laid down the composition of the Australian contingent, also stipulated that troops were to embark 'not later than 31 October'.[1] Why the British authorities should have wished to get the token forces of colonial irregulars to South Africa so quickly is a matter for conjecture; but one result was to put to the test colonial military organization and ministerial competence. Parliamentary approval for the despatch of troops was given between 5 and 19 October and, although preparations had begun before then, it is to the credit of ministers and military that 1200 men with horses and equipment were embarked for war between 28 October and 5 November.

The Home Government's request for units of 125 men (two units to come from the larger colonies and one from the smaller) freed the colonies of the need to attempt co-operation with one another, and accordingly they set about raising their separate forces. In the light of earlier military enthusiasm, this should have been an easy task, but in fact some colonies had difficulty in filling their units in the given time.

New South Wales, the leading military colony with 7788·on the muster rolls of its defence force at the end of 1898[2] had no trouble meeting its quota of 250 men although a majority of serving members chose not to volunteer at that stage. The difficulty lay in deciding which regiments would be represented, and competition for the relatively few places was so keen that the colony eventually sent a force of 450.

The officers commanding the New South Wales Lancers, the New South Wales section of the Royal Australian Artillery, and the New South Wales Army Medical Corps were very anxious that their regiments should experience active service and, in response to their initiatives in offering detachments,[3] Lyne took steps to determine the composition of the New South Wales contingent. In a cable of 7 October to the Colonial Office he confirmed the offer of the Lancer squadron at Aldershot subject to parliamentary approval. Four days later, under pressure from General French, an artillery officer himself, Lyne offered a field battery.[4] On 13 October he offered the medical detachment, subject to the approval of parliament.[5]

Had these units alone formed the first contingent, the great majority of the defence forces of New South Wales would have been without representation. Apparently this did not concern Lyne who was attracted by the prospect of the Lancers being the first Australian unit to arrive in South Africa, and also by the cost factor. The pay and maintenance costs of the R.A.A. had already been provided for in the Estimates. When Lyne introduced the motion to send a contingent, he spoke in favour of New South Wales being represented by the R.A.A. and the Lancers on the grounds of economy.[6] George Reid scorned Lyne's preoccupation with cost, and drew his attention to the recommendations of the Colonial Office cable.[7] Probably Reid's attack, along with War Office rejection of the field battery offer and the agitation of other regimental commanders, led the New South Wales cabinet and French to plan a different contingent. On 21 October Lyne reported that the colony would send 125 mounted infantry, 125 infantry, 86 medical corps, and the squadron of Lancers.[8]

This permitted New South Wales to embark some of its keenest soldiers. The Mounted Rifles establishment was four hundred, located in eight half-squadrons at Molong, Bathurst, Picton, Camden, Bega, Forbes, Tenterfield and Inverell. The regiment was a militia unit, receiving twelve to sixteen days training a year at the rate of eight shillings for a full day's attendance. The government supplied arms and uniforms, the troopers their own horses and equipment. By 25 October 140 volunteers from this regiment had been given a local preliminary medical test and were on their way to Sydney. Only 100 of these were to be selected, for the remaining places in the mounted infantry unit were to go to the Australian Horse.[9] A list of the 129 officers, non-commissioned officers and men who formed this unit shows that only eight of the soldiers were married. The average age was twenty-six. Forty-two were farmers or graziers, with the remainder in essentially unskilled occupations, and of ninety-eight who stated religions, nineteen were Roman Catholic and

'An Ominous Start'—FEDERATED AUSTRALIA: 'And so my first national act is to back up a wanton deed of blood and rapine!'

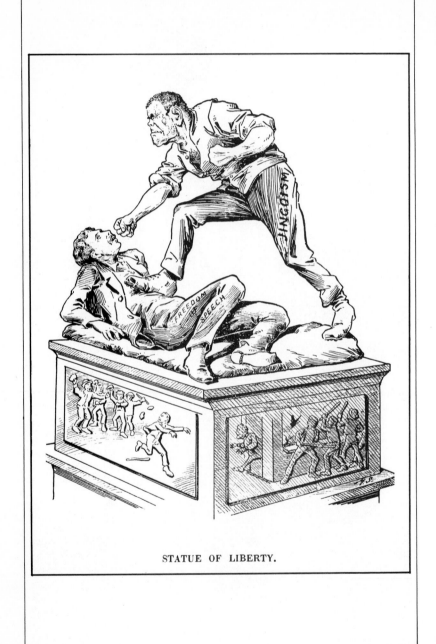

STATUE OF LIBERTY.

A cartoon from the Brisbane *Worker* depicting the threat to freedom of speech in Australia when war fever was at its height

the rest Protestant. With odd exceptions the men were country born and Australian born.[10] Neither the occupations of the men nor the addresses of their next-of-kin indicate whether they were country men or country town men, but when we consider that few town men in unskilled occupations would have been able to afford the upkeep of a stabled horse, it can be reasonably concluded that the majority of the mounted infantry unit came from the bush.

On the word of their commanding officer, the thirty Australian Horse members included in the unit were without doubt bushmen. Lieutenant-Colonel K. Mackay had described his regiment as 'purely a bush organization, the men being either shearers, station hands, farmers, or squatters, and the officers in nearly all cases, sons of old squatting families'.[11] The Australian Horse was a cavalry regiment with a strength of about 400 men, drawn principally from Goulburn, Quirindi, Mudgee, Scone, Gunnedah, Bungendore, Murrumburrah, Braidwood, Cootamundra, Gundagai, Michelago and Rylstone.[12] As a volunteer force its members were distinguished from militia men mainly by receiving no pay for attendance at parades and very little government assistance of any other description. The men were accomplished as horsemen but not as soldiers.[13]

The only other cavalry[14] unit in the Australian colonies was the New South Wales Lancer regiment. It had eight half-squadrons located at Sydney, Parramatta, Berry, Robertson, Maitland, Singleton, Lismore and Casino; but forty men of the squadron sent to Aldershot were from the Sydney and Parramatta units.[15] No particular mode of selection had been applied to the Aldershot detachment, the first 103 men to come forward with twenty pounds towards the cost of the trip being selected. One report stated that the majority of the Aldershot Lancers were married or had dependent relatives.[16] The average age of members of the detachment was twenty-four and a half years; the average height was five feet nine and a half inches. Only seventy-two Aldershot men got off at the Cape, and a draft of forty men was sent from New South Wales to make up the squadron.[17]

The army medical corps was to embark with a strength of ninety-two men, including twenty-three permanent drivers of the R.A.A.[18] This mixture of regulars and irregulars was drawn from the Sydney area. It made up in discipline, dedication and efficiency what it lacked in the fruits of bush experience.

The infantry unit was drawn mainly from Sydney, the location of four militia battalions totalling 2400 men. There were also 1900 volunteer infantry men from which to recruit, the majority of these being located in Sydney or Newcastle.[19] Volunteering from this numerous branch of the service was not up to expectations, and a large proportion of those who did come forward were rejected on medical grounds.[20]

Officers for the New South Wales contingent were approved by cabinet on the recommendation of French. Competition for the few places ensured a good standard of officer. All were colonial men, a fact which Lyne found most pleasing.[21]

The recruitment of the Victorian contingent was characterized by a marked discrepancy between the numbers volunteering for service in the event of war, and those who reported for attestation after Victoria had undertaken to send a contingent. New South Wales had experienced the same phenomenon, but with little effect on the raising of its contingent. In the southern colony the discrepancy made necessary the recruitment of infantry and mounted infantry units in part from sources other than those considered most appropriate.

When enrolment of Victorian volunteers began at Victoria Barracks, members of all branches of the service were invited to register, as well as citizens with previous military training,[22] and by 28 September 760 men of the defence forces and 280 civilians had volunteered.[23] But after 3 October, when Victoria committed itself to sending 125 infantry and 125 mounted infantry, the call for recruits became more specific. By 12 October 260 mounted men from a volunteer regiment of 800 and 250 infantrymen from a militia regiment of 1900 had registered. This was hardly an enthusiastic response to the call to arms, but worse was to follow. When called up for medical and military efficiency tests, only 128 mounted infantrymen and 107 infantrymen reported.[24] The medical examination also produced a surprise: forty per cent of the applicants failed to pass a test considered not strict. The failure rate among the Victorian Mounted Rifles might be explained by the fact that as a volunteer regiment its recruits were not subject to any medical examination; but the same excuse could not be made for the militia, and their failure rate was just as high.[25] To complete the numbers in both the mounted and unmounted units, the authorities called on the Victorian rangers, a volunteer infantry regiment; but still lacking five men for the infantry unit they gave the places to members of the permanent artillery![26] Victoria had set out to enlist preferably single men of twenty to forty years of age, and it is a further measure of recruiting difficulties that twenty-seven married men embarked for South Africa.[27]

It was common for press reporters to regard the Victorian contingent as being composed of bushmen, but that could not have been so for about eighty per cent of the infantry were recruited from Melbourne, with the remainder coming from Castlemaine, Ballarat and Bendigo. Only the mounted unit was filled from country areas. A summary of the occupations of the Victorian contingent shows a preponderance of town men, with rural areas being represented by landowners rather than rural workers.[28]

Selection of the officers for the contingent on grounds that ignored seniority was questioned in the Legislative Assembly, but defended by the premier who claimed that efficiency had been the criterion.[29] An *Age* report regarded the officers, who had been selected from 'numerous volunteers', as 'young, intelligent and enthusiastic',[30] but when one considers the favourable connections of several of them, another factor in their selection seems likely. A biographical summary of the officers is given on p. 40. It indicates possible sources of influence, but more importantly, it gives an idea of the type of leader who sailed with the first and second contingents. All the Victorians were colonials and in personal and professional details they appear fairly typical of Australian militia officers of the time.[31]

Queensland's problem was to produce the 250 mounted infantry promised to the Home Government by Dickson in July; not an easy task if press reports and parliamentary criticism can be considered informed. Although enrolments could not be finalized until the government gave its sanction to the contingent on 18 October, recruiting did proceed, the object reportedly being to raise twenty men out of the fifty who comprised each of the twelve half-companies of mounted infantry.[32] During the debate on the contingent, an opposition member claimed that the officer commanding the Queensland Mounted Infantry had reported to the military commandant on 27 September that he had sufficient volunteers, although press comment indicated that recruiting was

Name	Age	Occupation	Education	Army service	Stated social connections
Major G. A. Eddy	39	permanent officer	—	14 yrs as c.o.* Military courses in England, 1898-99	—
Lt T. M. McInerney	30	barrister	St Patrick's Coll. & Melb. Univ.	8 yrs as c.o.	brother of warden of Univ. Senate
Lt H. W. Pendlebury	29	public servant	Victoria Coll.	5 yrs as c.o.	—
Lt A. J. N. Tremearne	—	medical student	Geelong Grammar	4 yrs as c.o.	—
Capt. D. McLeish	—	grazier	privately educated	13 yrs as c.o. English tournament exp. 1891	—
Lt R. W. Salmon	35	grazier	Amherst C. of E. School	14 yrs service, 9 as c.o.	brother of M.L.A.
Lt G. F. Thorn	—	businessman	—	4 yrs as c.o.	—
Lt T. S. Staughton	—	—	Melbourne Grammar	3 yrs as c.o. and other mil. exp.	son of M.L.A.
Lt G. G. F. Chomley	23	grazier	Melbourne Grammar	3 yrs service 1 yr as c.o.	nephew of a judge & of Cssr of Police
Lt J. C. Roberts	—	medical student & qualified engineer	Carlton Coll. & Melb. Univ.	5 yrs as c.o.	—

— information unavailable

*commissioned officer

going on as late as 17 October.[33] Other members quoted alleged incidents which suggested pressure recruiting. Captain Harry Chauvel had enticed recruits from the Warwick half-company by assuring them the war would be 'a grand picnic' with 'very little risk' and no expense.[34] Similar cajolery was used at Roma by Lieut-Colonel Hutchinson, who promised a change from 'the humdrum of ordinary everyday life' at no greater risk than getting on a horse.[35] On 10 October Colonel P. Ricardo addressed the Q.M.I. at Toowoomba and secured twelve volunteers.[36] According to a member of the legislature, Ricardo's approach was to direct the paraded members thus: 'Those who are willing to go to the Transvaal stand on the right of Sergeant McLennan and those who are going to stop and grow pumpkins stand in the ranks'.[37]

If the recruitment of other ranks required effort, that of the officers did not. There was a scramble for places. The ramifications of that scramble can be deduced from a speech in the Assembly when a member interceded on behalf of four officers who had missed selection. The member complained that while an ex-Imperial officer had gained a place, two colonial officers with Imperial training and another two who were regarded as superior marksmen were passed over. The member had made pressing requests to Colonel Ricardo, the officer commanding the Q.M.I., on behalf of one of the men, and had followed this up by introducing the supplicant to the premier, who had personally recommended the officer to Ricardo. But still the man did not gain a place.[38]

Volunteering for South Australia's infantry unit of 125 men proceeded so slowly that a Sydney newspaper used the headline, 'Apathetic South Australians', and noted that military authorities were considering the need for an active recruiting campaign.[39] At that stage only about 150 men had volunteered and authorities estimated that one-third of these would be rejected medically.[40] One call to a parade of 200 infantrymen in Adelaide yielded twenty-five volunteers.[41] On another occasion the roar of the elements proved stronger than the blasts of the bugles of war, for only twenty men out of a company of 100 turned up at a recruiting parade, 'the smallness of the number being largely due to the wet night'. Ten of the men registered.[42] Eventually 250 volunteers came forward, but not all were from the 1250-strong South Australian defence force, a number being civilians with some previous military experience.[43] At the last moment the officer selected as the senior subaltern had to withdraw as he was detained by pressing private business.[44]

Tasmania's contingent of eighty infantrymen was drawn from 180 volunteers in a defence force of 1945.[45] Western Australia's infantry unit of 125 was recruited without obvious difficulty, the only extraordinary thing being its composition. Fifteen were West Australians by birth, thirty were from Britain, and the rest were from the eastern colonies.[46] Command was given to an Imperial officer, the commander of the Albany garrison artillery.

From existing sources, fragmentary though they may be at times, there emerges a reasonably clear picture of the men who were to lay the foundations of Australian military tradition. They were predominantly unmarried men, on an average in their mid-twenties. The average physique was probably a man five feet eight and a half inches in height, ten stone twelve pounds in weight, and thirty-five inches around the chest.[47] This suggests a tallish, lithe soldier, and the suggestion is supported by numerous contemporary references to the Australians' admirable physique. If members of infantry units, the volunteers were most likely to have come from the cities; if members of mounted infantry and cavalry units they would have come mainly from country towns and rural areas. They would have had a liking for the military life, a modicum of discipline, but only a limited knowledge of the science of war.

How could they have been accomplished soldiers? As militia or volunteers their periods of training were almost negligible. The Queensland militia were supposed to do eighty hours drill a year, but most of this would have been completed in an annual eight-day camp. The volunteer forces had to complete sixty-six hours of drill a year but attendance at camp was not compulsory. In South Australia a minimum of thirty-six hours of training was required for the militia. Each member of Western Australia's volunteer force was required to attend twelve parades and fire forty rounds a year to qualify for an efficiency allowance of thirty shillings. These figures are representative of all Australian colonies.[48]

Drill occupied most of the limited parade time. There was some training in musketry but the weapons used were obsolete or obsolescent. The main Boer armament was a .276-calibre magazine Mauser. Against this the British were preparing to match their .303 magazine Lee-Metford and Lee-Enfield.[49] In Australia at the outbreak of war the only unit equipped with the Lee-Metford was the New South Wales infantry militia. Elsewhere the single-loading .303 Martini-Enfield had only recently taken over from the old .450 Martini-Henry.[50]

Shortcomings in the training of Australia's part-time soldiery were accentuated by the limited service of many members of the forces. The Aldershot detachment averaged only two and a half years service per man, and troopers of the recently formed Australian Horse would have had a maximum of one and a half years service. The brief period at the disposal of commanders before the first contingent sailed was not sufficient to rectify these deficiencies. There were drills and route marches and shooting practice, and Victoria even tried to simulate battlefield conditions by firing volleys in the midst of the mounted force, but the fact remains that the contingent went off to war ill-prepared. Its personnel were saved by the fighting style of their enemy, for they could not possibly have coped in a conventional war.

While the first contingent filled its ranks and sailed away to war, the three most articulate groups in colonial society raised their voices in defence of the expedition. From pressman, preacher and politician came utterances designed to mould an honourable cause for the soldier, and to denigrate his enemy in the field and his opponents at home. The way of the warrior was acclaimed.

An *Argus* reporter was so impressed by the sight of young Victorians embarking for war that he described the occasion as 'an event worthy to signalise the closing of the century, and one which will not be forgotten when the century which follows is being put to bed'.[51] Another opinion looked beyond the present conflict, regarding it as a preparation by the military forces of Britain and her colonies 'for the mighty struggle that a few brief years may witness'.[52] There were many similar accounts of the idealized function of the soldier, but the press was generally hesitant about praising the martial qualities of the untried Australians, though the *Age* made reference to 'the flower of our manhood'[53] and the *Argus* claimed that in training, discipline and physique the men were comparable with the auxiliary forces of any country.[54]

The press was particularly severe on the enemy. In South Australia the *Register* and the *Observer* set out to depict the Boers as a cruel and fanatical race.[55] The *Singleton Argus* regarded them as an inferior people who must be brought down by the sword to 'the humiliating position of serfs, dragged down because of their own tyrannical acts'.[56] The *Manaro Mercury* attributed the war to Boer 'swagger' over the defeat of the British at Majuba.[56] The *Western Argus* regarded the enemy as 'a somewhat brutal and very ignorant race'.[58] The *Age* quoted 'the eminent war correspondent', Villiers, on the Boers. He was said to consider them 'some of the lowest types of humanity . . . unprogressive in every way', and prone to live 'like pigs'.[59] So widely propagated was this unsavoury and uncivilized image of the Boers that Australians must have initially accepted their soldiers as crusaders for a higher civilization.

Criticism of the contingent by Labor parliamentarians and others evoked from the conservative press responses that were often as intemperate as the attacks. Under the heading of 'A Pro-Boer Councillor', the *Age* carried the story of a Ballarat town councillor who had remarked on the great disparity between the opposing forces and suggested that some Australian volunteers had gone to war for the sake of four shillings a day and not out of loyalty.[60] In an editorial two days later the councillor was bitterly attacked. He had a 'huckster's mind'; he was prepared to 'sneer' at the men of the contingent; and he was willing to see the Boers, who 'live like pigs . . . lording it over men of Australian birth'.[61]

On the other hand, the radical *Catholic Press* wrote disparagingly of the 'valiant volunteers of the colonies',[62] and the Brisbane *Worker* strongly attacked the contingent. Following Dickson's offer of troops in July the *Worker* had ridiculed the (non-existent) 250 mounted infantrymen as 'swashbucklers', but by late September it had to accept that there was volunteering from the ranks of the workers 'either through necessity or through blind ignorance'.[63] The paper could not resist a final word to the departing troops, and in an open letter it asked how many had inquired into the right or wrong of the war. It also suggested that their views were derived from press falsehoods, and wanted to know if they would hand over their country to 'a mob of Jew and foreign exploiters'. Better to stay home and grow 'the peaceful pumpkin'.[64]

Australia's ashamed of ye, living or dead,
And the man of the pumpkin is honoured instead.[65]
The contingent went to war fortified by the blessing of the churches. The Anglican Synod in Victoria demonstrated 'quite a warlike enthusiasm', and promised every facility to Church of England chaplains who might be called to the Transvaal to perform their duty 'to God, their Queen, and their country'.[66] The Victorian Congregational Union offered up prayers for peace but if war should proceed 'were equally fervent that the British nation, the upholder of righteousness, should triumph'.[67] The New South Wales Congregational Union showed a little more Christian apprehension over the conflict. At its annual session it expressed the hope that the war would bring an extension of popular liberty and the uplifting of native peoples, but it deleted from the original motion a clause expressing trust in the justice and humanity of British statemanship.[68] The Moderator of the Presbyterian Church in Victoria admitted to ignorance of the factors involved in the war, but considered that he could trust in the wisdom of British statesmen.[69] A lesser figure of the same church regarded the war as 'unnecessary and unrighteous', and for his pains was made the subject of an editorial attack in the *Age*.[70] The Jewish faith in Australia expressed its loyalty through a prayer 'appointed by the Chief Rabbi of the British Empire to be read in Synagogues every Sabbath during the continuance of the War'. The prayer offered supplications 'on behalf of the brave men, who pass through seas, armed for War in a far-off land, in obedience to the command of our beloved and venerated Queen and the bidding of her counsellors'.[71]

The Roman Catholic Church remained relatively aloof from the fervour of the October days. When the Church's acknowledged spokesman in Australia, Cardinal Moran, did speak it was to assert that true Australian patriotism was to stay home and defend one's own country. He felt that the troops had the colony's sympathy, however, because 'they had received orders to go'.[72]

Individual churchmen, like their political brethren, seemed to regard the war as a grand opportunity to have their voices heard throughout the land. Bishop Green of Armidale described the enemy as a 'brutal, obsolete, cruel and tyrannical oligarchy', but his attempts to join the contingent as a chaplain were confounded by the diocesan council of Grafton/Armidale, which was not convinced that his reasons for wanting to go outweighed his duty to his diocese.[73] The rector of St Luke's at Burwood regretted the war but recognized that in the present conflict England stood for justice and the integrity of the Empire.[74] Archdeacon Gunther at Parramatta prefaced his views with the same sop to Christian pacifism and claimed that the war was a defensive one.[75] At a public farewell to Bendigo volunteers, a cleric advised the men to 'keep their sight clear and their powder dry, to turn to God, and to fire straight'.[76] At a send-off in Newcastle to a part of the first contingent, the bishop of the city, in seconding the mayor's toast, said the men 'had actually consecrated the streets of Newcastle by having trodden them with the feet of their loyalty and patriotism'.[77] The most ungodly statement came from a minor clergyman on a minor occasion, but such was the order of things that it received prominence in the press. At a farewell to a Swallow and Ariell employee in Melbourne, the Reverend E. James stated that Britain would not tolerate injustice and oppression and 'he asked in all sincerity that God would speed the bullet for the liberty of the world'.[78]

Despite their general support for the war, the churches did not figure prominently in the official farewells to the contingent. There was no religious service associated with the march through Melbourne streets. In Sydney there was a valedictory religious service at Victoria Barracks before the farewell march began, but Cardinal Moran was not pleased with what he called 'the ridiculous Protestant service' which Catholics were obliged to attend.[79] The spiritual needs of the soldiers were better served in Adelaide where an 'immense crowd' attended a public church parade at the Jubilee Exhibition Building. Great enthusiasm prevailed throughout the service and at the conclusion of the sermon the gathering rose and sang the anthem and cheered wildly.[80]

The mixture of sacred and profane was to become commonplace in the weeks and months ahead, but one of the most glaring examples of religious impropriety occurred at the annual diocesan festival of the Church of England at Ballarat. The governor, Lord Brassey, was there, revelling in the early victories of the British army; Trooper Cherry sang 'Rule Britannia'; a brace of bishops expressed their thanks to God for British military successes; and the Bishop of Ballarat called for cheers for the Empire and the Queen, during which Lord Brassey vigorously waved a miniature red ensign in vice-regal glee.[81]

No provision had been made to send a chaplain with the contingent. This led to numerous protests by the churches to the relevant authorities in several colonies. In New South Wales a deputation of Anglican, Wesleyan and Presbyterian churchmen waited on the minister for defence, and he and General French permitted an Anglican clergyman to accompany the contingent.[82]

The Queen's representatives in Australia were to play a significant part in events connected with the departure of the colonial contingents. Most prominent was Lord Brassey, who seemed bent on justifying Britain's intervention in the Transvaal. The Victorian governor, a great proponent of the concept of an imperial naval reserve drawn from the colonies, must have been delighted to witness a situation that gave credibility to his scheme. 'If the Empire were really in danger these colonials would make great efforts', he confided to Chamberlain.[83] But while he acclaimed the potential of the colonial soldier, he usually saved the greater praise for the British regular. In his farewell speech to the troops, Brassey assured them that they were 'worthy to stand shoulder to shoulder with that band of heroes' already fighting in South Africa.[84] And he repeated the sentiments when he stood with Lord Beauchamp during a Melbourne farewell to a part of the New South Wales contingent.[85]

If Brassey privately considered the Empire to be in no danger, it was understandable that he should show a preoccupation with publicly justifying British belligerency. In a lengthy speech at the Grand National Show at Maryborough, his main theme was the justice of the British cause,[86] and he dwelt on the issue again at a mayoral banquet in Melbourne.[87]

Beauchamp was not nearly as active as Brassey, but his perceptiveness led him to take a course of action which probably had more effect on Australian loyalty than anything the Victorian governor said or did. On 24 October he telegraphed the Colonial Office: 'Venture to suggest for your consideration that spontaneous expression of thanks from H.M. the Queen for troops going to S. Africa would be very deeply appreciated in Australia'. Chamberlain acted quickly. A draft telegram was sent to the Queen at Balmoral for approval, and a cable of thanks was on its way to the colonies at 3.30 p.m. on the day of Beauchamp's request.[88] The Australian press did the rest, and Australians revelled in their monarch's gratitude.

In South Australia Lord Tennyson also played an active imperial role. He addressed the colony's troops as 'Men of the South Australian Contingent of the British army in South Africa', and applauded their 'alacrity in obeying the summons of the old country'. He had a lot to say about the importance of discipline, but he considered that the men would prove competent soldiers after a little military experience.[89] During their brief training period Tennyson visited the troops in camp several times. He had the entire contingent to lunch at Government House and then capped a fine vice-regal performance by marching with Lady Tennyson at the head of the contingent to the docks.

Their profound deliberations in the colonial legislatures completed, politicians turned to enjoy the fruits of their labours. It was a time to bathe in the reflected glory of the departing troops. It was a time to appear on platforms at farewells to individual soldiers, and to take part in the embarkation parades in the capital cities. William Lyne, despite his apprehension that the Victorian contingent might be first to the Cape, enjoyed himself immensely. He took part in the valedictory religious service at Victoria Barracks; he spoke with patriotic fervour at a luncheon given to five hundred citizens by the owners of the troopship *Kent*; he formed part of the great march through the streets; and he followed the troopship up the harbour in a launch adequately equipped for the convivial hour.[90] At a Patriotic Fund meeting in the Town Hall a few days later, he was so carried away that he promised another contingent of 10 000 men.[91]

Many politicians had surrendered principle to expediency in matters relating to the war, but Sir George Dibbs represented the prime case of hypocrisy and opportunism. In 1893, when Dibbs was premier and Colonel E. T. H. Hutton had just been appointed colonial commandant, the former cut the military estimates by £30 000, the sum needed to run the essential Easter encampment. In a press interview Dibbs described the camp as a luxury and spoke of putting Hutton in his place.[92] Yet at the departure parade for the New South Wales contingent, Dibbs marched proudly at the head of the scarlet-coated National Guard, a small body of rather ancient reservists who could hardly be reckoned part of the military establishment.

One New South Wales politician who was prepared to ignore the heroics of the occasion was P. Crick, the Postmaster-General.

He refused military leave to married men for service in South Africa, on the grounds that there was another duty besides loyalty to Empire and that was loyalty to a man's wife and family.[93]

In Victoria parliamentarians joined in the novel entertainment surrounding the dispatch of the contingent. Thirty of them, accompanied by a hundred friends, visited Flemington showground to watch the V.M.R. unit carry out battle exercises.[94] A reception in their home town for the seven Bendigo members of the contingent attracted, among other people, two M.L.C.'s and three M.L.A.s.[95]

Parliamentary patronage of the Melbourne farewell, self-indulgent though it might have been, was a further assurance to the troops that they were part of an extraordinary happening. Members and their wives watched the parade from a vantage point at Parliament House, whence they were taken by cabs to the docks to board the *Monowai*. The vessel had been made available by the Union Steamship Company, and M.P.s had a 'merry meeting in the saloon' at the expense of the company while following the *Medic* to the heads.[96]

The occasion of the mayor's farewell to the contingent lifted Sir George Turner quite out of his usual character. It was reported that 'no one would have recognised in the fiery orator of last night the cold arithmetician of the Government'. The premier was greeted with cheers when he assured the volunteers that they would not be 'mere hewers of wood and drawers of water' (a possibility suggested by Labor speakers during the debates).[97]

The Victorians received further assurances when they reached Adelaide. Charles Kingston, the South Australian premier, at a civic reception to Victorians and Tasmanians aboard the *Medic*, told the men that 'they went to fight for Queen and country, and constitutional freedom from a serfdom worse than death'. But the only proof he offered of the justice of the cause was that Lord Salisbury, the British prime minister, had the support of the opposition parties.[98]

Later the *Bulletin* was to regret that politicians had not seized the opportunity to stand against the tide of ignoble militarism; the Hour had not found the Man.[99] Few, indeed, had stood with any resolution against involvement during the October debates. Who would stand against war now, when all articulate agencies had accepted the cause as just and the volunteers as patriotic and romantic figures? The politicians had acted throughout with little regard for the higher values of young Australian nationalism. Instead, in accepting militarism and imperialism, they were accepting Old World values that they had generally regarded as alien to Australian democracy. The *Bulletin* could be excused for bemoaning the fact.

> We had a dream—it seems but yesterday—
> That dream is dashed—to direst darkness hurled;
> For where our Commonwealth—a virgin lay,
> A Wanton fronts the world . . . [100]

The men of the first contingent had been told by press editors, parliamentarians and other public figures that what they were doing was right. But only when the hitherto inarticulate masses expressed their approval at public concerts and during farewell parades did the volunteers realize their new importance. Soldiers' letters and diaries frequently testified to the exhilarating effect of the roar of the crowd. But not only were the departing troops affected by the tumult of the street. It also inspired others, citizen and militiaman, to emulate the action of the volunteers. As an observant trooper put it: 'The streets were full of citizen soldiery, and still more full of civilians burning with the zeal which creates citizen soldiery'.[101]

If the crowds were a motivating force in later enlistments, what motivated the crowds? Nationalism and a desire to identify with the greatest power in the world were paramount factors. *The Times History* regarded the enthusiasm as a manifestation of national rather than imperial sentiment, with national self-consciousness being stirred by the sight of troops to whom their country's credit was entrusted. Imperial sentiment and love of the mother country were there too, 'but as the emotional setting . . . to the no less intensive national feeling'.[102] That same observant trooper saw the wild enthusiasm of the farewell as

> the manifestations of a people mad with the excitement of their first taste of war, the first shedding of blood in which they had an interest of their own . . . What Australians for the most part wished, was that England should recognize her willingness to share the burdens of Empire as fully as its advantages, and this thrill of emotion—war fever, jingoism, national insanity, or whatever it be called—was merely the inarticulate expression

of the delight with which the acceptation of their proffered aid filled the colonies.[103]

The *Argus* explained: 'We are proud of our racial kinship and heritage. Our interests are bound up with Britain's high place among the powers and the integrity of her empire'.[104] The Sydney *Daily Telegraph* interpreted public enthusiasm for the war as proof that the people wished to become 'working partners, for better or for worse, in the foreign policy of the British Empire'.[105]

A modern scholar, Donald C. Gordon, has also emphasized the growing-up process:

> It was national sentiment in Canada and Australia which demanded that they share in the dangers of empire as well as the benefits they had long known. Self-appreciation would no longer permit colonial peoples in such advanced areas to feel that they could make no significant contribution to the war in which Britain was engaged.[106]

Troop farewells invariably began at the local level. Quite often they were civic affairs, for aldermen and councillors were as keen as politicians to appear on platforms with the men of the moment. The pattern of activities was common. The volunteer was honoured at a suitable function (frequently a smoke concert for males only), where he was the subject of speeches and a presentation. Later there was a parade through the streets, ending at the local railway station or coach depot. From there the hero departed to war amid cheers, martial music and singing, and the songs they sang were: 'The Girl I Left behind Me', 'When Johnny Comes Marching Home', 'Auld Lang Syne', 'The Minstrel Boy', 'Rule Britannia', 'Sons of the Sea', and above all 'Soldiers of the Queen'.

Less intimate but no less flattering to the volunteers were the great farewell parades at the points of embarkation. The functions were assured of maximum popular support by the actions of the civil and military authorities, who either scheduled the parades for non-working days or proclaimed special holidays. The Queensland and Victorian contingents paraded on Saturday afternoon. The New South Wales contingent sailed in three sections which embarked on different days. Those leaving on the *Kent* marched through Sydney streets on Saturday afternoon. Those embarking on the *Aberdeen* marched through Sydney on

Friday, though every effort had been made to delay the departure of the vessel to permit a Saturday farewell. A half-holiday was granted to government employees for the occasion. A public holiday was declared for Newcastle and the Hunter River district when the third New South Wales section left from the northern city. A public holiday was planned for Adelaide, but it did not eventuate because it was not known precisely when the *Medic* would berth to take aboard the South Australian contingent.

The Victorian government took additional steps to ensure the success of the Melbourne farewell by making available holiday excursion fares from all stations to the city. It also approved the issue of free rail passes to the immediate relatives of country members of the contingent.[107]

In Sydney the rain was heavy and continuous when the men embarking on the *Kent* marched through the streets on Saturday 28 October. But that did not quell the ardour of a crowd estimated at between 250 000 and 300 000 and thought to be larger than that which had farewelled the Soudan contingent. There were no distinguishing badges on the uniforms of the volunteers, so the escorting militia units were cheered as well. There was an embarrassing delay to the military procession as the troops swung down Park Street and across Elizabeth Street for no one had thought to stop the trams. From two o'clock until dark the excited populace cheered in the streets and at the docks and many retained their enthusiasm until well into the night. One reporter said of the march: 'It will surprise the mother country; it has even surprised ourselves! We knew we were loyal, but it required a stirring episode to provide such convincing proof'.[108]

Light rain fell on Friday 3 November when the *Aberdeen* troops marched through Sydney. The crowd was smaller but there was a greater show of bunting, including a banner across the intersection of Park and Pitt Streets which reflected the growing confidence of the public in their fighting representatives:

> Be copy now to men of grosser blood,
> And teach them how to war.
> *Henry V*[109]

The Newcastle demonstration was of a magnitude befitting a proclaimed holiday, but its conclusion was marred by an element of farce. The *Langton Grange* was not ready to receive the troops,

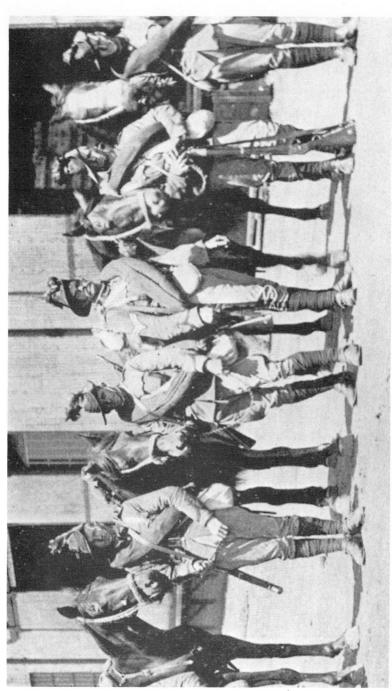

Men of the New South Wales Mounted Rifles waiting to leave Cape Town for the front

A Boer commando

so to conclude the great military display suitably at the docks the men went aboard a smaller steamer, not for foreign fields but for a trip around the harbour. Later they quietly disembarked and spent the night in a drill hall.[110]

The Victorian contingent was given a taste of the morrow by the crowds who thronged inside and outside the Melbourne Town Hall for the mayor's farewell. 'For the first time in the history of Victoria the thrill of patriotism vibrated through the nerves of the people', and their hearts were stirred by the colony's first plunge into 'the great deeps of international warfare'. After the ceremony the troops headed a triumphal procession back to barracks, and as the men disappeared within the gates the huge crowd sang 'Soldiers of the Queen'.[111]

The thronged streets were lined by 2000 school cadets for the march the following day, Saturday 28 October, and the contingent had an escort of 4000 members of the defence forces. Included in the column, and basking in a glory they must have thought gone for ever, were former Imperial soldiers, 'ambling but proud old wrecks', who wore the medals of Crimea and the Mutiny.[112] Lieutenant Tremearne, in writing of the occasion later, told of people, perfect strangers to him, rushing into the ranks with tear-filled eyes and murmuring, 'Good luck, old man'.[113] Followed by a flotilla of smaller craft, the *Medic*, the largest ship ever to enter an Australian port, sailed down the bay and turned to the open sea. Long after the cheering had died and the launches had turned back, Victoria continued to salute her first contingent with huge bonfires which blazed along miles of coastline.[114]

Other cities had farewell ceremonies just as spontaneous as those of Sydney and Melbourne, and before mid-November all troops for South Africa were on the high seas. The *Medic* carried the units from Victoria, Tasmania, South Australia and Western Australia. The men from New South Wales were aboard three ships, and the Queenslanders, possibly both by choice and from necessity, were still going it alone.

The Australian people had acted creditably enough during the first weeks of war. They had revealed elements of national immaturity in their behaviour, but nothing malicious. When the incident of the New South Wales Lancers occurred, however, a deplorable aspect of the Australian character was demonstrated.

Throughout the greater part of 1899 a squadron of Lancers had been training with regular British cavalry regiments at Aldershot. The officer commanding the detachment, Captain C. F. Cox, offered the entire squadron for service in South Africa when war seemed likely and the offer was accepted. But when the Lancers reached Cape Town in a ship bound for Australia, only 72 out of 101 men disembarked. The remainder went on to Australia.

The reaction was profound. The returning men were reviled in the streets and in parliament, and were forsaken by their regimental commanders. The unfortunate affair can be understood, if it cannot be condoned. The decision of the twenty-nine Lancers not to disembark for active service came at a time when the Australian colonies were flushed with self-esteem. England had accepted their offers of troops, and the men of the first contingent had received sufficient praise from notable people to make the colonists optimistic about their performance in South Africa. Much of this pride and expectation was threatened, however, by what Britain and the rest of the Empire might construe as cowardice or lack of loyalty.

An examination of the whole episode indicates that the handful of Lancers were neither cowards nor disloyalists, but were victims of the extraordinary times. Much of the bitterness directed at the returning Lancers rested on the belief that they had volunteered for active service, and then changed their minds before the eyes of the Empire. The issue was not so clear-cut, and a *Daily Telegraph* reporter who accompanied the Lancer squadron from London in the *Nineveh* gave a comprehensive account which raises doubts about the extent of volunteering among the detachment. Captain Cox explained to him that early in June he had been approached by 'the men', who said they were anxious to go to the Cape. Cox called the Lancers together and asked if this were so. Only one man demurred. Cox passed on the outcome of the meeting to Lord Carrington, honorary colonel-in-chief of the Lancers, and Colonel Burns, the officer commanding the regiment. When war was imminent, Cox spoke again with Carrington who notified the New South Wales government of the desire of the squadron to serve in South Africa. Cox had seen no necessity to consult the men again before his approach to Carrington, but on 7 October the War Office consulted them by ballot. According to information the reporter received, 'over 30 men' declined to volunteer.[115] War

Office action was obviously justified. But Cox, Carrington and the New South Wales Agent-General, Sir Julian Salomans, continued to play the part of the three wise monkeys.

On 10 October London gave the Lancers a wildly enthusiastic farewell. The streets were so crowded that all traffic was suspended along the route of the march. Amid this fervour, which would have swelled the pride of any colonial agent-general, Sir Julian vehemently denied a *Daily Chronicle* report that twenty-six Lancers had refused to volunteer. The statement was false, he said, and the entire squadron was burning with impatience to get to the front.[116] Meanwhile the War Office had made known its displeasure. Cox was called before the Aldershot authorities the night before the Lancers embarked, and shown a War Office letter expressing Lord Wolseley's indignation over Cox's having stated that all men would volunteer.[117] The ire of the commander-in-chief was understandable, for since its offer to serve in South Africa the squadron had been hailed by the English press as a symbol of Imperial solidarity. No official statement was made on the Lancers, and some authorities hoped that the dissenting troopers would change their minds by the time the *Nineveh* reached Cape Town.[118]

The dissenters, however, had good reasons for not changing their minds. Many claimed that they were not present when Cox made the inquiry in June. This would have been true, for twenty-five were taking part in a Dublin tournament at the time, and many more had measles and severe colds.[119] Others were in financial straits; some had been granted only limited leave by their employers; while others were in poor health.

The news that twenty-nine Lancers had failed to remain with their squadron had startling effects in New South Wales. In Parramatta one father announced that he would make his son return to South Africa immediately; and a mother said that if her son had returned she would have been at Circular Quay to shoot him.[120] The residents of Berry expressed great relief that ten of the town's Lancers had remained to fight, and only one man, who was ill, had returned.[121] Singleton waited anxiously for an official explanation why two medically fit men from the town's half-squadron had returned.[122] In the city that housed the headquarters staff of the New South Wales Lancers, 'self-possessed businessmen fumed over the slur cast upon Parramatta particularly', and in Parramatta streets small boys called out derisively whenever a Lancer uniform was seen. At near-by Carlingford, a schoolteacher was reported (wrongly) as coming home to a class that planned to stay away from school for two weeks as a protest.[123] And, in addition, the returning men received white feathers and abusive letters.[124]

New South Wales parliamentarians showed extreme embarrassment over the affair during question time in the Legislative Assembly. R. Sleath attacked the Lancers as men who had strutted around Sydney in their flash uniforms, got themselves off to England on a picnic, and then failed when put to a trial. 'They have, practically, brought disgrace upon the colony, and I am perfectly satisfied the people are disgusted with their action'.[125] The member for West Maitland feared that if a Lancer from his district, who 'should have gone' to war, returned to the area he would be tarred and feathered. He regretted that the action of a few should have spoiled the great pride New South Wales experienced when the Lancers volunteered and were treated so magnificently in London as representatives of the colony.[126] J. Cook felt that the affair had placed 'a big and deep stain on the escutcheon of the colony', for the men had passed right by the conflict but were not prepared to lend a hand.[127] A few members suggested that judgement should be suspended until each case was treated on its merits, but none took up the cause of the maligned men.

Following a military inquiry into the matter, General French reported that of the twenty-nine Lancers who had come home, nine were medically unfit for active service, eight were minors who had been ordered back from the Cape by their parents, and five had given satisfactory reasons for returning. He said nothing about the remaining seven. French considered that the men had no responsibility to volunteer but regretted that they had not done so. Colonel Burns passed judgement by observing, 'We have 72 heroes out of 92 men'.[128] So great was the odium attaching to the returned Lancers that all of the seven whose reasons had apparently been regarded as unsatisfactory were reported to have volunteered for service in South Africa by mid-December.[129]

Of these men, Corporal Ben Harkus emerged as a tragic figure. Harkus, a letter carrier on leave without pay, had taken his wife and two children with him to England, where he had been one of the most successful members of the detachment in tournament events. According to a letter from Mrs Harkus to the press, she had persuaded her husband to return home and put their domestic affairs in order before returning to the Cape.[130] Three months after rejoining his regiment in South Africa Harkus died of enteric fever at Bloemfontein.

If the public felt that he had made atonement there was no evidence of their compassion in the press. Only the *Bulletin* saluted him. An anonymous poet recounted Harkus's return home for his family's sake, the jeering he suffered, the white feathers he received, and his return to South Africa so that his children would not be maligned. The poem concluded:

> Sleep deep, Ben Harkus, sleep!
> Men true do mourn thee as a martyr
> To a curse.
> Not true unto thyself thou wert,
> But in thy very failure to maintain
> The cause thy heart deemed right,
> More truth is taught than
> Hadst thou been so.[131]

But Ben Harkus was not allowed to sleep in peace. Many years later his old commander, C. F. Cox, displayed a sad lack of sensitivity when replying in parliament to criticism levelled at the Aldershot detachment by a retired British general. Cox wrongly described Harkus as the only returned Lancer who was not under age, medically unfit, or with adverse family circumstances, and then went on to say that 'when he got back to New South Wales things were made so hot for him that he rejoined us in South Africa and died on service'.[132]

Even before the troopships bearing the first contingent had cleared Australian waters William Lyne took steps to send more troops to South Africa. The premier's motives must be suspect. At the time the advantage in the conflict appeared to rest with Britain, and if Australian participation was intended mainly as a gesture of loyalty that gesture had already been adequately made. Lyne had come under attack from George Reid for having been a follower rather than a leader among the colonies in the rush to arms, and his public statements throughout October had clearly shown that he wished to disprove such criticism. A successful initiative in raising a federal contingent would put his leadership beyond question, and might also please his Queen.

Lyne's move to organize an 'Australasian contingent' in the first days of November began with a telegram to the other colonial premiers:

> In view of complications which may arise, will you authorise me sending message to Secretary of State for the Colonies to the effect that if the British Government will accept, the colonies are prepared to send a second contingent, of an equal number of men, which might be called the 'Australasian Contingent'.[133]

The response must have been disappointing to the New South Wales premier. Of the immediate replies Victoria was prepared to send 250 men if needed, but Queensland thought that nothing more should be done unless further complications arose,[134] and South Australia declined to take part as it was felt that Australian loyalty had been sufficiently demonstrated.[135]

As it transpired, 'complications' did arise which put a completely different complexion on the war. In the words of a noted British historian of the conflict, the 'week which extended from 10 December to 17 December, 1899, was the blackest one known during our generation and the most disastrous to British arms during the century'.[136] The cause for gloom lay in three engagements. At Magersfontein, almost 1000 men were killed or wounded, most of them from famous Scottish regiments. At Stormberg, although fewer than 100 British soldiers were killed or wounded, over 600 were taken prisoner in a humiliating reverse. The final blow of 'Black Week' was administered at Colenso, when General Buller's force suffered 1200 casualties in a futile attempt to relieve Ladysmith. Amid the great wave of patriotic concern that swept the Empire, Lyne moved forward in another attempt to play his part as premier of the mother colony. But this time it was at the prompting of the *Times*.

Alarmed by the defeat at Magersfontein, the *Times* called for more troops, including more colonials, to reinforce the army in South Africa.[137] Lyne immediately cabled the Imperial government concerning the article in the *Times*, and asked if additional troops were required from Australia.[138] At the same time he sent a telegram to the other colonial premiers which read:

'In light of latest war news, should British Government desire colonies send more troops, have I your concurrence in offering an Australian contingent'.[139] The Colonial Office acted quickly on Lyne's inquiry. The Home Government would respond favourably to an offer of troops, and preference was to be given to mounted men who should 'be trained and good shots'.[140] It was generally accepted that the reference was to members of the defence forces, but a further cable from Chamberlain a few days later was taken as opening the second contingent to civilians.[141] The switch of preference to mounted men was inevitable, for the British infantry had fared badly against a fully mounted foe. And to get those horsemen quickly the War Office was prepared to enlist men with no previous military experience.

Parliamentary sanction for the second contingent was, a formality. The colonial executives had responded quickly and favourably to Lyne's inquiry, and had proceeded with their planning, confidently assuming parliamentary endorsement. In the New South Wales Legislative Assembly, only W. A. Holman continued to oppose the war.[142] On both sides of the House the sentiments were widely expressed that Australians were Britishers, that the Empire was in trouble and Australians were of the Empire, and that Australia could not expect help if she did not give help.

In the Queensland Assembly debate was grave and subdued. A. Dawson, the Labor leader and opponent of the first contingent, seconded the motion and dominated the short debate with his efforts to make his shift of ground credible. He spoke of Continental intrigue and hatred of Britain; he dwelt on the seriousness of British defeats; and he expressed concern at the extent of British naval preparations, which he felt could not be explained by a mere Boer threat.[143]

Debate in the Victorian Legislative Assembly was brief and uncompromising. A. McLean, the leader of a new ministry, drew attention to the changed military circumstances and the fact that the Empire was now engaged in a serious struggle.[144] A common opinion among members was that the Empire was at war and there was no room for debate. J. Murray of the Labor party was greeted with the cry of 'Traitor!' when he rose to say that he would not oppose the motion because it would be fruitless to do so.[145] As a diversion he attacked W. A. Trenwith, the Labor leader, whom he described as 'an Imperialist of the Imperialists' because of a patriotic speech delivered at the Town Hall.[146] Trenwith lived up to the title when he moved (but later withdrew) an amendment seeking the deployment of the contingent with Imperial forces anywhere in the world.[147]

Tom Price, the Labor leader in the South Australian Assembly, supported the motion to send the contingent on the grounds that England and the Empire were in trouble. Price had stood strongly against sending the first contingent, but the only ire roused in this debate was directed against William Lyne. One member deplored the action of the New South Wales premier which 'virtually pledged the whole of the colonies without first consulting the other Governments concerned'.[148] Thomas Playford was even more caustic, and possibly very close to the truth, when he denounced Lyne for having 'tried to steal a march upon the other premiers' and for trying 'to get the whole of the kudos for himself, following exactly in the steps of Mr. Dalley in connection with the Soudan'.[149]

The public recanting which took place in the colonial legislatures in December and January cannot be attributed solely to the stunning reverses of 'Black Week'. The defeats to British arms gave a depth and seriousness to the war, placing it beyond the popular idea of 'a promenade to Pretoria', but they could hardly affect the basic question of the tenability of the British cause. Previously dissenting politicians, however, so readily accepted the new military situation as justifying Australian involvement that one suspects they welcomed the opportunity to shift their ground to a position more in line with popular clamour.

William Lyne had taken the initiative in the matter of a second Australian contingent. In the weeks following, he sought to retain for New South Wales the lead he regarded as appropriate to the mother colony. But owing to his own tentative leadership, the rivalry between the two senior colonies, and British ignorance of or antipathy towards the idea, the New South Wales premier failed to organise the colonial units into a federal contingent.

Lyne and his cabinet established the contingent size at 1000 mounted infantry, plus 'A' Battery of the Royal Australian Artillery, which had been offered to the Home authorities for the second time, and half a field hospital, which had been requested by Britain.[150] It was tacitly accepted by the colonial premiers that representation in the mounted infantry force should be roughly on a population basis, with New South Wales making up any discrepancy in numbers. This arrangement promised numerical dominance of the contingent to the mother colony, for the artillery and medical units were both from New South Wales.

The premier was not so successful in taking transport details in hand, although he assured the press (and Lyne was eager to talk to the press about his plans) that his government would make all arrangements to embark the contingent.[151] When he made an offer to Victoria along these lines, however, McLean countered by asking why his colony could not make its own arrangements, seeing that the entire contingent could not go in one ship.[152] Without waiting for a reply, the Victorian premier went ahead with his own transport plan and notified Lyne accordingly. The New South Wales premier made a lame show of retaining control of the situation by telegraphing: 'If you are offered suitable transport of men and horses, then you had better accept. Please let me know what you have done'.[153]

Lyne made an attempt to achieve uniformity of dress for the contingent. In a telegram to McLean he put forward the New South Wales mounted infantry uniform as a possible pattern, and asked if Victorians could be similarly attired.[154] The Victorian reply noted that while the New South Wales uniform differed only slightly from that of Victoria, one important difference was that the Victorian uniform carried no tunic facings, a modification based on the experience of first contingent personnel who had removed all colour from their habiliments of war as a safety measure. It was suggested, therefore, that New South Wales adapt her uniform to that of Victoria.[155]

No communication passed between the two colonies on the sensitive subject of the command of the proposed federal contingent, although both gave much thought to the matter. Victoria did not covet the command. In fact she appeared to concede it to the senior colony. There was strong support in Victorian military circles for the appointment of Colonel Tom Price as leader of the Victorian section of the contingent, but this was regarded as possible only if New South Wales appointed an officer of high rank who could then command the entire Australian contingent.[156] New South Wales proceeded on the

assumption that the command was her right, and Lyne, with
General French in mind, cabled the Home Government seeking
permission for the military commandant to proceed to the front.
But the request was refused.[157] The War Office had not specified a
maximum rank for second contingent officers as it had done for
the first Australian force, when it ruled that no officer above major
could lead a colonial unit. But it would have had little desire to let
loose in South Africa a general with no war experience and
without a command, for the War Office had decided that the
Australians would not be grouped into a brigade.

Faced with so many difficulties the notion of a federal
contingent soon lost momentum, and was brought to a halt finally
by a Colonial Office cable which asked that the Australian
volunteers be organized into units of 125 men.[158] The request was
in line with War Office conditions for the first contingent, but it is
highly likely that Lyne influenced the decision, for the premier was
playing an odd game. On the one hand he sought a federal
contingent, initiated and organized by New South Wales and
commanded by her senior military officer. On the other hand he
sought to break up an Australian federal force which British
authorities had assembled at Enslin in South Africa under the
command of the senior Australian officer on the spot, a Victorian
colonel.[159] Lyne had acted on the reports of New South Wales
officers who complained that they were completely subordinated
to Victorians in what had been called the Australian Regiment. In
order to get his force out of this situation, the premier cabled
London requesting that New South Wales units in South Africa
be attached to similar arms of the Imperial forces.[160]

The time factor indicated a clear connection between Lyne's
action and the Colonial Office call for units of 125 men. The press
published the Colonial Office reply to Lyne and the Colonial
Office request for small units on the same day. The former
communication read: 'Referring to your telegram of 20 December
. . . There can be little doubt that your suggestion will be adopted.
The wishes of the government have been communicated to the
military authorities in South Africa'.[161] Lyne could hardly protest
at the fragmentation of the contingent into small units readily
assimilable into British brigades, and the other colonial premiers
did not mourn the passing of his project.

William Lyne had come to power late in his parliamentary

career, but he laboured hard to make the most of opportunities provided by the war after he assumed the premiership in September 1899. He had not been impressive in matters concerning the first contingent, but after the force had sailed Lyne moved with unnecessary haste to take the initiative in sending more troops. His first attempts were treated coolly by other colonial premiers, but the misfortunes of 'Black Week' gave him his opportunity for personal aggrandizement. His ambitious plan deservedly failed, for his motives appear dishonest in the light of his attitude to the Australian Regiment. But Lyne's motives were not scrutinized in England, and the man who led the Australian colonies in a further act of loyal assistance in the troubled days of December was knighted by his Queen in mid-1900, after only nine months as a political leader.

The heights of egotism reached by this opportunist politician as a result of his war-time role were revealed during question time in the Legislative Assembly. After a member had remarked on the leadership of the makeshift Australian Regiment going to a Victorian, Lyne quite seriously added, 'General Buller has had the temerity to do this without consulting me'.[162]

The second contingent was not raised easily although adversity had brought to the war a more heroic complexion, and volunteers could expect even greater public adulation than the first contingent received. It was harvest time in Victoria when the call to enlist went out through the pages of country newspapers to the men of the part-time defence forces, the majority of whom belonged to country units.[163] Recruiting officers looked first to the Victorian Mounted Rifles for volunteers. The V.M.R., the only mounted regiment in the colony, was the obvious source for 250 mounted infantrymen, but the unit's volunteering record for the first contingent had been poor. Major-General M. F. Downes, the new military commandant, hoped that the likelihood of being led into battle by their peace-time commander, Colonel Tom Price, would encourage more to volunteer for the second contingent, but after two weeks only 119 candidates had come forward out of a V.M.R. strength of over 600. Sixteen of these failed a medical test, and of seventeen married men among the remainder, thirteen were rejected because they had more than two children.[164] Therefore only ninety members of the Victorian contingent were drawn from the elite Mounted Rifles. The minimum age limit for enlistment of twenty years would have excluded some from volunteering, and the preference for single men would have excluded others, but the response from men who had shown a liking for military life was disappointing. Perhaps the martial needs of the bushmen of the V.M.R. were satisfied by a horse and a uniform. Whatever the reasons for the poor turn-out of mounted riflemen, the military commandant was moved to deplore publicly the performance of what he called 'the pet regiment of the colony'.[165]

With 160 places left to fill, the military authorities were obliged to turn for volunteers to the part-time foot regiments. The personnel of these numbered thousands but they only produced 257 candidates. Medical, riding and shooting tests and family limitations reduced the aspirants to the number required.[166] About 700 civilians with some military experience had volunteered, but the authorities decided to enlist serving members of the forces only.[167]

A press report gave a good generalized account of the second Victorian contingent. The average age was 'about 24'; the volunteers from the V.M.R. were 'mostly drawn from the agricultural districts' and were 'sturdy young farmers and graziers'; men from the Victorian Rangers, a volunteer infantry regiment, were 'mainly from the Gippsland districts . . . and from the dry districts of the Wimmera and the north-western parts of the colony'; among the volunteers from the militia infantry battalions were 'a large sprinkling of country bred Australians and a proportion of smart young mechanics from . . . Melbourne and the provincial cities'; and there was a handful of professional soldiers from the permanent artillery garrisons of the capital.[168]

The military efficiency of the improvised mounted unit was questioned by a press correspondent who advocated a delay in its departure for further training. His suggestion was discussed by the minister for defence and Colonel Price, and the latter issued a statement which branded the press report as highly coloured, and claimed that not more than twenty of the contingent could be classed as indifferent horsemen.[169] Price's statement merely confirmed press suspicion that military authorities had gone close to the bottom of the barrel to get their 250 mounted infantry.

New South Wales had far more places to fill than Victoria, for Lyne made no attempt to limit the colony's contribution to its proportional share of the mounted infantry force. His government decided on a force of 810 men, and this was raised without much difficulty, although with the aid of civilian volunteers. 'A' Battery of the Royal Australian Artillery would take 175 men; 92 would go with the half field hospital; the cavalry arm would be represented by 104 members of the Australian Horse and 15 New South Wales Lancers, the latter serving as reinforcements for the Aldershot squadron; there would be three companies of mounted rifles, totalling 399, and an additional 25 men to reinforce the 1st N.S.W.M.R. in South Africa.[170]

As soon as Lyne had made the offer to the Home government, French issued a general order to officers commanding units to supply the names of volunteers.[171] There was no trouble filling the artillery unit from the keen professional soldiers of the R.A.A. The half field hospital also gathered its complement quickly, for who could resist the honour of being called to war by a British general?[172] The main recruiting effort involved the raising of the three companies of mounted infantry and, to a lesser extent, the squadron of cavalry. In the terms of French's general order, volunteers for the mounted infantry, including civilians, were to be 'well trained, good shots, good riders, and medically fit for active service, between the age of 20 and 40, unmarried preferred'.[173]

By 11 January 1900, 1279 recruits claiming to meet those requirements had sought positions. The total was made up of 470 men from the defence forces, 52 police, and 757 civilians.[174] Of those, 484 passed the required medical, shooting and riding tests. The elimination of a further 84 candidates meant that only one man in every three who volunteered was selected.

This process should have ensured a good standard of entrant, but there is some doubt whether all the candidates were genuine aspirants for the contingent. Volunteers were paid from the time they went into camp to undergo elimination tests, but it was considered that this situation was being exploited by some who merely sought a few days pay. So it became the practice to subject men to medical and shooting tests on the day of enrolment, with the result that on some days half the applicants were dispersed by nightfall.[175]

The New South Wales cabinet had favoured the Australian Horse over the other cavalry regiment, the Lancers, on the ground that the latter were already represented in South Africa by a squadron, but the embarrassment caused the government by the Aldershot 'rump' probably influenced the decision.[176] By 11 January 177 troopers out of an Australian Horse strength of 600 were in camp undergoing tests that would reduce them to 104.[177] The Australian Horse was self-regarded and generally accepted as a regiment of bushmen, but good markmanship was not necessarily a corollary of bushmanship. The cavalrymen shot poorly. On one occasion 150 of the volunteers were tested and over 50 rejected on a trial which required a score of only 18 out of a possible 56 points for acceptance.[178] When French farewelled the squadron, he praised its horses and horsemanship but commented unfavourably on its carbine work.[179]

There were 107 applicants for 28 commissions in the New South Wales contingent. Disregarding specialists like chaplains and doctors, the number without military experience was negligible. This would have ensured the selection of a decent type of leader. Biographical sketches of the men selected show that with odd exceptions they were Australian-born or had been in the colonies for many years. Most had been educated at secondary colleges and all were of good social standing.[180] But the man chosen to lead the contingent was an Imperial officer, Lieut-Colonel G. C. Knight, who was to prove an unpopular leader but who initially distinguished himself by refusing to enlist in the mounted infantry any applicant with a foreign accent, so great was his fear of sabotage after an alleged attempt to burn the troopship *Maori King* at Brisbane.[181]

In South Australia disappointment was expressed at the slowness of the mounted arm to volunteer. Of a half-company of fifty men said by their captain to have volunteered, only five turned up for a medical, and other companies showed a similar reluctance.[182] Finally, military authorities enrolled 118 men, from whom they were to select 100, but it was found that many had misrepresented that they could ride and shoot. So the organization of the contingent was held up while officers sought more recruits from both military and civilian sources.[183] The final contingent relied considerably on the latter, forty-four of whom gained selection.[184] Other colonies went through similar difficulties in raising their contingents.

As with the first contingent, there was no rush to enlist by the defence forces. Civilian volunteers showed some degree of enthusiasm, and if Chamberlain had not left the way open for their participation, military authorities would have had to pursue a far more active recruiting campaign to fill the contingent from the ranks. Of the military men who did enlist, many came from foot regiments. Add to these the civilian volunteers, with or without military experience, and you have a hotchpotch mounted infantry force which, in part, lacked any real appreciation of the function of the mounted arm. Nor was this deficiency remedied by training, for the contingent embarked without benefit of any significant military instruction.

In general, press support for the second contingent echoed the note of solemnity and purpose that characterized parliamentary debate. Most newspapers used the war in its recent and adverse stage to point out the emergence of a new Imperial relationship in which the colonies proudly assumed their share of responsibility for the defence of the Empire. The radical press, however, made its last protest before lapsing into resentful silence until the peak of war fever passed. The *Catholic Press* expressed alarm at the decision to send another contingent. William Lyne, it claimed, had been 'intoxicated by the cheers of the thoughtless crowds', and while the journal accepted that it was the duty of professional English soldiers to obey orders, it could not countenance the action of the volunteer.[185] It printed verse that ridiculed the Australian soldier:

> You're a lazy lot of beggars, and you run from work that's hard,
> Seeking "glory"—dressed in khaki and in feathers.

But it was sympathetic to the Boers:

> Let go thy plough—thy rifle seize!
> The plunderer seeks our soil![186]

The same paper attacked another prominent Roman Catholic organ, the *Freeman's Journal*, for 'profession of her loyalty to Judas Chamberlain'.[187]

The *Bulletin*, known widely as 'the bushman's bible', held that 'as a whole' the sentiment of the bush was against the war.[188] It showed its disdain for the city crowds who had farewelled the first contingent by suggesting that if a public holiday was proclaimed for the exhibition and export of a three-legged calf there would be just as many people to see it go. As for the volunteers, they 'would go just as readily to shoot parrots, or Paraguayans, or polar bears, if they had the same amount of Government and newspaper backing, and the same pay, and the same chance of sport'.[189]

Very little war writing found its way into the pages of the *Bulletin*, and when it did it was anti- British. Perhaps this was the result of editorial policy, or perhaps the usual contributors had no stomach for the conflict. Henry Lawson certainly did not, and his theme that bush boredom led to enlistment, as expressed in the satirical 'Blessings of War',[190] was taken up by other *Bulletin* poets.[191] It was unfortunate that Australian blood was first spilled on foreign soil in pursuit of a dubious cause, for this situation denied to the strongly nationalistic literature of the time a stimulating subject.

All but one of the major religious denominations had clearly demonstrated their support for the war at the time the first contingent was raised. The Roman Catholic church had been more circumspect. But as the conflict became more serious its attitude, as expressed by the leading Catholic prelate in the country, became more sympathetic to Australian commitment. Cardinal Moran remarked at the time of the departure of the first contingent that true patriotism rested in staying at home to defend one's own country.[192] He repeated this sentiment at the end of the year, and was non-committal when asked where his sympathies lay in the conflict.[193] But he could not remain silent in the face of the public tumult that surrounded the departure of the second contingent, and he spoke out for the British cause though his expressed reasons were decidedly sectarian. The Boers, he said, were the greatest enemies the Catholic church had ever known, but with the inevitable victory of British arms and a united South Africa the church would have 'freedom to pursue a mission of enlightenment and beneficence'.[194]

Cardinal Moran never enthused over the war in the manner of Anglican spokesmen. Very few Catholic clergy did. This reserve evoked criticism of the Irish-Australian population, and the extent of that criticism is suggested by Catholic reaction. At a public farewell to Father Patrick, the Catholic chaplain to the second contingent, the honoured guest gave two reasons for going to war. One motive was to serve God, and the other was a desire 'that by his action he should give denial to the calumny put forward by the press regarding the attitude of the Irish in Australia'.[195] Archbishop Carr of Melbourne also found it necessary to remind people that Catholics were as vitally involved in the war as any of their fellow citizens.[196]

The churches were permitted to play a much bigger part in the departure of the second contingent. This was probably the result of clerical protests at the omission of the Christian element from the official farewells to the first contingent; and it may have owed a little to the greater need since December for the help of the Almighty in fighting the Boers. There was an impressive church parade for the Victorian unit in the grandstand at Flemington racecourse, where a crowd of 8000 sang the old martial hymns and prayed for the soldiers who 'were going to South Africa in a spirit of patriotism and loyalty, which had called them from their homes to fight for their country'.[197] There was a high mass at St Patrick's cathedral for Catholic volunteers,[198] and Jewish patriotism was demonstrated by a service in the Bourke Street synagogue, where a patriotic address and prayers for Victorian and Imperial troops was climaxed by an enthusiastic rendering of the Anthem and an appeal for the Patriotic Fund.[199]

In Sydney church parades were held at St Andrew's, St Mary's and Centenary Hall. Thousands of citizens flocked to the entrances and when the volunteers were admitted 'the sea of humanity surged in at each building, fighting at the doors like beasts to gain admission'. Women and children were trampled underfoot at St Andrew's.[200] The Anglican archbishop in his address claimed that the war had been forced on Britain, which was striving for 'principles of liberty and justice'. The congregation sang 'Onward Christian Soldiers' and the Anthem with great fervour. The Catholic archbishop moralized on the need for piety and fidelity in the warrior, and the congregation sang '*O Salutaris, Tantum Ergo*', and the 'Hallelujah Chorus'.[201] If the Catholic church was to go along with the war, it would do so with dignified restraint. The most intimate of the Christian farewells occurred in Western Australia, where Anglican and Catholic volunteers breakfasted with their respective bishops after valedictory services.[202]

Other demonstrations associated with the departure of the second contingent showed a continuing interest in the war by the people and their political and vice-regal masters. The enthusiastic public farewell in Melbourne on 13 January was taken as proof that the send-off to the first contingent was no mere passing spasm of patriotic fervour.[203] After personal good-byes ('little family tragedies') at Victoria Barracks, the men were addressed by General Downes. The commandant praised them as soldiers of the Queen and of Victoria who were going to stand shoulder to shoulder with British regulars against a gallant foe. He knew that they would act up to the traditions of their British forefathers but he feared their lack of discipline. Then it was on to Government House where the governor and the premier addressed them. Lord Brassey eulogized their patriotism and thanked them on behalf of the Queen, 'the old country' and 'the United Empire'. McLean, who had a son in action with the 1st V.M.R., spoke with obvious feeling when he wished the men a safe return to their 'dear native land'. But it was the crowd in the streets on that fine Saturday afternoon which provided the heady wine in the feast of adoration. As the contingent swept into the streets with an escort of 4500 members of the defence forces, the crowd went wild. People waved 'clouds of Union Jacks', they cheered, and young ladies broke from the throng to kiss sun-tanned heroes. Colonel Tom Price, proud leader of the contingent and no longer the legendary scourge of striking unionists, was treated to cheers and handshakes. Above the marchers were stretched silent tributes—huge banners which proclaimed: 'For Queen and Empire'; 'Soldiers of the Queen—God Speed'; 'Victoria's Sons will do their duty'; and 'The Empire one and undivided, the world we defy'. On then to Port Melbourne pier and embarkation, with a vast crowd outside the gates cheering and singing, and otherwise diverting themselves by hanging an effigy of Kruger.

A 'myriad small craft' followed the *Euryalus* down the bay. One specially chartered launch carried the Harbour Trust commissioners, Melbourne City councillors, and their families and friends. A larger vessel carried the official party of 400—parliamentarians, public service and military notables, and their families and friends. No one had thought to invite members of the Legislative Council on a similar trip to farewell the first contingent, but they had not been overlooked on this occasion. 'There was scarcely an absentee member of the Council, and they showed they could appreciate the good things of a Parliamentary trip with the best of the Labor party'. From a vantage point on the official vessel, McLean led 'three cheers for the brave fellows of our contingent' as the troopship moved out to sea.

On the way home the government whip took up a collection for the Patriotic Fund which yielded five pounds. A similar benevolence towards the dependants of those who would be maimed or killed in the service of the Empire was displayed by the huge crowds which witnessed the march. Thirty-six firemen and naval brigade members were employed on an incentive basis to work the thronged streets for donations to the Patriotic Fund. They collected £126 2s 11½d.[204]

Sydney said farewell to the New South Wales contingent on Wednesday 17 January. The sun shone and the wind blew on crowds that had been boosted by a government half-holiday for the occasion and a voluntary closure at one o'clock of most businesses. In the words of a leader writer, the send-off was 'a popular demonstration of national unity and enthusiasm which Sydney has certainly never witnessed on the same magnificent scale before'. The streets were gay with flags and with banners that carried patriotic slogans. There was a cheer for Sir George Dibbs who once again marched at the head of the National Guard, and cheers for parliamentary ministers who formed part of the great martial procession in their carriages. William Lyne won his due acclaim and he responded by vigorously raising his hat. Earl Beauchamp was there in the uniform of honorary colonel of the Australian Horse. But despite all the pomp and circumstance, the march soon turned into a most unmilitary spectacle as friends mingled with the marching columns and 'all order was annihilated'. Civilians carried soldiers' kits and rifles (the latter often ornamented with flowers), and soldiers imbibed freely the liquid gifts of elated citizens.[205] The *Bulletin* carried an account of the event that was exaggerated in style rather than in content: 'The march began decently, but in its latter moments it was just as orderly as the downhill rush of the Gadaren [sic] swine, and the evil spirit of Hot Beer was in it, and it knew not where it went, or why'.[206]

Enthusiasm did not stop at the docks, for a multitude of small craft followed the troopships down the harbour. Forming part of this small fleet were three vessels carrying an official party of over 2000, made up of members of both Houses, senior public servants, military officers and other dignitaries, and their ladies.[207] Somewhere amid the tumult of the day Lyne was able to promise the troops glory amid the hardships of war. 'You will make a name for us such as rarely falls to the lot of a youthful country', he said, and he assured them that 'a generous Government and a generous public' would take care of the loved ones of those who fell.[208]

In Adelaide a half-holiday for schools helped swell the crowd which was reckoned at 'quite 50 000'. The display of enthusiasm 'was unparalleled in the history of the colony'.[20] Lord Tennyson bid the troops God-speed in the name of Queen and Empire and South Australia. Lady Tennyson shed a 'womanly tear' at the impressive sight of bronzed young men marching off to fight the Empire's battles. The minister for defence assured the volunteers that they were going to fight for the liberty of their fellow men and for the defence of their country and their Queen.[210] In Western Australia the colony's unit paraded through the streets of Perth with the men from New South Wales and South Australia. 'Patriotism ran rampant' and the soldiers were feted for two days.[211]

Regarded superficially, the second contingent and the war for which it was bound had the enthusiastic support of virtually all Australians. Even the radical press was beginning to temper its traditional anti-Imperialist viewpoint in the light of the threat to Imperial prestige and the public pressures that followed thereon; and the Roman Catholic church had accepted the military expedition to South Africa. But beneath all the cheers and patriotic cliches there existed misgiving over the war. The extent of this attitude is difficult to assess for the vehemence of the pro-war forces soon stifled it, but evidence suggests that it was of significant proportions. In the first six months of the war, particularly the three months following the shocks of 'Black Week', there were numerous instances of individuals, the press, local government bodies, and governments laying complaints or taking action against alleged pro-Boer sympathizers. Admittedly, many allegations were based on the flimsiest of grounds, but when all allowances are made there remain reasons for believing that many Australians were opposed to the war.

The *Grenfell Record*, when describing reports of alleged Boer cruelty to women and children, considered that the 'indignation of even the anti-Britisher and Boer sympathisers in our midst must be aroused'.[212] The *Daily Telegraph* printed an item from Gundagai which claimed that the amount of sympathy shown in the district for the Boers was 'anything but creditable to a British community'.[213] The *Sydney Morning Herald* saw fit to publish resolutions of the Durban Church Council justifying the war because of the view 'in certain quarters' that the war was unjust.[214] Following on a sermon by the rector of St Andrew's, Goulburn, which opposed Australian participation, it was reported that the sentiments expressed 'caused a great deal of discussion in town . . ., by no means altogether antagonistic to the preacher'.[215] A pro-Boer demonstration was actually held in the Sydney Domain but was broken up by opponents who assaulted the speakers.[216]

The electoral fate of some politicians who opposed the war was used by sections of the press to show the reaction of the public to 'Boer sympathizers'.[217] But electoral results can be used to indicate widespread support for men who refused to countenance the war in any way. In the 1898 election for the seat of Grenfell, W. A. Holman beat his opponent by 1115 votes to 892.[218] When Holman faced the electors again in 1901, after uncompromising opposition to the war and consequent denigration by the press, he retained his seat by 1289 votes to 1200.[219] H. B. Higgins was defeated in the Victorian elections of November 1899, but the figures show he was well supported.[220] And when he stood for Northern Melbourne in the first federal elections he was elected by what he claimed was the largest majority over a second candidate achieved by any member in the new parliament.[221] J. Murray was returned for Warrnambool in 1897 by 860 votes to 629.[222] Although he led the Labor party in bitter opposition to the first contingent and was attacked both inside and outside parliament for 'disloyalty', he retained the seat in the elections of November 1899 by 1035 votes to 990.[223]

It was easy to point to reduced winning margins as proof of public disapproval, but the simple fact remains that a majority of voters in certain electorates favoured candidates who were unequivocally opposed to the war. Other factors may have influenced their support: perhaps the war was not a major issue with them. This would indicate apathy towards Australian involvement, and a fair inference could be that the three major political opponents of the war were returned by people who thought as the candidates did or did not care that they thought as they did.

Repressive action taken by a whole range of persecutors from governments down to individuals seemed to indicate widespread disaffection over Australian participation, if it did not indicate primarily a state of war hysteria. The phenomenon was remarked upon by the *Sydney Morning Herald*. A leading article noted 'something resembling a heresy-hunt' which revealed itself in 'a tendency to suspect people of disloyalty because they happen to express themselves freely about the war'. It also noted that it was usually public servants, especially schoolteachers and policemen, who were singled out for attack and mostly on 'trivial charges of disloyalty'.[224]

The New South Wales government was not slow to move on reports of 'disloyalty'. Its main inquisitor was J. Perry, the minister for public instruction. Perry, acting on information that 'several' schoolteachers had expressed disloyal sentiments, began an independent inquiry into a case he considered worthy of investigation.[225] A fortnight later he reported that there was no foundation for the charge.[226] But he considered that his zeal had not been in vain. When unveiling a memorial tablet to the second New South Wales soldier to die at the front (a schoolteacher), he spoke of rumours which accused teachers of telling pupils that the war was unjust. 'He had felt strongly on the subject, and at once put a stop to anything of this kind, and he believed that there was now in his and all the departments a unanimous feeling of loyalty to the Empire'.[227]

Further government action which may have encouraged this 'unanimous feeling of loyalty' was directed against a Newcastle policeman. Following a Police Board of Inquiry the constable was dismissed from the force on the grounds that, while in uniform, he 'loudly protested in public places, including the railway station and tram cars, against the action of Great Britain in regard to the Transvaal war and applauded the Boer victories'.[228]

An Adelaide newspaper reported that claims were frequently made that South Australian public servants were disloyal in their attitude to the war. The government investigated all such reports and warned of instant dismissal if 'disloyalty' occurred again.[229] The Western Australian government was said to be investigating treasonable utterances among railway, customs and police employees at Albany.[230]

W. McCulloch took a strong line against Victorian 'disloyalty'. In a discussion in the Legislative Council he called attention to action taken by other colonial governments, and asked the premier to proclaim that summary dismissal faced any Victorian public servant guilty of uttering disloyal expressions. McCulloch based his move on a conversation with the stationmaster of a 'large central country station' who stated that the place 'was seething with disloyalty'. He was informed further that a similar state of affairs existed at another large country station and at several smaller ones. He also received letters complaining of disloyalty at Flinders Street, Spencer Street and Prince's Bridge stations. Other informants had reported that a police constable in a large Gippsland town had expressed the hope that the Boers would win, that two disloyal men in an office at the Education Department were constantly jeering about the war, and that a schoolteacher was advocating the Boer cause.

The responsible minister assured McCulloch that 'if any Boer sympathisers came under the notice of the Government, whether they received Government pay or not, the Government would know how to deal effectively with them'. The government, he said, had received a few anonymous letters but inquiries had revealed little substance in the charges.[231]

The heresy hunt bore fruit when a public meeting of civil servants was held in Melbourne to express sympathy with Great Britain and to raise funds for the third contingent. The seconder of the loyal motion admitted to 'a small leaven of disloyal persons in the service', who had been quietened, however, by the weight of public opinion.[232] Some Victorian police likewise became zealous contributors to patriotic funds as a defensive gesture against public criticism[233]

Local government authorities also felt it their duty to respond to activities they considered disloyal. At Ballina, in New South Wales, the council resolved to employ no person who was known to be disloyal to the British cause in the present war, or expressed pleasure or satisfaction when the British suffered reverses.[234] A number of instances of local government activity in support of the war occurred in Victoria. The Eaglehawk Borough Council resolved to dismiss any employees 'proved to have used disloyal expressions towards Her Majesty and the troops in South Africa'.[235] The Warrnambool Water Trust did likewise,[236] and so did Prahran Council.[237] Kew Council allowed a similar motion to lapse because if passed it would have reflected on the body of council employees, but discussion indicated that any offenders would be dismissed.[238] All but one member of Mudlawirra South District Council walked out and refused to serve with the chairman, A. Both, because of alleged pro-Boer utterances. Mr Both denied having said that one Boer was equal to nine Englishmen.[239]

Unofficial groups of citizens also took action. Loyalists posted placards around Stawell requesting 'that all true British subjects . . . should boycott any person, whether in the Government service or in business who . . . makes bold to openly avow themselves [sic] Boer sympathisers'.[240] Horsham and Mt Gambier carried out the same exercise against 'disloyalists',[241] and residents of Charlton formed an 'Anti-Boer League' pledged to boycott businesses whose proprietors expressed pro-Boer sentiments.[242]

An overflow meeting at Murwillumbah, New South Wales, resolved:

> That in view of the reported disloyal utterances of persons in receipt of Government moneys in this district this meeting requests the heads of departments to make the fullest investigations into the same with the object of procuring the instant dismissal or disqualification of such traitors.[243]

And a meeting of raspberry-pickers at South Wandin in Victoria resolved not to pick for any grower with pro-Boer sympathies, and to duck in the creek and drive from the field any picker with similar feelings.[244] But for an individual effort in what passed for patriotism none could beat the proprietor of a steam thresher, who announced that he would not employ anyone with Boer sympathies, and then set out through the Victorian countryside with a Union Jack flying from the engine funnel.[245]

Sections of the German population in Australia may have expressed some sympathy with the Boers, or they may simply have remained aloof from the patriotic excesses of the time. Whatever the case, they aroused the ire of bodies of citizens. At Natimuk, in Victoria, a sports meeting was halted while German-born residents and those who resented their alleged Boer sympathies fought an hour-long battle.[246] In South Australia 4000 Moonta residents paraded to mark their disapproval of 'the Pro-Boers of Moonta . . . mostly Germans'. The crowd sang patriotic songs, made patriotic speeches, and burned effigies of local citizens who were regarded as being sympathetic to the enemy.[247] And in Broken Hill the German Club was stormed by stone-throwing mobs.[248]

In just four months from October 1899 the Australian colonies had pledged and re-pledged themselves to fight for the Empire, and had honoured those pledges amid scenes of wild and apparently unqualified enthusiasm. But what was the depth of real support for the war? By December parliamentarians were almost unanimously in favour of the war, although the sincerity of some of them could be questioned. The press, with a few notable exceptions, was for it. The churches were for it, with the Catholic church running a poor second to the Protestant churches in enthusiasm. But there are good reasons for believing that a lot of ordinary people passively opposed the war, although the extent of that opposition is hard to estimate. The indifferent response of the defence forces to the call to arms, something which is very difficult to explain, could have been partly the result of a grass-roots distaste for the war, because public acclaim of the volunteer is a necessary condition for successful recruiting. During the war Australia sent eight contingents totalling about 16 000 men, but that number represents too small a percentage of the available manpower to indicate a major war effort. The exuberant scenes in the streets could be taken as mass support for the war, although it is more likely that they represent a bored population's craving for novelty, for in turn the crowds went wild about and then lost interest in the public farewells, the receptions for invalids, and the receptions for returning contingents. The Mafeking celebrations of May 1900 and the welcomes to the returning first contingent in December 1900 were the last big public demonstrations, and they were more notable for acts of larrikinism and over-indulgence than for displays of genuine patriotism.

The campaign against the 'pro-Boers' certainly pointed to the existence of a body of opposition, for the attacks were too widespread not to have had some factual basis, and were so virulent that their purpose must have been to intimidate persons who were or might become sympathetic to the Boer cause.

Intimidation certainly had its effect, because after the wild accusations of the early months of 1900 no one gave the heresy-hunters any further cause for concern; and with all dissent effectively silenced the magnitude of opposition to the war became quite unmeasureable.

3 The First and Second Contingents in the Field

When war broke out in South Africa, no one with any inkling of the respective military strengths of the protagonists would have envisaged a conflict lasting more than two and a half years, but then no one could have foreseen that the superiority of the British Empire in treasure and in men would be countered in part by factors peculiar to this war.

During the course of the struggle, Britain and her colonies committed 448 435 troops. The Transvaal and the Orange Free State, supplemented by rebels from Cape Colony and small numbers of mercenaries from America and several European countries, committed an estimated 87 000.[1] To take a more specific figure, by November 1900, 195 000 British troops faced an estimated 30 to 50 000 Boers.[2] This numerical superiority was more apparent than real, for the British force was predominantly infantry while the Boer army was fully mounted. A preponderance of foot soldiers was appropriate to a conventional war, but the South African War turned out to be anything but conventional, although British generals did their utmost to employ traditional military tactics in the early months of the conflict. This brought into confrontation two fundamentally different military systems, and it was the Boer system which prevailed in so far as the British had to adapt to it as best they could. Frontal attacks on concealed Boer positions by stolid infantrymen marching in close formation had to be abandoned, for the British had to face the scourge of the modern high-powered rifle. The highly efficient .276 German Mauser was the standard Boer weapon, and it could kill at 2500 yards. Boer tactics were geared to the Mauser. A rifleman could conceal himself on one of the many kopjes (small hills) which dotted much of the landscape of the battle area, and at a safe distance take unhurried aim at the enemy advancing over open country. Nor would his firing reveal his whereabouts, because smokeless powder was then in common use. Having taken toll of the oncoming force, the Boer would abandon his position and, superb horseman that he was, would scamper to safety. The Boer soldier despised unnecessary self-sacrifice and scorned the heroics of war, thinking it more sensible to live to fight another day. His readiness and ability to break off an engagement when it suited him completely spoiled British tactics. It also greatly irritated his enemy, including the Australians, who deplored the fact that the Boer would not stand and fight. The bayonet was not a part of Boer equipment, so there was no chance of the toe to toe combat that Australian soldiers fancied themselves at.

The British army found it difficult to adjust to Boer methods of warfare, for according to *The Times History* it was not composed of very adaptable material. The common soldier was recruited mainly from the ranks of the unskilled town labourer, and in physique and intelligence was below the nation's average. Officer training was stereotyped and failed to develop initiative, and the majority of the generals were incompetents who had risen through seniority, or a successful expedition against native forces, or by social influence. 'Regarded as an institution . . . the British army of 1899 was undoubtedly a success' said the critic, but 'as a fighting machine it was largely a sham'.[3] Any war would have created problems for the Imperial military structure, but its troubles were multiplied by the novel character of the South African War.

One section of the Imperial forces which found adaptation to the Boer fighting style relatively easy, however, was the colonial component. During the course of the war 30 628 volunteers were drawn from the overseas colonies and an estimated 52 000 from South Africa.[4] These men were better able to endure the rigours and disease of veldt warfare, and better able to find their way in the vast land and live off its resources. Above all, they were horsemen and as such they doubled the mounted force in an essentially equestrian war, although they comprised only twenty per cent of the South African Field Force. The colonials, therefore, despite their limited military training, were able to make a contribution to the war quite out of proportion to their numbers.

The South African volunteers, formed into some ninety different corps, were not uniformly good. The overseas colonials won a much more favourable reputation and Australians, numbering 16 378 men, comprised more than half of this category. The six Australian colonies sent their troops to South Africa in eight contingents (see Appendix C) but it was the men of the first two contingents who did most to create an image of the Australian soldier. Drawn mainly from the part-time defence forces, these 3000 volunteers took part throughout 1900 in the great sweeping manoeuvres of Lord Roberts which reduced the war to purely guerrilla operations. Their work was almost completely separate from that of the third and fourth contingents. These were the corps of Bushmen, raw citizen soldiers who arrived in Africa hot on the heels of the first contingents, but who were destined for operations peripheral to Roberts's thrust into the Boer homelands.

The voyage to the Cape took about four weeks from the eastern colonies, and life aboard the transports was arduous for the mounted men in particular, for they were in almost constant attendance on their horses. The infantry fared better, but for all troops there were parades, drills, lectures and occasional shooting practice at boxes thrown into the sea. The men accepted the routine readily enough, for the great majority had received the benefit of some military training and were keen to get on with the business of war.

The monotony of the Indian ocean was broken for the men of Queensland's second contingent when an attempt was made to set the *Maori King* on fire. There had been a previous attempt to burn the ship before it left Brisbane. This time the incendiarist came closer to succeeding when he poured kerosene on hay in the hold and ignited it. Luckily the fire was detected early and tragedy was averted. Much to the disappointment of many, who had regarded German crew members as potential saboteurs, the culprit turned out to be a Briton.[5]

Unfortunately there was widespread theft of personal equipment aboard the transports. A propensity among Australians to regard items of government issue as fair game was aggravated by regular kit parades, which led to disciplinary measures against soldiers with deficient kits.[6]

Despite the strained relationships which must have resulted from the high incidence of petty theft, harmony generally prevailed aboard the transports. There was one inter-colonial incident, however, which cast its shadows ahead.

Shortly after the *Medic* sailed from Melbourne, Major G. A. Eddy of the Victorian infantry unit made a move to assume responsibility for the Tasmanian contingent in addition to his own command. Eddy was acting under Queen's regulations which gave command of troops on a transport to the senior officer, but Captain C. Cameron of the Tasmanians wished to retain separate command of his unit.[7] When informed of the situation, the Victorian minister for defence suggested to the premiers of Tasmania, South Australia and Western Australia, the colonies sharing the *Medic*, that there was no need for any officer to interfere with the unit of any other colony. But should the occasion arise when a decision of the senior officer was required, the parties involved should defer to Colonel J. C. Hoad, a Victorian among a small group of Australians known as Special Service officers, who were proceeding to South Africa for experience with British forces. At the same time McCulloch instructed Eddy to restrict his command to the Victorian force.[8] McCulloch's recommendations were accepted by the other colonies, and the Australian forces aboard the *Medic* proceeded to South Africa under four distinct commands.

The first contingent arrived at the Cape just before 'Black Week'. At the time Britain had four armies deployed. General Sir Redvers Buller, commander-in-chief in South Africa, was bogged down in Natal before the main Boer thrust which had succeeded in investing Ladysmith. General Sir W. Gatacre was operating in north-eastern Cape Colony against a Boer invasion which aimed at inciting rebellion among the Dutch population. General John French was facing a similar invasion in the Colesberg district of northern Cape Colony. In the west Lord Methuen was moving uncertainty towards besieged Kimberley. The British were on the defensive, although the Boer advances had lost much of their momentum through the investment of Mafeking, Kimberley and Ladysmith.

The second week of December confirmed what the first weeks of the war had suggested: that British generalship was deficient and that British scouting was all but non-existent. Out of the catastrophes of Magersfontein, Stormberg, and Colenso some good did come, however. The Empire drew closer together, and Lord Roberts was appointed to take over from the indecisive Buller.

The events of December were important to the Australians for they exposed the limitations of the professional British soldier and his leaders. The obvious inference was that unorthodox tactics were called for, and in this type of warfare the colonial irregulars felt they had a peculiar competence. The whole situation was a boost to their confidence. The appointment of Roberts also favoured the colonials, for the new commander advocated flanking movements and stressed the need for better scouting. Both these tactics demanded good horsemen, and the best horsemen were colonials. But Roberts did not sail for the Cape until 23 December 1899, and the men of the first contingent were to see some action before they came under the command of the charismatic field-marshal.

The New South Wales Lancers from England were the first colonial troops to land in South Africa, thus fulfilling the ardent hopes of William Lyne. On 2 November seventy-two of them went ashore, lacking horses and adequate equipment. These deficiencies were remedied sufficiently to allow twenty-nine Lancers to go forward and join Lord Methuen's force at De Aar, where it was poised for the drive north towards Kimberley. The remaining forty-three, when horsed and equipped, joined French's cavalry brigade in the Colesberg area, where they were reinforced by a detachment of thirty-six Lancers from New South Wales in early December.

The rest of the first contingent were initially located at points along the western railway. The N.S.W.A.M.C. opened a hospital at Orange River Station. The Q.M.I. went to Belmont, the N.S.W.M.R. to De Aar, and the V.M.R. and all infantry units to Enslin. To many of the troops it seemed that their worst fears were realized. They were relegated to a line of communications role while the real action was going on in Natal and with Lord Methuen's force towards the Modder River. The Colesberg area was also regarded as a minor front.

The first Australians to see action were the twenty-nine Lancers who had joined Methuen's column.[9] The general moved out from the Orange River on 21 November with a force of 8500 men, only 850 of whom were mounted. His objective was to relieve Kimberley but the imbalance of his column, poor scouting, and poor tactics led to Methuen's having to turn back on his heels after a troubled advance of three weeks duration. At Belmont a

Boer force of about 2000 attacked the British flank, inflicted sharp casualties, and then broke off the engagement. Methuen's cavalry and mounted infantry were unable to halt the retreat and bring the Boers to battle because of their limited numbers and because their horses were exhausted from reconnaissance work prior to battle. The fight at Graspan showed a similar deficiency in the mounted arm. At Modder River, Methuen made an unwise frontal attack on a strong Boer force which retreated with impunity after leaving seventy-one British dead on the field. The battle of Magersfontein emphasized Methuen's tactical incompetence and resulted in even heavier casualties before the British force retreated to the Modder.[10]

The troop of New South Wales Lancers could hardly have been expected to play a significant part in Methuen's advance, because its numbers were negligible in a mounted force which itself was almost completely ineffectual. But partisan accounts capitalized on the fact that the men had been exposed to shot and shell. One writer stated that their part in the advance had brought the Lancers 'into great prominence'.[11] Another claimed that Methuen 'repeatedly complimented them in person on their steadiness under heavy fire', and said that the British regiments gave them the title of the 'Fighting Twenty-Nine'.[12] And another wrote that they had won the acclaim of military critics for their effort at Graspan where, operating at the rear of the Boer position with twenty British regulars, they looked like being cut off by the Boer retreat but remained steady and diverted the enemy with their fire.[13] The troop went south to the Colesberg area after Magersfontein and joined up with the remainder of the squadron serving under General French.

Methuen's defeat marked the beginning of 'Black Week', and as the year drew to a close, gloom settled over the Empire and the South African Field Force. Then came an event, a mere skirmish, which was given acclaim far beyond its due because it represented a British victory after weeks of defeat and stalemate. This time Australians formed the most significant part of the British force engaged.

On 1 January 1900, Colonel T. D. Pilcher, an Imperial officer and commander at Belmont, led an attack on a laager (camp) of Cape Colony rebels at Sunnyside, to the north-west of Belmont. His force consisted of 200 men of the Q.M.I., 100 Canadian

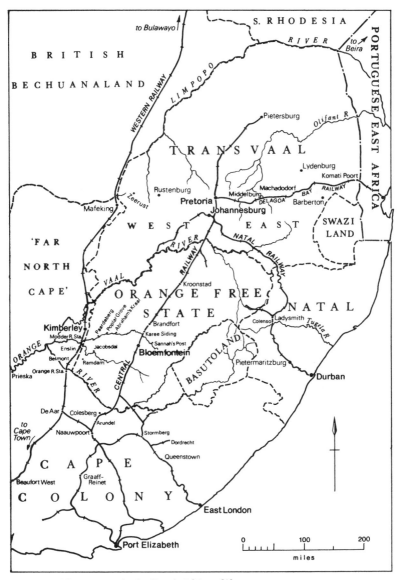

Theatre of Operations in the South African War

infantrymen, 40 British regular mounted infantry and artillery support.[14] The first casualties came when five Queenslanders on scout duty rode into strong Boer fire. The horses of Lieutenant Adie and Private Victor Jones were killed under their riders. Adie was wounded but carried from the field by a comrade; Jones was mortally wounded and died where he fell, the first member of an Australian contingent to give his life on the South African battlefields.[15]

Pilcher then began his attack. He sent the Canadians and the regulars straight at the laager, and deployed the Queenslanders in an enveloping movement on the Boer right flank, where they worked from ridge to ridge so skilfully that they surprised the enemy. Another young Queenslander, Private McLeod, was killed in the exchange of fire before the artillery helped bring the fight to a conclusion. The Boers retreated but the men of the Q.M.I. swept forward and took 41 prisoners. The wounded on both sides were tended by three ambulances of the N.S.W.A.M.C. which had been detached from the Orange River hospital for service with the Queenslanders.[16]

As the victorious troops returned to camp, the Canadians sang 'The Maple Leaf' and 'The Niagara Camp Song'.[17] One wonders what the Australians sang. Was it 'Soldiers of the Queen'? Perhaps this was the very first occasion when Australians felt the dire need for a national song.

The brief engagement at Sunnyside had important consequences. *The Times History* saw the victory as one of considerable strategic importance, helping to check rebellion in the area, securing Methuen's line of communication from attack from the west, and lifting British morale after a succession of reverses.[18] The stocks of the untried Australian soldiers rose sharply because of the wide and favourable publicity given to the event. Under the heading of 'Colonial Gallantry' the *Advertiser* published a London cable which stated that the 'Queenslanders behaved magnificently throughout the engagement, and while under fire chatted and laughed together with the utmost sangfroid'.[19]

At least three contemporary histories of the South African war owe much to this report, each of them stressing the nonchalance of the Queenslanders under fire.[20] But the *Catholic Press* observed sourly that 'in spite of the efforts of the daily press to swell the skirmish into a British victory it was clearly a small beer affair'.[21]

Another consequence of the Sunnyside skirmish is not well documented but one might presume that it came to pass. Rudyard Kipling gave it some substance in an article called 'Hospital Train Number Three'. The piece referred briefly to numerous occupants of the train, one of whom was a Queenslander who 'blew' furiously over Sunnyside.[22]

The action of Pilcher in giving the Q.M.I. the key role in the Sunnyside attack when he had a company of regular mounted infantry at his disposal (they were held in reserve), showed that a British commander was prepared to treat the colonials no differently from the regulars.[23] But there is little reason why he should not have placed his trust in a unit of confident and dashing irregulars in a small fight against a group of rebel farmers.

Two days after Sunnyside the New South Wales Mounted Rifles also moved against the Cape Colony rebels as part of a force commanded by Colonel E. Alderson, another Imperial officer. But theirs was a futile affair. Marching on Prieska, the column easily dislodged the few rebels who commanded the town, and eighty troopers of the N.S.W.M.R. and twenty-five South African irregulars were left in occupation.[24] A week of cricket matches and general fraternizing with the loyalists of Prieska followed, but Captain Antill of the N.S.W.M.R. led his men hurriedly out of town on hearing that a large rebel force was grouping. The Boers occupied the town an hour after Antill's departure, but were driven out when Alderson came up with 1000 troops to reinforce the former garrison. However, the column merely marched into and out of Prieska and back to the Orange River station in a fruitless demonstration of the British presence. The rebels quickly re-occupied Prieska and ordered the loyalists out because of their collaboration with Antill's command.[25] Not even the most partisan of correspondents could have turned the Prieska episode into a tale of military prowess, and the N.S.W.M.R. had to wait many weeks for an engagement that lent itself to such treatment.

The Australian infantry units had to undergo trial and tribulation before they saw action. When the foot soldiers from Victoria, South Australia, Western Australia and Tasmania arrived in South Africa, together with the V.M.R., the British command at the Cape decided to form them (and the New South Wales infantrymen when they arrived) into a force that became known as the Australian Regiment. It is not clear why the British authorities decided to depart from their original intention of attaching each colonial unit to a regular regiment as an extra company, but expediency could have been a factor in the decision. What readier way was there to dispose of five companies of colonial irregulars than to leave them in the grouping in which they had proceeded to the seat of war? Accordingly, the loose command structure which had prevailed aboard the *Medic* was formalized and extended. Colonel J. C. Hoad was given command, although as a Special Service officer he had proceeded to South Africa in the vague expectation that he would be given a place on General Buller's staff. Major G. A. Eddy of Victoria was made second in charge. Captain G. R. Lascelles, an Imperial officer accompanying the South Australian contingent, was made adjutant; and Sergeant A. W. Johnson of South Australia was appointed regimental sergeant-major.[26] William Lyne's hopeful boast that the New South Wales contingent would beat the Victorians to the Cape had not been fulfilled, and the result was that officers from the mother colony, arriving late, received no regimental appointments. The rancour that ensued placed in jeopardy the concept of a federal regiment.

The Australian Regiment stayed only briefly at Cape Town, where the men's physique and soldierly bearing brought favourable comment from Lord Milner, the British high commissioner, and others.[27] Some attention had to be given to the regiment's uniforms, which were not federal in appearance although several colonies had achieved a basic uniformity of field service dress by 1899. The changes effected, however, were more in the interest of safety than of uniformity. In deference to Boer markmanship, coloured facings were removed from tunics, as were all insignia and badges of rank; and the distinctive Western Australians had to discard their blue jumpers and blue putties in exchange for khaki gear. The superior physique of the Australians became very evident when it was found that most of the British clothing stock would not fit the colonials. An important armaments change was the substitution of the magazine Lee-Metford rifle for the Australians' single-loading Martini-Enfield.[28]

The regiment arrived at Enslin just in time to watch the yellow lyddite shells splashing on the hills of Magersfontein, twenty miles to the north, as Methuen's Highlanders were locked in combat with General Cronje's force. And as all fell quiet on the western front the Australian Regiment took up an important but uneventful existence as one link in the chain of garrisons which protected Methuen's communications from De Aar to the Modder. 'Guarding the jam' was hardly an operation to satisfy the military aspirations of the Australians, however, and discontent with the state of affairs became a factor in the inter-colonial dissension which developed at Enslin.

When the regiment had passed through the Orange River station on its way north, Colonel W. D. C. Williams of the N.S.W.A.M.C. enthused over the formation of the federal force. 'We have sunk all provincialism and have driven another nail for the military federation of the colonies', he wrote.[29] But that was before the New South Wales infantry company joined the regiment at Enslin.

As soon as the unit arrived at the Cape its commander, Captain J. G. Legge, expressed disappointment at the amalgamation of the Australian military companies, because his corps was thus 'prevented from gaining experience with an Imperial Battalion'.[30] But after a few days at Enslin Legge's disappointment turned to envy and chagrin because, according to him, the Victorians were 'outrageously favoured in everything, even rations'. So the New South Wales company commander sought to forward through Colonel Hoad a letter to British authorities asking that his unit be attached to an Imperial regiment, but Hoad refused to pass on the request.[31] There was evidence that discontent at Enslin was not confined to Captain Legge, nor to New South Wales officers.[32] But while the plea from several officers was for service with British battalions, complaints were invariably directed at Victorian monopoly of senior commands in the Australian Regiment. Letters from New South Wales other ranks at Enslin at this time voiced no dissatisfaction with the organization of the regiment, thus adding to the impression given by the statements of disgruntled officers that the main motive for discontent was professional jealousy.

Amid the discord Colonel Hoad tried hard to make his command succeed and to engender into the sceptics his belief in the significance of the very first federal military force. Typical of his leadership was his visit to every tent on Christmas Day to speak to the troops.[33] And at a combined colonial concert on 26 January he reminded an audience of Australians, Britons and Kaffirs of the new role of Australia as a partner in Empire.[34]

The military situation in South Africa was changing rapidly, however, and circumstances were to cast the Australian Regiment back into fragments, thereby either denying the force the chance to show what a group of Australians of battalion size could do, or else saving it from the ignominy of more serious internal strife.

Lord Roberts arrived in South Africa in mid-January 1900 and immediately set about evolving a new strategy, aided by the mistakes of Buller and Methuen and his own more astute military mind. The field-marshal's first priority was to increase the mobility of his field force. He did this principally by raising as quickly as possible irregular mounted units from among the Cape colonials, and by ordering those regular infantry battalions that had not already done so to provide a mounted infantry company. Roberts knew that the Australian and New Zealand second contingents were due to arrive in February, but he looked to further help from the antipodes in the form of the Australian Regiment at Enslin. Why not convert the five companies of foot to mounted infantry? So began the horsing of the Australians. At the first call for volunteers for conversion 450 men responded out of 580. The remainder soon changed their minds and Colonel Hoad was able to offer the entire regiment as a mounted force. A war correspondent stated that 'few of the men were without equestrian experience of some sort'[35] but, nonetheless, Enslin camp became the scene of much activity as the Australians practised their horsemanship, bareback on transport mules because there were no horses available.

Their 'training' completed, the regiment moved south to the Colesberg area on 2 January where their physique again won praise, this time from a British general.[36] But the Australians were in no mood for compliments because they considered themselves to have been cast into the military wilderness, away from the advance on Kimberley and the rumoured invasion of the Orange Free State from the west. Little did the men of the Australian Regiment realize that the Colesburg operations were to provide them with ample opportunity to become acquainted with war. But before they spilled their blood upon the veldt, the

Australian cavalry were to feature in an incident which did little for the embryonic military reputation of the Australian contingent.

By the end of 1899 the troop of New South Wales Lancers who had been attached to Methuen's force rejoined the rest of the Aldershot men near Colesberg. As reinforcements from New South Wales had already joined the unit the squadron now stood at full strength. The Lancers formed part of the command of General John French, whose function was to prevent a Boer invasion of Cape Colony and protect the flanks of Methuen and Gatacre. Also included in this force were two troops of Australian Horse who had formed part of the New South Wales mounted infantry unit of the first contingent, but who now found themselves part of the cavalry arm to which they claimed to belong.

At dawn on 16 January 1900 a mixed patrol of fourteen Lancers and seven Australian Horse, commanded by Lieutenant W. Dowling of the latter regiment, set out to reconnoitre Boer positions at Slingersfontein near Rensburg.[37] Perhaps the colonial cavalry were keen to the point of indiscretion; perhaps their proficiency was countered by colonial brashness and inexperience. Whatever the reason, the Australians did not exercise the great caution needed in hostile country and, as they proceeded across a plain surrounded by small kopjes, they fell among a party of wrathful Boers. A. B. Paterson, the war correspondent attached to French's force, was able to piece together a good account of the ambush and its tragic consequences. Dowling, when surprised, led his men towards a near-by kopje with somewhere between forty and a hundred Boers in pursuit, only to find the position occupied by another party of the enemy. At that it was a case of every man for himself, but a wire fence hindered escape and only six troopers were able to break out of the trap. Of the remaining sixteen, one man was killed, another mortally wounded, and fourteen were taken prisoner, including several wounded men.

When the news of the disaster got back to camp, the wildly excited Australians wanted to set out immediately in the hope of aiding their comrades, but the Imperial brigade commander refused because of approaching darkness. At daylight next morning an Australian party set off for the scene of ambush, and there, amid noisy vultures that feasted on the carcases of slain horses, lay two forms. One was the body of Sergeant-Major Griffin of the Australian Horse. The other was the mortally wounded Corporal Kilpatrick of the New South Wales Lancers. Kilpatrick's lower jaw had been shattered by a bullet, and he had also been shot through the lungs. His wounds had been roughly bandaged by the Boers. It is not difficult to imagine the pain endured by the teacher from Leichhardt Superior Public School during the long night alone on the veldt, but his suffering was emphasized by the word 'cold' written in the dust by the finger of the dying Lancer. Griffin was buried where he had fallen. Kilpatrick died before the day had passed and was buried alongside two New Zealanders on a slope above Slingersfontein farm.[38]

One contemporary historian regarded the episode as 'another lesson as to the need of watchfulness and most careful scouting'.[39] Another suggested that the disaster 'might have been averted if Lieutenant Dowling had shown little less pluck and made up for the deficiency in caution'.[40] But the criticism loses some of its point in the light of a discovery by Paterson when visiting the scene of the fight a few days after the event. A Boer pony acquired by the correspondent broke away and was chased by a trooper. Soon both the pursuer and the pursued dropped out of sight on the open veldt, hidden by a depression which concealed forty grazing mares and their foals. It was from this point that the Boer attack on Dowling's troop had originated.

Following Slingersfontein, the Australian cavalry were retired to a rest camp at Arundel. 'The loss of Dowling and his troop had cast a gloom over everything', wrote Paterson, 'and it looks as if the authorities are afraid of risking any more losses to the volunteers than they can help'.[42] Colonel Porter, the British brigade commander, inquired into the incident and held that the ambush had been an accident and that no one was to blame.[43] The Lancers and Australian Horse saw no more action in the Colesberg area, however, and by early February had moved north to the Modder with French's cavalry, leaving the defence of northern Cape Colony to General Clements and a force that included the Australian Regiment. French had done well, and *The Times History* specifically praised the competence of the horse artillery, 'the steadiness of the Berkshires' and 'the gallantry of the New Zealanders'.[44] The Australians received no honourable mention. After all, they had blemished the record of the British army's premier cavalry commander.

A. G. Hales, an Australian war correspondent who later met the wounded Dowling in a Boer hospital, wrote an account of the Slingersfontein skirmish which showed that the affair was not without gallantry on the part of the Australians. Dowling would not discuss his contribution to the fight, but Hales got it from a Swede who had been with the Boer force. In the first fusillade of bullets Dowling's horse was shot from under him and several of his men wounded. Urging the unscathed members of the troop to ride for their lives Dowling turned his rifle on the attackers, but he was soon down with a bullet wound in the head. Then he was on his feet again, only to be felled by a shot which blew off his thumb. But he rose again, firing away with his revolver. 'He looked like a gamecock as he stood in the sunlight, his face all bathed in blood . . . and his shattered hand numbed beside him', recounted the Swede. Two bullets in the legs dropped him by his dead horse, but it took a blow on the head with a rifle butt to finally quieten the Mudgee lieutenant.[45]

An important consequence of Dowling's misfortune was the beginning in Australia of a more tolerant attitude towards the Boers. When he returned to Sydney early in May Dowling spoke of the kindly treatment he had received as a wounded prisoner of war and testified that the Boer, in the main, was an admirable foe.[46] Two days after the publication of the officer's views, the *Sydney Morning Herald*, in an editorial comment, praised the humanity of the Boers and noted a changing attitude in Australia which was beginning to recognize 'the better personal qualities' of the enemy and 'his splendid courage and constancy in a desperate cause'.[47]

Paterson had written in January that the British military authorities would be happy to get more colonials because of the way the Queenslanders and Canadians had fought at Sunnyside and the New South Wales Lancers elsewhere.[48] Knowing the modest character of the military operations involved, one might suspect Paterson of exaggeration, but the use made of the Australian Regiment as soon as it was mounted indicated British faith in the colonials, as well as a shortage of Imperial cavalry and mounted infantry.

When General French relinquished his Colesberg command to General Clements and moved north to the Enslin area to assume a position for Roberts's invasion of the Orange Free State he took with him all but two squadrons of his cavalry. As Clements had brought with him into his new command an essentially infantry force the new Colesberg column relied heavily on the Australian horsemen who numbered 691 in a force of 6600.[49] Boer equality in numbers and superiority in mobility placed an added responsibility on the men of the Australian regiment. And for Clements and his force the price of failure would be great: the cutting of the supply line for Roberts's gathering invasion force.

The British column took up its position along a 35-mile front which straddled the Naauwpoort-Norval's Point railway line. The left wing, under an Imperial officer, included the Wiltshire infantry, and mounted infantry from New South Wales, South Australia and Victoria. The right wing, also under an Imperial officer, included the Worcester infantry, and mounted infantry from Western Australia and Tasmania.[50] Ahead lay an estimated 7000 Boers, so firmly positioned in the Rensburg hills that the British could do little more than show a presence and hope that the enemy would not realize too soon that the force was inferior in numbers and mobility to that commanded by French. A fight was inevitable, and in a week of severe skirmishing Clements's force was pushed back down the line to Arundel.

The South African conflict was the first war to be fought under the probing eye of the press. Therefore it was not inappropriate that the first Australian to die in Clements's campaign should be a journalist, W. J. Lambie, who wrote for the *Age*, the *Advertiser* and the *Daily Telegraph*. Lambie had been wounded when in the Soudan with the New South Wales contingent. He died in South Africa, partly out of indiscretion and partly out of an earnest desire to record the way in which Australians conducted themselves in battle.

Lambie was killed on 9 February while accompanying a small force on patrol in enemy-dominated territory. With him was A. G. Hales of the London *Daily News*. The patrol was surprised by a party of Boers and in the melee that followed Lambie was shot dead and Hales taken prisoner. As war correspondents, both men were uniformed in the manner of British officers, and Hales was told by members of the Boer party that their dress, and the fact that they retreated so hastily, led to their being fired on.[51] W. T. Reay of the Melbourne *Herald* was accorded every facility by General de la Rey to visit Lambie's grave and to obtain what information he could concerning the correspondent's death. It was the great Transvaaler himself who talked with Reay and expressed deep regret that Lambie was killed through being mistaken for a combatant.[52]

In those few days of skirmishing among the Colesberg kopjes, the men of the Australian Regiment displayed an aptitude for unorthodox mounted warfare. They showed courage and a keeness to join battle with the enemy, and these qualities often manifested themselves in audacious patrolling which led to situations from which the Australians only extricated themselves by fearless riding across the bullet-splashed veldt. Two episodes stand out in those days of baptismal fire. The first concerned the West Australians at Slingersfontein, where a stand was made which did much to atone for Dowling's defeat at the same location a month earlier.

At daylight on 9 February a troop of W.A.M.I. under Captain Moor and a squadron of Inniskilling Dragoons moved out from their camp on reconnaissance. Almost immediately the force made contact with a Boer commando of 300 to 400 men. The regular cavalry took up a defensive position and the West Australians were ordered to the flank, where they made a stand on a kopje which stood at the entrance to a horseshoe formed by a string of other kopjes. In an endeavour to turn the British flank, the Boers attacked the West Australian position from the hills on three sides. From sunrise to sunset the little band of twenty men defied a force of several hundred. As they day drew to a close the enemy came close enough to call on Moor to surrender, but although the troop had lost one man dead, one mortally wounded, and five others wounded, the answer from the colonials was a defiant display of bayonets and a challenge to come and get them. The troop eventually retired in twos and threes, running a gauntlet of fire as the daylight faded.[53] General Clements recognized the value of the Western Australians' stand in a brigade order:

> The General Officer commanding wishes to place on record his high appreciation of the courage and determination shown by a party of 20 men of the Western Australians, under Captain

Moor ... By their determined stand against 300 or 400 men they entirely frustrated the enemy's attempt to turn the flank of the position. [54]

Rolling up the flanks of the tenuous British line became a major Boer objective, and it led to the other significant episode involving Clements's Australians. The engagement at Pink Hill was the logical outcome of the shaky strategic position of Clements's force, and Australian cockiness. Pink Hill was a little Anzac. It was a defeat which led to a major withdrawal from the area; it involved proportionately high casualties; and it was praised as a great display of Australian courage and honour in war.

On 12 February the Boers attacked both British flanks. Situated on the extreme left, at Pink Hill, were seventy-five Victorians, twenty South Australians, fifty Inniskillings, and fifty Wiltshires. Major Eddy had assumed command of the post that morning from an Imperial officer, who had moved off with the artillery to another position. The enemy attacked in considerable numbers just before noon, and for two hours Eddy's force defended grimly from among the rocks of Pink Hill. It soon became obvious that the position could not be held and the Wiltshire infantry were evacuated first, with the mounted men remaining to cover their retreat. Throughout the battle Eddy had moved among his men, encouraging them and directing their fire, but no sooner had he given the order for the final retirement when he fell with a bullet through the head. The Australian casualties were severe: six killed and twenty-three wounded, of whom ten were taken prisoner. [55]

The right flank having also been turned, Clements withdrew his wings to the centre and fell back upon Arundel, where he assumed a defensive position until Boer pressure was relieved by Roberts's move on Bloemfontein. An Australian war correspondent regarded 12 February as 'a calamitous day for the British cause' and 'a glorious but a fatal day in the history of the Victorian contingent'.[56] The official report acknowledged the value of the 'assistance rendered to their dismounted comrades of the Wiltshire Regiment by the Victorian Rifles',[57] but other views of the minor engagement were less restrained. The *Argus* called for 'a beautiful and stately monument' to the gallant dead, which would 'tell to all future generations of Victorians the story of a deed which they could never surpass but from the heroic measure of which they must never decline'.[58] The *Advertiser* stated that Australians would be proud that they had not looked in vain to their representatives on the field of battle for a display of the highest military qualities, and added, 'Plainly wool and wheat are not our greatest products![59] *The Times History*, not given to high praise, noted, 'As an exhibition of resolute courage on the part of comparatively untrained troops, this performance of the Australians is worthy of mention'.[60] The highest praise came from the pen of Arthur Conan Doyle, who wrote that the Australians 'proved once for all [sic] that amid all the scattered nations which came from the same home there is not one with a more fiery courage and a higher sense of martial duty than the men from the great island continent'.[61]

But amid all the praise for the Pink Hill defence, which even more than Sunnyside was taken as marking the 'arrival' of the Australian soldier, there were critical murmurings that perhaps reputation had been achieved at the unnecessary expense of life. It was considered that Eddy should have given the order to retire much earlier.[62] But caution was not part of the make-up of the former school teacher who had found soldiering so attractive that he had made it his career. The night before he fell, Eddy had stood on the very spot where he was to die the next day and had remarked to friends that the position was superb for a last stand and that he would, in fact, like to make a last stand there.[63] Add to this heroic inclination Eddy's stated contempt for the Boer,[64] and we have a situation where discretion was unlikely to be regarded as the better part of valour.

Whether or not Major Eddy aspired to glory, he did achieve it in the short-term, for flags flew at half-mast in his honour in all those Victorian towns that had some claim to him.[65] And although his body, together with those of his comrades, was to lie among the blood-stained rocks of Pink Hill for three weeks, he was eventually buried in a manner befitting a hero. Because of the British withdrawal from the area, no action had been taken to inter the dead, but there was supposedly an understanding between British ambulance men and the enemy that the Boers would bury the fallen on Pink Hill. This had been done in an inadequate way, although in a manner in which the Boers often disposed of their own dead, the bodies being roughly covered with boughs or rocks to protect them from the scavengers of the veldt. When it was heard that the Victorians had not been properly interred a burial party went to the scene. Major Eddy was the first of five Australian dead to be honoured in Christian burial. Chaplain Wray, clad in full clerical vestments, conducted the service and the members of the burial party raised a huge mound over his grave. A simple head-board served to identify the lonely tomb of a man who had fought with defiant courage.[66]

While the Australian Regiment was being put to the test on the hazardous field of Colesberg, elements of the second contingent were arriving in South Africa. Most of these units moved up to join Roberts's invasion force at various points on his drive to Bloemfontein, but the units from Victoria and Tasmania were directed to the Colesberg area. Before they made contact with the Australian Regiment, however, Colonel Tom Price of the V.M.R. was accorded an honour, however brief, that was denied all other Australian officers throughout the war. He was given a command of his own. The Victorians and Tasmanians had been de-trained at Hanover Road while en route from Cape Town to Naauwpoort, and were brigaded with several units of British regulars and South African irregulars to form the Hanover Road Field Force under Price. The objective of the hastily organized force was to protect Hanover Road from a Boer commando reported to be in the vicinity. Despite alarms the enemy did not appear, and Price went forward with the mounted section of his command, about 350 men, to join Clements at Arundel. Here he fought an engagement that he later recounted with pride. The objective was Kuilfontein kopje, a position crucial to Clements's march on Colesberg. On the left of the advancing British force was Colonel Page Henderson of the Inniskilling Dragoons, on the right was General Clements himself, and in the centre was Tom Price and the H.R.F.F. But most flattering of all was the presence of Kitchener as an observer.

The fight was sharp but unsuccessful despite the extensive use of British artillery, and the attackers retired. Two days later Price led his force in another assault on the kopje and took it without opposition. The Boers had begun their withdrawal to meet the main invasion threat, and the entire Colesberg force moved slowly behind them towards Bloemfontein. By this time, however, Price's command had been narrowed down to the Victorians only. Even that was something of a distinction, for the other Australian units moved north under Imperial officers. Price regretted the limiting of his command but the fact that he was the only Australian officer honoured with a separate command during the war remained a great source of pride to him. He was inclined to attribute the reluctance of British authorities in this matter to the existence of inter-colonial jealousies. Perhaps Price had a point, because the bickerings of colonial officers at Enslin would not have been lost on British authorities.[67]

On the day that the Colesberg force began its withdrawal to Arundel the invasion of the Orange Free State began. Roberts had gathered together near Enslin an army of 45 000 combat troops, made up of four infantry divisions and one cavalry division, each of 7500 men, and a force of 3600 mounted infantry. Servicing the whole was a transport wing of 4000 drivers, 11 000 mules and 9600 oxen. Included in this formidable array of British military strength were about 500 Australians, men from the Q.M.I., the N.S.W.M.R., and the Lancers, all of whom were merged with French's cavalry division.[68]

Roberts's plan was to move to the Modder River and then strike east towards Bloemfontein, but before doing this he wanted to use French to relieve Kimberley. A morale booster was needed both in the field and at home, for Buller had blundered again in the tragic battle of Spion Kop in Natal. Roberts was also aware of 'the disastrous political effect' which the fall of Kimberley would have, so he placed great importance on the relief of the diamond town. [69] The brief campaign by which this was achieved was quite spectacular, and it filled with pride the small group of Australian citizen soldiers who were privileged to ride with men of illustrious Imperial regiments. To begin with, there was an inspiring address by the revered 'Bobs' himself, who spoke after the fashion of a great Shakespearean warrior king: 'You will remember what you are going to do all your lives, and when you have grown to be old men, you will tell the story of the relief of Kimberley'.[70] Then there was the move-out, when French led his 6000 men in formation away from the main force and towards the Modder at dawn on 13 February. An English soldier was awakened by the sound of the movement of the largest British mounted force in history, and he watched in awe at what he described as one of the finest sights he had ever seen.[71] Even the prosaic Colonel Ricardo of the Q.M.I. was touched by the 'glorious sight' of the sun rising on the thousands of troopers.[72]

After French crossed the Modder he encountered stiff Boer resistance, but used some of his crack regiments to clear the way.

No Australians were involved, but in the ensuing dash to Kimberley on 15 February the squadron of New South Wales Lancers was among the vanguard. The Q.M.I. also took part but the N.S.W.M.R. were not among the 5000 men who relieved the town. According to one of their number, General French asked the unit to accompany him, but their horses 'were too much done up'.[73] A bearer company of the N.S.W.A.M.C. added to the excellent reputation the corps had already built up through its field hospital at Orange River and its ambulance work at Sunnyside, by being the only medical unit to keep up with French's cavalry in the horse-killing ride to Kimberley. This distinction won for its leader, Lieutenant C. A. Edwards, a mention in French's dispatches.[74]

A. B. Paterson accompanied the Kimberley relief force, and the occasion prompted him to write one of his twelve ballads on Boer War themes. The poem did not celebrate a heroic battle, for there wasn't one. But it did celebrate an event that assumed heroic proportions for Paterson and his compatriots; that is, the emergence of Australian soldiers as apparently equal and integral parts of an Imperial force of elite corps and famous commanders.

> And in the front the Lancers rode that New South Wales had sent:
> With easy stride across the plain their long, lean Walers went.
> Unknown, untried, those squadrons were, but proudly out they drew
> Beside the English regiments that fought at Waterloo.[75]

During the time that Lord Roberts had been gathering his invasion force together near Enslin, General Cronje with an army of 6000 Boers had been sitting athwart the railway at Magersfontein in the belief that the activity to the south indicated the reinforcing of Methuen's shattered force and a renewed British advance on Kimberley. But French's sweep northwards and Roberts's easterly movement perplexed the old Transvaal general, and he decided to shift his force closer to Bloemfontein. On a bright moonlight night he passed unobserved just three miles to the north of the invasion army, earning for that force the opprobrium of *The Times History* which considered British scouting to be once again at fault.[76] Roberts now set out in pursuit of Cronje, his plan being to halt him with his mounted men and then crush him with his infantry.

The N.S.W.M.R. had missed out on the glamorous ride to Kimberley, but they were given the opportunity of a more demanding role as part of a force of 2000 mounted infantry under Colonel Hannay, which tried to hold Cronje's commandos as they headed up the Modder River. The British force encountered stiff opposition, however, from the Boer rearguard and fell back before accurate light artillery fire, in their confusion racing over a steep bank into the river. 'The incident was a single object-lesson in the deficiencies of the improvised force and of its leading', observed *The Times History*.[77] The reference was to the regular infantry who had recently been mounted, but the New South Wales men, deservedly or undeservedly, had to share in the odium of the retreat. Being brigaded with British regiments could bring acclaim, as the New South Wales Lancers had found when they rode along to Kimberley with French's cavalry. But there was another side to the coin, and the fine enthusiastic horsemen of the N.S.W.M.R. found this out when they were made a subordinate part of an inferior British mounted unit. Hannay's force was re-formed as well as possible and brought back into the attack, but again they 'fell back in some confusion'.[78] Despite the shocking condition of French's horses after his dash to Kimberley, the cavalry were ordered into the race to head Cronje. The one day of operations involved in the relief of Kimberley had cost French only five men killed, but sixty-eight chargers had died, mainly from exhaustion.[79] The animals were to suffer even more the following day in the chase after Cronje, scores dying under their riders to become what were popularly known as 'French's milestones'.

The British cavalry succeeded in forcing Cronje to laager at Paardeberg Drift, thus recording one of the rare instances during the war when a Boer force was out-manoeuvred by a far less mobile enemy. But the distinction was of dubious merit, for Cronje had been slowed up by the presence in his convoy of numerous families which had joined the force while it waited at Magersfontein.

Paardeberg was the last major battle of the war. It was also the decisive battle of that conflict, but Australians played little part in the action. The Queenslanders had remained behind at Kimberley at the request of Colonel Ricardo who considered they were in need of a spell. For ten days the Q.M.I. men and horses enjoyed the comfort of the De Beers stables which Cecil Rhodes had made available to the Queensland commander.[80] Those members of the N.S.W. Lancers whose horses were fit accompanied French from Kimberley but played no part in the battle of Paardeberg. The N.S.W.M.R. were more involved, being engaged with Colonel Hannay's force of mounted infantry in skirmishes on the periphery of the main Boer force, until Hannay received orders from Kitchener which implied the rushing of the laager. The charge was cut short, however, by the death of Hannay, who had ridden recklessly at the head of his men, probably smarting from Kitchener's criticism of the poor performance of his force during the preceding days.

From this point the battle became, of necessity, an infantry and artillery affair for horses were of little use against a besieged enemy. Of the colonial troops, it was the Canadians who won glory. They formed an infantry force of battalion strength which had been retained as a unit at the insistence of the Canadian government; and it was their turn to man the front line on the day of the final assault. They made the most of their opportunity, winning high praise from Roberts and from their prime minister, Laurier, who claimed that Paardeberg had revealed to the world that a new power had risen in the west.[81]

It was after the final assault of Cronje's position by Canadian and regular infantry that Major Fiaschi of the N.S.W.A.M.C. figured in an incident that was soon exaggerated. While Fiaschi and members of his corps were picking up wounded Canadians close to the Boer lines, a group of 209 of the enemy displayed a white flag, filed out of their positions and offered their surrender to Fiaschi, the senior officer of the ambulance party. He accepted, and his single-handed 'capture' of a large force of Boers became one of the rare Australian legends of the South African War. At the same time as Fiaschi was supervising the stacking of Boer arms General Cronje was surrendering his force of 4000 men to Lord Roberts, and very soon the New South Wales men were in the Boer laager tending enemy wounded.[82]

Fiaschi had earlier won the attention of Roberts by asking to be excused from meeting the great man during an inspection of the Australian hospital. The doctor was busy operating. When news reached Roberts of Fiaschi's 'capture' of the Boers, he recalled the incident and directed that the Australian be given a D.S.O.[83]

The efficient work of the New South Wales medical unit at Paardeberg was recognized by Roberts when, in eulogizing the Canadians, he referred to the New South Wales field hospital which was treating their wounded as one of the best-equipped he had seen anywhere in the world.[84]

Paardeberg was a notable engagement in a number of ways. It demonstrated some of the humane gestures between the combatants which earned for the conflict the title of 'the last of the gentlemen's wars'. During the siege the Boers would hold their fire while the British filled their water-bottles at sundown; British medical corps tended the Boer wounded both during and after the engagement; and when the dejected Cronje, portly and unkempt in a slouch hat and bottle-green overcoat, appeared before the trim and distinguished looking Roberts, the latter extended his hand and said: 'I am glad to see you. You have made a gallant defence, sir'. Whereupon the two men sat down to breakfast together, prior to the beginning of the long journey which was to end for Cronje and his men at St Helena.[85] For the Boers, Paardeberg was a humiliating defeat that was made worse by the fact that it took place on the anniversary of Majuba. It meant the capture of the most famous general in South Africa, along with 4000 burghers, and the demoralization of 14 000 others who were positioned on the periphery of the engagement and who now retreated in disorder towards the east. But it also meant the birth of new tactics; never again would the Boers attempt to hold a position against overwhelming odds, but would make use of their superior mobility to attack and withdraw. The capture of Cronje, along with the death of Joubert, who had commanded in Natal, also meant the eclipse of the old leaders and their replacement by younger and more able men like de la Rey and Christian de Wet. For the Empire, Paardeberg was a badly-needed victory which Roberts had successfully contrived on the anniversary of a Boer victory over British arms.

Australian reaction was jubilant. There was wild cheering when the lieutenant-governor announced the surrender during the Sydney farewell to the third contingent, and the Primitive Methodist Conference at Goulburn rose and sang the Anthem when the news broke. In Adelaide the bells of the town hall rang out and sharebrokers, after a patriotic demonstration, sent a congratulatory cable to Roberts.[86] The Wesleyan Conference in

Melbourne responded with cheers and the Anthem, and in the New South Wales country town of Walcha the surrender was celebrated by a street procession which included 'clergymen, aldermen and school children'. The affair was suitably capped by Lord Milner who sent cables to the colonial governors congratulating them on the noble part played by their troops in the surrender.[87] An editorial in the *Sydney Morning Herald* the day after the report of Milner's cables called for a memorial to the event, and acclaimed the success of the Australian soldier on the verdict of commanders like Lord Roberts and Major-General French, as well as the testimony of the Queen and her Ministers of Parliament and of the Press'.[88] The war was only young but the highly self-conscious nationalism of Australians had already begun to create a favourable image of its military representatives, principally from the courteous and calculated utterances of Imperial figures.

Paardeberg marked the end of a fruitful fortnight for the invasion force. Things had looked black for the British cause when Roberts left Enslin but now the tide was running Britain's way. Kimberley had been relieved, the main Boer army outside Natal had been captured or scattered, and Clements at Colesberg, Gatacre at Stormberg, and Buller in Natal all found their opponents melting away before them as the Boers moved to meet the greater threat of Roberts. According to Conan Doyle, 'a single master-mind had in an instant turned England's night to day'.[89] Small wonder that Australians considered it an honour to serve under such a man, and were thrilled to the core just to see him ride by.[90]

In terms of numbers the Australian colonies played a more significant role after Roberts moved on from Paardeberg, for most of the second contingent went up to join the main force as soon as they arrived in Cape Town. A reorganization of mounted infantry brought all units into four brigades commanded by four British colonels. Irregulars formed about half of each brigade, the idea being that the colonials with their scouting ability and better horsemanship would leaven the raw lump of improvised horsemen who had so recently been taken from the ranks of regular infantry. The first and second N.S.W.M.R. formed a half brigade, as did the first and second Q.M.I. and the second contingent units from all other Australian colonies except

Victoria. A squadron of Australian Horse and the Lancer squadron were brigaded with the regular cavalry. At this point over 1000 Australians were included in Roberts's force of 34 000.[91] But the men were to see very little action in the drive on Bloemfontein, for the defeat of Cronje had lowered Boer morale and shattered the loosely-knit Boer military organization. An estimated 14 000 burghers streamed to the east in disarray. If French and his cavalry could have headed them and held them for the infantry divisions, the war may have been finished there and then. French's horses were too weary and under-nourished to effect an encirclement of the mobile enemy, however, and President Kruger was no more successful in getting the commandos to stand and fight. Therefore the engagement known as Poplar Grove amounted to no more than skirmishing between the Boer rearguard and the British cavalry.

The squadron of Australian Horse was accorded a considerable honour when the army moved out from Poplar Grove. They were sent ahead to find a ford over the Modder and to guide the main force across. Paterson stated that this might seem an easy task, but he claimed that the average 'Tommy' could not have done the job. The assignment indicated that Australians had already won recognition for their scouting ability.[92]

The burghers did make a stand at Driefontein, however, despite continuing desertions. Kruger and General de Wet were influential in getting the Boers to make a fight of it, but the decisive factor was General de la Rey, who had cut short his successful campaigning in the Colesberg area to hasten back with a small force to oppose Roberts. No more than 7000 Boers faced Roberts at Driefontein, but the British suffered sharp casualties in an unsuccessful attempt to contain them. The *Official History* noted some Australian participation in the battle. The two squadrons of cavalry from New South Wales were among the units used by French in an attempt to turn the Boer flank, and when the enemy had been forced into retreat by the British infantry they joined in a pursuit made fruitless by tired horses. The mounted infantry brigade that included the Queenslanders was engaged in holding an outlying kopje throughout the day. Once again it was the infantry which bore the brunt of the fight. Out of 87 killed and 347 wounded only 17 wounded were not infantrymen.[3]

The Australians received a favourable press despite their modest contribution to the battle. The London cables read: 'The New South Wales Infantry [sic] did splendid service' and 'The New South Wales Mounted Infantry Regiment made a gallant attempt to capture the Boer guns'. There were no details to spoil the favourable impression the public would have gained.[94]

There was no further opposition before Bloemfontein and on 13 March, just thirty days after he had set his invasion force in motion, Roberts entered the capital city of the Orange Free State. In that short time the war had swung dramatically in Britain's favour. The *Official History* attributed the change to the strategy of Roberts and the confidence the troops had in their leader; and to two additional infantry divisions and the 'assistance of the Colonial contingents'.[95]

The Australians had sustained minimal casualties in their first month with Roberts,[96] but they and their horses had undergone severe physical hardship. The horses, in particular, had suffered. For weeks they had survived on a half-ration of two and a half pounds of oats a day and what herbage they could find on the parched veldt. This lacked nutrition, being equated by an Australian officer to Bryant and May's matches.[97] To make the situation worse, the Australians' horses were given no acclimatization period in South Africa. The mounts of the greater part of the second contingent had joined Roberts's column twelve days after disembarkation, three of which were spent on a train.[98] Within a month of landing only 50 horses out of the 2nd Q.M.I. total of 170 were still with the unit.[99] The rest had died from exhaustion or sickness, or were recuperating in depots run by the Remount Department of the British Army, from whence they were allocated as remounts to any British or colonial unit. Few would have found their way back to Australian units. None of them returned to Australia because of quarantine regulations. So the 40 000 horses that went to war from Australia, either with the contingents or as remounts, were usually destined for an early and cruel death on the desolate veldt. Paterson, the horse-lover, spoke with feeling of their plight in a poem called 'The Last Parade', in which he described their privations and imagined them pleading to be returned to their native land—

> Home to the Hunter River,
> To the flats where the lucerne grows,

Home where the Murrumbidgee
Runs white with the melted snows.[100]

Close by the entrance to the Sydney Botanical Gardens there is
a plaque honouring the Australian horses of World War I. One
might hope that in some corner of an Australian city there is a
memorial to the greater-suffering horses of the South African
War.[101]

Australian soldiers were better able to endure the privations of
the drive on Bloemfontein than their horses. Despite reduced
rations (the result of the inability of the transports to keep up with
the movement), heat, violent thunderstorms, and no shelter of
any kind, the Australians displayed a fortitude and a capacity to
'make do' that won praise from Paterson. The Australian war
correspondent regarded them as quite different from the English,
'in that they were always providing for their own wants in
mysterious ways'. The night after Driefontein, the troops got into
their bivouacs in darkness. Units were all mixed up but Paterson
came across two Lancers with a couple of ducks and sufficient
firewood (a scarce commodity) to cook them. They soon made
themselves comfortable for the night, not worrying in the least
about being separated from their squadron. 'This capacity to shift
for themselves', noted Paterson, 'has been a great feature of our
troops all along the march'.[102]

Roberts was compelled to stay in Bloemfontein for seven weeks
to rest his men and horses, to await remounts and supplies of
clothing, and to secure the railways. It is unfortunate that he had
to delay his advance because Bloemfontein, the 'fountain of
flowers', belied its name and became a pest-hole of enteric fever
and other illnesses. The unclean water at Paardeberg, polluted by
dead horses and human waste from Cronje's laager, had infected
the army and the disease had completed its incubation stage by
the time Roberts entered the capital.[103] Conan Doyle regarded
the epidemic as 'the greatest misfortune of the campaign',[104] and
an Australian soldier wrote feelingly of a tragic episode which
cost more than 1000 lives.

There is no forgetting the carts that rumbled through the
street, loaded with those stiff, blanket-shrouded shapes which
had been vigorous men—the dwindling squadrons, the
crowded sick tents, the unfed, unwashed, unhappy men who
filled them, will never cease to linger in one's memory.[105]

Initially the medical facilities to cope with the outbreak of enteric were inadequate, but the inadequacies served to increase the value of the contribution of the N.S.W.A.M.C. The second medical unit had arrived in South Africa in February, and had joined Gatacre in his advance from Cape Colony to Bloemfontein. Fourteen nursing sisters had sailed with this draft. Both medical contingents now came together to form a well-trained, well-equipped corps of about 240 personnel, with an immediate task of attending the sick at Bloemfontein.[106]

Colonel Williams took over the Free State Artillery barracks and soon had an efficient hospital functioning. In the early weeks of the epidemic the sick lay on the floor in their clothes with one blanket to cover them and little more than Bovril and tinned meat for food. An 'all pervading faecal odour' so filled the make-shift wards that it was considered necessary to divert to other hospitals the wounded brought in by New South Wales ambulance men from skirmishing on the outskirts of town.[107] Admission to the N.S.W.A.M.C. hospital was never limited to Australians. The fact that the sick and wounded from any regiment were taken in if space was available was regarded by an Australian war correspondent as something that distinguished the colonial medical corps from the Imperial.[108]

At Bloemfontein and in the field, prior to the onset of the epidemic and after, the N.S.W. hospital won a reputation that became a legend. It was claimed that 'Tommies went about with tickets sewn into their tunics bearing the words "If sick or wounded, please take me to the N.S.W. Hospital" '.[109] A Lancer noted, 'They have a splendid name here, and Lord Roberts sends his wounded officers to them in preference to the English Corps'.[110] Others wrote in similar vein.[111]

General E. T. H. Hutton, the former New South Wales commandant, paid tribute to the work of the corps in a message to the New South Wales premier: 'Their praises are in everybody's mouth, and I am told that every sick and wounded soldier . . . hopes that Providence may place him under the care of the N.S.W. Ambulance'.[112] In drawing attention to the ambulance function Hutton was referring to the outstanding section of the New South Wales medical unit. The Principal Medical Officer of the British Army in South Africa, in his evidence before the Elgin Commission, freely recognized the superiority of the New South Wales ambulances. He attributed this to the fact that the colonial unit had its own transport and was not reliant on the army transport pool as the Imperial ambulance units were. The P.M.O. praised the efficiency of the Australian medical officers and said, 'Their transport was the thing for us to imitate'.[113] Colonel Williams explained the superiority of his ambulances in an interview given on his return from South Africa. He dismissed rumours that the Imperial medical corps was to be remodelled on the N.S.W.A.M.C. and said that what distinction was claimed for his corps was due to a light and mobile waggon service which was an integral part of the unit. In treatment, organization, and other equipment, the colonial and Imperial corps were identical. When in the Soudan with the New South Wales contingent, Williams had noticed the shortcomings of the Imperial system and had effected the appropriate modifications for the N.S.W.A.M.C.[114]

It is difficult, however, not to see Williams as the factor which won for the medical unit pre-eminence among the Australian corps sent to the South African War. He had raised the unit and brought it to a high standard of efficiency, and the superior quality of his leadership soon became obvious in South Africa. In quick succession he held the post of P.M.O. for the Australian and New Zealand forces (the first Anzac command, surely), for General Ian Hamilton's mounted infantry division, and finally for Sir Archibald Hunter's force of 35 000, an appointment which Williams claimed to be the largest medical command of the campaign.[115]

When a medical force was raised to accompany the Australian Commonwealth Horse to South Africa, Lord Kitchener asked that Williams should command the unit. But he was needed at home to develop the army medical services of the new nation. As with most other Australian officers, Williams was eager to serve well in the campaign, for in addition to being a patriot who wished to win an identity for his country,[116] he held a higher loyalty. Amid the death and hardship of Bloemfontein, Williams was able to report to his commandant in New South Wales: 'We know nothing of what is going on in the outside world, nor even in our own immediate neighbourhood—but one and all work on, sternly and quietly . . . having in view only one object — the Empire'.[117]

The occupation of Bloemfontein brought considerable numbers of Australians into close contact with Imperial troops for the first time in history, and the comparisons drawn by Paterson favoured the colonials, whom he described as 'long-legged young fellows, brown and hard-faced, and all with the alert wide-awake look that distinguishes the Australian soldier from the more stolid English "Tommy" '.[118] Paterson was also impressed by their keenness to involve themselves in the skirmishing that was going on around the town. On one occasion he met fifty de-horsed members of the N.S.W.M.R. who were walking to an engagement fifteen miles north of Bloemfontein in the hope of getting into action.[119] The bulk of that regiment did see service in this area, however, and returned to Bloemfontein after a month's patrolling to the north, with their ranks greatly depleted through enteric and dysentery and their horses in ghastly condition. By contrast, Ricardo's Q.M.I. experienced only one sharp engagement which added nothing to the lustre of Australian arms. East of Bloemfontein, Christian de Wet had rallied sufficient burghers to take the initiative from Roberts's immobilized army, and at Sannah's Post inflicted a stinging defeat on General Broadwood's column. The Q.M.I. and Imperial units went to Broadwood's aid, but were forced to retreat after being pinned down for hours. Ricardo comforted himself by blaming the entire affair on poor British scouting, and tried to dissociate the Queenslanders from the defeat by holding to a rumour that Roberts was to mention the unit in his dispatches.[120]

It was not until the end of May that de Wet's depredations on the British supply lines were brought to a temporary halt and arrangements were completed for the march on Pretoria. Of great importance to Australians was the creation of a mounted infantry division. There had been some talk of an Australian mounted infantry brigade, 'but it had not amounted to much, because of the intercolonial jealousies among our officers'.[121] The two New South Wales cavalry squadrons were motivated to resist inclusion in an Australian brigade by other factors. Although the distinction between cavalry and mounted infantry had largely vanished, the men of the New South Wales Lancers and the Australian Horse considered there was 'a certain amount of éclat in being brigaded with troops like the Scots Greys or Inniskillings'.[122] So the Australians remained part of French's elite cavalry division, the only colonial troops to be so honoured. The mounted infantry division of two brigades was formed under General Ian Hamilton, with General E. T. H. Hutton and Colonel C. P. Ridley as brigadiers. Hutton's command comprised all the Australians, the Canadians, the New Zealanders, and four battalions of regular mounted infantry. The Australians numbered 2000 in a brigade of just on 6000, and the pioneer company and medical corps were Australian units. Four of Hutton's eight staff officers were Australians.[123] With a large 'A' sewn on the left side of their helmets to emphasize their identity, and being dominant numerically in three of Hutton's four corps, the Australians were for the first time in a position to make an impact as a national force. But the opportunities for military achievement were quickly diminishing. The Boers were no longer prepared to fight the pitched battles that created heroes and, in any case, the mounted infantry were to continue to play a subordinate role to the cavalry until the tedious and unheroic guerrilla phase of the war began. Hutton was delighted to have the Australians in his command. 'Such fine looking workmanlike men', he called them,[124] and he had high hopes for them and for the other colonials in his brigade. Hutton considered the men from Canada and Australasia as representative of all that was best in 'the young and vigorous manhood' of the colonies. He wanted them to win prestige for their colonies through military success but considered they were 'ignorant of their own value'.[125]

On 3 May, with bands playing, Roberts led his army out of the pestilential city. His command actually extended through a series of British forces reaching from Kimberley to Ladysmith, and now this Imperial host of 110 000 men made independent but converging progress towards Pretoria. On the right wing was Buller, moving his force of 45 000 out of Natal with irritating slowness. On the left were Hunter and Methuen with 20 000 men, and in the centre was the main strike force of 45 000 men, including 2500 Australians. Confronting the British advance was an estimated force of 30 000 Boers, who were in a state of disorder.[126] In the words of Conan Doyle, the record of the army's progress from Bloemfontein to Pretoria was 'rather geographical than military',[127] but occasionally the enemy made a tentative stand and in the ensuing skirmishes Australians usually played a part.

The spirits of Hutton's colonials were high as the force moved northward, for the anticipated capture of Pretoria was regarded as the conclusive and crowning achievement of the war, and the mounted infantry were appointed to play an important part in the operation. One historian honoured the Australians with the title of 'the eyes and the ears of the army of invasion',[128] and they did play a significant part in the advance, forming protective screens for artillery, infantry and supply columns. By day they patrolled far ahead of the slower and more vulnerable corps and closed in to the main force at night. So essential was this scouting function that Hutton's force soon became widely dispersed, the N.S.W.M.R. and W.A.M.I. even passing under the direct control of Ian Hamilton at Kroonstadt.[129] Yet, despite their importance, Hutton's men were obliged to play second fiddle to the cavalry. The mounted infantry brigade operating under Ian Hamilton had relative freedom of movement and operated with effect on the right wing of the advance, but Hutton's brigade was operating with and under French and he would not permit the mounted infantry to advance in front of the cavalry, much to the chagrin of Hutton.[130]

The mounted infantry did not always operate in the shadow of the cavalry, however, and on the occasion of the first Australian skirmish in the advance northwards the cavalry were conspicuously absent. At Karee Kloof, out from Bloemfontein, three hundred Victorians under Colonel Tom Price were detailed to lure a Boer force from a series of kopjes for destruction by the artillery and cavalry. But the Boers were concealed in long grass on a plain and very successfully ambushed the Victorians and a company of Cornwall mounted infantry, chasing them over two and a half miles of flat country. The dreaded pom-poms[131] were also brought into use, causing death and panic among the horses, and it was in this situation that the Victorians partly redeemed themselves by carrying to safety de-horsed comrades. Amid the confused retreat a message was received advising Price to delay the operation for two hours to permit the cavalry to come up! Victorian casualties were light: three prisoners taken and one man injured by a fall from his horse, and Victorian achievement was nil, but Price was able to convey to his discomfited men the praise of the divisional general for 'the masterly and soldier-like retreat' they had made.[132] An Australian historian blamed the debacle on poor Imperial leadership and tactics,[133] but a Victorian trooper who took part in the 'engagement' attributed the rout to poor scouting by the V.M.R.[134] By contrast, the next skirmish involving Australians brought great credit to the men of the N.S.W.M.R. On Sunday 5 May[135] Hutton's force attacked Boer positions at Coetzee's Drift on the Vet River in what was to be the only engagement in which the colonial brigade operated as a unit. The enemy, numbering an estimated 1000, were positioned along the right bank of the river with their artillery covering them from a kopje beyond. The Royal Horse Artillery softened up both positions, and then Hutton sent in the N.S.W.M.R. The *Official History* gives a glowing account of their work:

> They delivered their attack with determination, rushing the drift despite heavy fire and lack of cover . . . Nor did the New South Wales men stop at the northern bank, but pushed the enemy at the point of the bayonet, not only from the Vet river, but headlong over a spruit [watercourse] which offered a second sunken position to the riflemen.[136]

Later in the day, after an artillery bombardment, the kopje was cleared of Boers by a composite force of Queenslanders, New Zealanders, regular mounted infantry, and the men from New South Wales.

Roberts was highly delighted at the result of the operation and congratulated the mounted infantry on 'their fine day's work'.[137] The men of the N.S.W.M.R. were elated;[138] and Hutton's joy was boundless. He was particularly proud of the men he had used as shock troops, for was he not their honorary colonel? And had he not laid the foundations of their efficiency when military commandant of New South Wales? 'Your fellows are terrors to fight', he told their commanding officer,[139] and in a more private moment he sought from the Almighty 'the discrimination and the insight to know when and how to best utilize such grand material'.[140] The only casualties suffered by Hutton's force were four men wounded (none from New South Wales). This was attributed to the Boers' being disconcerted by the vigour of the attack, and to inaccurate artillery fire and defective shells.[141]

The Zand River gave promise of being the location for a major battle, for Kruger and Steyn had agreed to make a stand. But although the engagement was the most important in the drive on Pretoria, it could not be dignified with the name of battle. Had the British forces made a frontal attack on the Boer positions, the Zand River could have been another Colenso or Magersfontein. The lessons had been learned, however, and the British strategy was a pincer movement, with French's cavalry moving in on one of the enemy's flanks and Bruce Hamilton's infantry on the other. Afraid as always of being encircled, the Boers retreated and offered no further significant resistance until after Roberts had entered Pretoria.

During French's flanking movement, disaster befell a section of his force through poor scouting. Three squadrons drawn from the Australian Horse, the Inniskillings, and the Scots Greys were ordered to silence a Boer artillery position, but were ambushed by a force of enemy horsemen whom they had assumed to be British mounted infantry. The cavalry detachment took shelter in a near-by cattle kraal until forced by the Boers into wild retreat. Many horses were killed in the engagement, and many more stampeded. British casualties were high although no determined stand had been made: fourteen killed, thirty-six wounded and twenty-seven taken prisoner. No Australians were killed but twenty-one of their thirty-five horses were. The 'Kaalong disaster' brought no credit on the Australian Horse.[142] The other Australian cavalry squadron, the New South Wales Lancers, did make amends, however, when the cavalry division was moving through Kalkhevvel Pass later in the advance. The 6th Dragoons, who were leading the division, were ambushed and began a mad gallop towards the rear. The Inniskillings and New South Wales Lancers, next in line of march, were almost overwhelmed in the retreat, but they responded to a call from Major E. Allenby to stand fast. Their example rallied the disorganized squadrons and imminent panic was averted.[143]

The irresistible British legions rolled on, taking Johannesburg and Pretoria with ease. Yet Roberts's achievement was illusory, for the Boers had been virtually untouched by the British advance.[144] On the other hand, the loose military organization of the Boers had failed completely. The future of the war effort of the two republics seemed to rest with independent commandos using guerrilla tactics and led by enterprising leaders like Christian de Wet. This type of warfare had already been practised against

Roberts's eastern flank as he moved on Pretoria, and it was to become the pattern. Roberts was confident that the war had been won when he entered the Transvaal capital. In reality, he had only determined its character for the next two years.

British battle losses were understandably light on that great drive; Hutton's brigade, for example, lost only one man killed and thirty-five wounded.[145] But another type of casualty, the de-horsed mounted soldier, occurred in numbers that rivalled sickness and disease as the scourge of the army. Roberts had covered the 300 miles from Bloemfontein in five weeks. But his horsemen had travelled much further than that on reconnaissance and screen duties. The result was that three of the four cavalry brigades lost 30, 40 and 60 per cent of their strength respectively. The mounted infantry lost 18 per cent of a comparable number.[146]

Australian losses were so high through illness and horse wastage that after Pretoria the components of the first and second contingents almost ceased to exist as viable units. The Queenslanders, in particular, suffered. Colonel Ricardo claimed that of the original 520 men of his command, only 192 got to Pretoria, the rest either being wounded or invalided.[147] A trooper wrote that only forty men of the 1st and 2nd Q.M.I. reached Pretoria, and of these only fifteen had horses in a fit state to go on. 'Lots of our men are sick', he noted, 'some gone home to England and Queensland, some left behind on duty and crowds of poor beggars walking, having no horses .[148] The active strength of the Q.M.I. was further reduced by British recruitment for police and railway duties. A question in the Queensland Legislative Assembly regarding the decimation of the Q.M.I. brought no concerned response from the premier,[149] and by the time the military commandant wrote his report for 1900 he could state that the first and second Queensland contingents had practically ceased to exist 'as such'. A 'large number' of men had succumbed to enteric and 'upwards of 100' had accepted employment on police and railway duty.[150]

The N.S.W.M.R. losses were also considerable. An officer of the unit claimed shortly after the fall of Pretoria that the regiment could only parade eighty men out of six hundred. Some, he said, were dead, some sick and wounded, and 'others scattered generally over South Africa'.[151] When allowances are made for the cracking pace set by Roberts, the phenomenon of de-horsed troopers might be explained in terms of poor horses or poor horsemastership. And evidence before the Elgin Commission suggested that Australia was guilty on both counts. A British expert rated Australian horses as 'very bad', although on the grounds of their not being acclimatized, a process which took up to nine months.[152] Many Australian horses had been wasted by Bloemfontein, however, and big sections of the first and second contingents had been re-mounted for the drive on Pretoria. Many of these remounts were also unsatisfactory, particularly those imported from Argentina. The Q.M.I. were supplied with this breed before heading north, and their horse losses were extremely high. It was General John French himself who rated overseas colonials as 'good horsemen, but bad horsemasters' and he cited the squadron of Australian Horse as an example. In its first three weeks of duty with the cavalry brigade, the squadron (about 100 horses) was reduced to only ten horses fit for duty, while in the same period the Scots Greys, with whom they were brigaded, were reduced to about thirty horses per squadron.[153] Campaign conditions which wrought such havoc on man and beast must have been extremely rigorous. It is fortunate that Trooper Steel of the N.S.W.M.R., an intelligent and perceptive diarist, should have written a full account of conditions in the field. Hardship was a constant. Steel noted that up to the time he was hospitalized at Johannesburg through a fall from his horse, he had slept always on the ground and beneath the stars, had never been completely undressed, and had never been free from vermin. When the force reached the Valsche River, Steel had been without a wash for twelve days and had not changed any item of clothing. But there he indulged in ablutions with 2000 other Australians and Canadians, using sand and gravel in place of soap. Along the banks, Tommies, with their legendary aversion to water, played cards and watched the frolic.[154] Lice were a major problem, and their eradication from the person was a continuing task. One novel method was to remove the clothing and place it on an ants' nest where the ants devoured the lesser insects, but Colonel Tom Price urged calm acceptance of the nuisance. Addressing the V.M.R., he said, 'Why . . . I'm lousy, the Padre's lousy, Lord Roberts is lousy, and the dear old Queen would be lousy too if she were here'.[155]

Lieutenant G. B. Forster of the New South Wales Mounted Rifles. Because the supply columns could not keep up with mounted troops, soldiers frequently had to live off the land.

A patrol of New South Wales Mounted Rifles crossing the Orange River

Inadequate food for both man and beast greatly hampered the efficiency of Roberts's army. The full daily ration for troops was four biscuits, a tin of bully beef, and a small quantity of coffee or tea, but frequently on the march to Pretoria this was reduced to two biscuits and little or no meat. Quite often the biscuits were consumed with the aid of water only, because firewood was so scarce.[156] Under such unsatisfactory commissariat conditions the urge to live off the land was great, and led to what was euphemistically known as 'commandeering'. Farmhouses were searched for chickens, eggs, vegetables, stock and horse fodder. It was not an unusual sight to see a trooper ride into bivouac with sheaves of hay strapped to his saddle, a fence post balanced across the pommel, a chicken attached to his person, and the horse's nose-bag full of eggs. Steel reported that from farms showing no signs of belligerency, soldiers took what they wanted but left receipts for the items; where ammunition was found or males were thought to have recently been under arms, goods were taken without receipt; and where farmhouses were in areas of active belligerency the buildings were burned.[157] Conan Doyle painted an idealized picture of Tommies living on foul water and bully beef while tramping through a land of fat geese and other abundance which they dare not touch because of Roberts's stern attitude towards looting.[158] But there can be no doubt that the practice was widespread. Paterson stated that it was generally accepted that to acquire sustenance for man and horse was no crime,[159] but, unfortunately, looting did not stop at the essentials. Australians became particularly adept at the art.[160] When the N.S.W.M.R. reached Pretoria they were informed by their commanding officer that they faced banishment to the lines of communication if British authorities received any more complaints over looting.[161]

If there was hardship on that 300-mile drive, there was also spectacle sufficient to thrill the citizen soldiers of the Empire. What could have been more exciting than to form part of a great British army as it prepared to move over the Zand River, and against the assembled Boer remnant, in what would have been the last battle of the war had the enemy stood his ground. Then there was the vast veldt, a pall of smoke by day and a sea of flame at night as the Boers used the fire stick to impede the progress of their pursuers, and to create a landscape that acted as a foil to the hitherto camouflaged khaki figures. The sweep into Johannesburg with its gum trees and wattles—the place where it had all begun—was exhilarating; and so was Roberts's grand review of his army in Pretoria. But perhaps the greatest spectacle of all occurred on the night of 24 May as the army waited to cross the Vaal River. During the evening there had been singing around the camp fires, and then on the order 'lights out!' regiment after regiment took up the national anthem. Steel estimated that 40 000 men would have joined in 'the homage of the fighting Army on the last birthday of Queen Victoria'.[162]

The capture of Pretoria did not end the war, and in the months that were to pass before they completed twelve months service and were allowed to return home, the men of the first and second contingents played various parts in a conflict that no longer merited the name of 'the last of the gentlemen's wars'. There was an occasional good scrap, as at Diamond Hill; there were exciting horse-killing 'hunts' after the elusive de Wet; and there were lazy days in the saddle while acting as escorts to supply columns; but for the most part the Australians found themselves involved in the unsavoury duties connected with what was termed 'pacification' or 'police duty'.

While the army was still at Pretoria, some corps fought an engagement against a determined force of 5000 Boers led by General Louis Botha. The location was Diamond Hill on the Magaliesberg, a few miles to the east of Pretoria, and General Jan Smuts was to regard the fight as the last great defensive battle fought by the Boers.[163] Against Botha, Roberts sent 14 000 men and a strong artillery force. In the middle advanced the infantry, and on the left and right flanks respectively were the sadly depleted ranks of Ian Hamilton's mounted infantry and French's cavalry. The latter force included ten men of the Australian Horse and thirty-five of the New South Wales Lancers—all that were left of two squadrons! French, moving against the enemy, sent a troop of Lancers ahead as scouts, but they were shelled by British artillery who thought the Australians were Boers joining their comrades. Luckily no one was hit, but French faltered and waited for the infantry to come up and take the position.[164]

On the other flank the mounted infantry were doing much better. The N.S.W.M.R. in particular were in the process of winning further distinction. Ian Hamilton had come up against a heavily defended Boer position on Rhenosterfontein kopje, against which he directed Colonel De Lisle's force of 6th M.I., N.S.W.M.R., and W.A.M.I. De Lisle, after softening up the enemy with two pom-poms, ordered the 6th M.I. to dismount and work up the hill. The N.S.W.M.R. were sent as support troops and the W.A.M.I. were held in reserve. As soon as De Lisle saw that the British regulars had gained a footing on the hill, he let loose the men from New South Wales. They stormed onward in open order and against brisk fire, fighting their way up the steep hill and bursting over the crest with fixed bayonets. But there was none of the hand-to-hand fighting that the Australians always loved to contemplate, for the Boers had retreated from the kopje. De Lisle's men had in fact captured the key to Botha's position, for the way was now clear for Ian Hamilton to bring his artillery on to Diamond Hill plateau, from whence he could shell the Boers at all points. Hearing of De Lisle's success, Botha withdrew his force.[165]

The courage and dash of the N.S.W.M.R. was reminiscent of the Vet River engagement, and it pointed forward to Gallipoli and Flanders. But it was yet another occasion when Australian officers displayed a tragic recklessness. As the men moved forward on their stomachs up the hill, Lieutenants Harriot and Drage stood up and urged the troopers forward by name. In foolhardy defiance, they even stopped to fill their pipes although their men implored them to take cover Both men were soon struck by bullets. Drage was shot through the head, but it took four troopers to restrain the dying man from stumbling forward against the Boer position. Both officers died, as did two troopers.[166] De Lisle's corps was complimented by Roberts and Ian Hamilton and De Lisle was himself ecstatic over the work of the N.S.W.M.R.[167] When General Ridley paraded the corps in recognition of its fight, the Gordon Mounted Infantry sought and gained permission to give the New South Wales men three cheers.[168]

After Pretoria Roberts had two objectives in mind. He wanted to complete the crushing of the Transvaal by a drive along the Pretoria-Delagoa Bay railway to Komati Poort, a town on the Portuguese East African border. This would rid him of the temporary seat of Boer government at Machadodorp, and the army of Louis Botha. And he wanted to crush Free State opposition which, inspired by President Steyn and Christian de Wet, was threatening his supplies and communications. He gave scant consideration to enemy activity in Western Transvaal, where another breed of Australian soldier, the Bushman, was making his presence felt.

The drive to Middelburg passed with little event, as Botha was prepared to risk rearguard skirmishes only, and French had been instructed by Roberts to avoid bloodshed wherever possible. At that point Roberts broke off his advance to send nine columns fruitlessly chasing after de Wet for a month. In late August the drive began again. Roberts had been joined by Buller's Natal army, and September found Buller and French forming the wings of a fan-like movement with the railway as its centre. By 23 September about 25 000 British troops had pushed Botha's 5000 Boers into a trap on a border lined with flags and Portuguese soldiers. Half the Boer force sought refuge in Portuguese territory; the other half eluded the British to fight another day. President Kruger had also retreated into Portuguese East Africa and on 19 October he sailed for Europe in the Nederlands cruiser, *Gelderland*. The war seemed to be over. Lord Roberts thought as much and informed the Home government that some troops could be withdrawn.[169] He, himself, sailed home to England and an earldom and the Order of the Garter, after handing over command to Lord Kitchener on 29 November 1900.

The war was far from over, however, and the unfortunate nature it was already assuming owed much to the policy of Roberts, although history was to accord him very little criticism. The field-marshal had at first treated the enemy with great rectitude, forbidding entry to houses and damage to property, and seeing that all stores were paid for at market prices. When de Wet and other commanders began to attack his supply lines, however, he retaliated with little discrimination. On 16 June 1900 he had proclaimed that farms adjacent to telegraph cuts or train derailments would be burned. On 18 November he modified this to decree the destruction of houses which were used as firing or supply bases.[170] Roberts found the latter proclamation necessary because, with the towns and railways lost as sources of supply, the farmsteads were now the life-line of the Boer cause. Their destruction became an avowed military aim and, because the displaced families could not be left to starvation or the Kaffirs, the concentration camp became 'the inevitable corollary of the policy of devastation'.[171] So after Komati Poort—even after Pretoria to some extent—the work of the army lacked excitement and was without glory. Of the 210 000 men Kitchener had at his disposal when he assumed command almost 100 000 were guarding the railways. The sick and the straggling and the non-combatants accounted for tens of thousands of others. The remainder were organized into fourteen columns which were engaged in breaking up small bodies of the enemy, searching for arms, burning farms and bringing in refugees, and collecting or destroying resources such as grain and stock.[172]

The history of the first and second Australian contingents during the period after Pretoria is not a happy one. It is a tale of lack of action, diminishing numbers, disillusionment, and a desire to go home.

The advance to Komati Poort is well documented by Australian diaries and letters, but none of their authors is able to make out a case for Australian military achievement although such was their usual desire. In the first place, the mounted infantry played a minor role, and the cavalry did little more. Much to Hutton's annoyance, his force (which now included no Australians but the N.S.W.A.M.C.) was frequently used on the lines of communication. 'The Mounted Troops seem to have done little', he said, and attributed this to the fact that the cavalry would not close with the Boers and the mounted infantry were not given the chance.[173]

Amid such restricted military opportunity the Australians were further hampered by depleted numbers. The two cavalry squadrons had been so reduced that Paterson left French in late June to view the war from the point of view of Ian Hamilton's mounted infantry.[174]

The N.S.W.M.R., with an original strength of 650, made an attempt to re-form at Pretoria after chasing de Wet during July and August, but found themselves sadly deficient in horses as well as men, all their Australian mounts having been expended. Reasonable horses were found for 130 men but another 130 had to wait because their commanding officer would not accept Argentine remounts. The drive to Komati Poort went on ahead of the N.S.W.M.R. In October they were chasing de Wet again, with everybody so fed up that an officer feared mutiny.[175] The

Q.M.I. almost ceased to exist about this time. Colonel Ricardo had few men and no horses, and no hope that he would obtain horses. He wrote: 'We all feel that the war is over and cannot get up any excitement but we *do* wish they would send us home'.[176] Ricardo had proved himself a poor leader and much of the blame for the disintegration of the Q.M.I. must rest on him. He accepted an administrative position in occupied Pretoria and ceased to show any real interest in his regiment. 'Ricardo is a rank failure and coward', claimed one of his men, 'and has been the curse of the Q.M.I.'[177] By contrast, Colonel Tom Price of the V.M.R. stuck to his depleted command and led it ragged and hungry into Komati Poort.

Australian disillusionment over the end of any real fighting was deepened by the nature of the new war against the civil population. Paterson publicly expressed his repugnance at the conduct of the war. At Bloemfontein he had 'lightheartedly' advocated the burning of farms, but when he saw it done, with crying women struggling to remove their possessions from doomed houses in the fifteen minutes allowed them, he was disgusted. All Australians, he stated, were sick of the war and wanted to go home. There was no honour or glory in chasing a few Boers from hill to hill and burning homes over women's heads.[178]

Even Captain Hubert Murray, whose personal correspondence indicates a deep and abiding concern for himself above all, could manage some feeling for the enemy. In July he was engaged in 'breaking up wagons and collecting horses', an occupation he described as 'not very pleasant' because he was 'continually surrounded by weeping women'.[179] In September he took up an appointment as Provost-Marshal with a British brigade, accepting that his principal work would be 'burning farms and turning out women and children to starve'.[180] A little later he noted that he hated the whole business but would 'have to see it through'.[181] And in October he was in Cape Town trying to get leave to go to England because there was nothing to do at the front but 'steal cows'.[182]

The desire to rid themselves of South Africa was widespread among both officers and men. Most just wanted to go home. Others wanted to go home by way of England. Some wanted to go to the Boxer Rebellion. Lord Roberts made the majority preference possible when in October he issued an order allowing 'such officers and men of 1st Contingents from overseas colonies, who have urgent reasons for desiring to return to their homes, to do so at once'.[183]

According to *The Times History*, the decision was taken in order to avoid grievance and 'to do nothing to discourage the patriotic ardour which had called these men to the ranks'.[184] But one result was to promote considerable grievance among men of the second Australian contingent who felt they should be allowed to go home with their comrades. Roberts and Kitchener could not accede to their requests, however, because a further reduction in the mounted force was considered risky. They had to wait until the anniversary of their arrival in South Africa, although there was no obligation on the part of military authorities to release them after twelve months service. The usual term of enlistment for colonials was twelve months and such time after as they might be required.

Perhaps it was the advice of Lord Milner, added to colonial complaint, that secured the early departure of the Australians and other irregulars while the great bulk of the British army laboured on. In a letter to Joseph Chamberlain, Milner expressed grave concern at the war-weariness and discontent of the South African and overseas colonials. They need to be humoured, he suggested, so release them at an early date 'with cordial thanks' and just hope that some will return to the field.[185]

Before closing the story of the work and worth of the first and second contingents in South Africa, something should be said of an Australian unit which never experienced the exhilaration of marching with Roberts, but which languished on the western perimeter of the theatre of war. This was 'A Battery of the Royal Australian Artillery, the only body of professional soldiers to represent Australia in the South African War. The New South Wales military commandant had expected more of 'A' Battery than of any other unit from the mother colony, but the men of the permanent artillery were never given a chance.

The activities of the battery over a period of eighteen months were recorded in reports by its commanding officer, Colonel S. C. Smith, to the New South Wales commandant,[186] but the tale told is one of frustration. The unit arrived at Belmont ten days after Roberts had begun his advance from that area, although it is not clear that Imperial authorities intended the battery to join the invasion force. Very soon the unit was split into three sections of two guns each and scattered throughout the rebel country of north-western Cape Colony. From then on Smith battled in vain to retain for his command some identity as a unit and to get them into action. In despair, he offered the battery for service in the Boxer Rebellion and for the grand review which, according to rumour, the Queen was to hold after the war. The old Imperial officer's reports ended on a highly expectant note as he waited at Prieska with a fraction of his force for the ubiquitous de Wet. But Prieska was too remote even for that itinerant gentleman.

Without benefit of a war correspondent the battery completely passed from public view, and on two occasions the New South Wales premier was questioned in parliament as to its whereabouts. But Lyne could only answer that it was in South Africa.[187]

Australians acted more like imperialists than nationalists in 1900, so the essential thing to them was the supremacy of British arms. Therefore, they could react with almost unbelievable fervour to the relief of Ladysmith, although no Australian unit had been within hundreds of miles of Natal.[188] And they could turn the relief of Mafeking into a riotous public holiday, although the only Australians connected with the event were one hundred Queensland Bushmen who arrived on the scene just as the siege was lifted.[189] They were also ready to revere Roberts and Baden Powell above Tom Price and Charlie Cox. It was natural for colonial and municipal leaders to shower thanks and compliments on the great commander of the South African Field Force, but the fuss made over Baden Powell[190] was hardly merited. He had done very little apart from remaining in ineffectual command in besieged Mafeking.

When the occasion presented itself, however, Australians were ready and willing to show their pride in their own fighting men, who had advanced as equals with British regulars in Roberts's great victories, and whose worth had been recognized by the field-marshal himself. As the relatively small casualty lists came through from South Africa, memorial services were held in suburbs and towns and hamlets, and flags were flown at half-mast. But it was when the invalids came back, and the first contingents marched home again, that the nation rose to express itself. And generally what it expressed was relief that its representatives had not failed the test of fire, and a conviction that the soldiers had brought the country nationhood and world acclaim.

From May 1900 onwards groups of invalids returned to Australia at approximately monthly intervals.[191] The rank of the statesmen and military officers receiving the invalids, and the size and enthusiasm of the welcoming crowds, had declined to humble proportions by August 1900, but the reception of the first group in May was worthy of the men who had sacrificed their health for the Empire in enteric-ridden Africa.

In Melbourne on that occasion the lieutenant-governor, the premier, and enthusiastic crowds welcomed forty-nine invalids from the eastern colonies.[192] The men from Queensland, New South Wales and New Zealand went on to an even greater reception in Sydney. Earl Beauchamp, Lyne and French all spoke comforting words and the men were taken through the crowded streets in triumph. Beauchamp told them to speak freely about their wants and French assured them that their injuries were all treasured by the people of New South Wales. Lyne said that there had been nothing so glorious in the history of Australia as their volunteering to help the British cause and their display of courage, which was equal to that of any other troops in the campaign.[193] An editorial comment noted that Australians could no longer be regarded as mere volunteers and amateurs for now they had 'a tried and attested value'.[194]

Individual invalids were also given enthusiastic receptions in their local areas, notable instances being a mile-long procession and mayoral reception for a Windsor trooper,[195] and a welcome home at Rylstone for Lieutenant Dowling of Slingersfontein fame who was greeted by a reception committee which included General French.[196]

The men of the first contingent came home in December 1900 and January 1901 to a people flushed by the new nationhood, by apparent British victory in South Africa, and by recent praise from Roberts for the colonial troops. The commander-in-chief had sent eulogistic cables to each of the colonies in November. All were similar in content and tone, for Roberts always was loath to make distinctions that would offend any section of the first Imperial army, which he so proudly led.[197] Of the men from New South Wales, he said: 'They have rendered invaluable service to the mother country, and can pride themselves on having won golden opinions from all ranks. I cannot praise them too highly or thank them sufficiently for the gallant work they have done in South Africa'.[198]

The returned soldiers were given a series of welcomes as the *Harlech Castle*, carrying men from all colonies, made its way around the south-eastern coastline. Adelaide provided the first reception. Amid huge Saturday crowds, Colonel Tom Price led the sun-burned and gaunt veterans in procession. Lord Tennyson was too ill to review the troops but the premier and other ministers proclaimed their worth. The chief secretary called upon the testimony of Lord Roberts as proof of the men's courage.[199]

The Melbourne reception was under-written by a half-day public holiday and a full-day school holiday, although what took place was hardly children's fare. The *Age* described the welcome as a 'lamentable fiasco' and something akin to the 'saturnalia' of Mafeking Day. It suggested that 5000 members of the defence forces who marched in the procession should have been used to control the crowds.[200]

The units marched off the pier to the tune of 'When Johnny Comes Marching Home' and went on up through the humble dwellings of South Melbourne where pictures of 'Bobs' and B.P., cut from illustrated periodicals, adorned doors and windows. But the lines of veterans soon lost all their military order as young women and others mingled with the heroes.

A luncheon presided over by the premier, Sir George Turner, gave many notables an opportunity to praise the men and assess the significance of their service in South Africa. The lieutenant-governor, Sir John Madden, stated that Australians stood a far different people from what they were a year before, and all because of the work of the soldiers in the field. 'It is you who have broken the sod of our glory, and you will be remembered as Scotland regards Bannockburn, as Ireland regards Limerick, as Holland remembers the men who fought with (sic) Alva'.

Turner remarked that the contingent had gone away as untried men but had returned with the praises of 'the best soldier in the British Empire', and McCulloch claimed that Australia had proved that she 'could produce children equal to any other in the world on the cricket, the battle or any other field'. At this point Major Cameron of the Tasmanians, an ex-Imperial officer, thought it necessary to remind everyone that the Australians weren't the only people in South Africa and that it had been the British army which had borne 'the heat and battle of the day and did the lion's work'.

That night, amid fireworks and illuminations and revelry of 'young men of riotous instincts', the veterans were 'shouted' by the populace, who paid no heed to Roberts's request to the Empire not to press alcoholic beverages on to returning men.[201]

Huge crowds also filled the streets of Sydney to welcome the troops from New South Wales, Queensland and New Zealand, although it was a working day and no holiday had been proclaimed. Both Lyne and J. See, the chief secretary, assured the veterans that they had done much more than Australia had dared to expect; and they dwelt at length on those 'sleeping in South Africa'.[202] When more troops returned on the *Orient* early in January 1901, Lyne was obliged to say much the same things again, but Edmund Barton, the first prime minister of Australia, was moved to a more generous utterance: 'The deeds they have done', he said, 'were worthy of the company in which they were done and of the brave enemy they fought'.[203] Meanwhile the man who started it all was lying on his death-bed. J. R. Dickson, the Commonwealth minister for defence and recipient in the New Year honours of the K.C.M.G., which his Labor opponents claimed he was seeking when he offered Queensland troops in July 1899, was dying within earshot of the revelry.

Only two colonial parliaments took steps to honour the return of the first contingent. South Australia, acknowledging the lead given by the New Zealand legislature, passed a motion tendering thanks to the troops and extending sympathy to the relatives of the fallen. The matter was completed with minimal discussion.[204] A motion in the Western Australian legislature was far more laudatory and was supported by considerable debate. It paid tribute to the valour and contribution of the Western Australian fighting men on the authority of 'the Commander-in-Chief and his Generals'.[205]

As the months rolled by other contingents returned, but never to the same public enthusiasm. In fact, the 'welcome homes' followed the same pattern as the 'send-offs' and the receptions to the invalids: diminishing crowds, diminishing stature of the official welcoming parties, and diminishing plaudits. All of which was perfectly understandable, for the basis of the lionization of the Australian soldier was very insubstantial. Political leaders could not continue to make flamboyant speeches whose justification was no more than the polite praise of Lord Roberts. And the Australian crowds soon tired of a recurring spectacle. Continuing enthusiasm for the departure and arrival of troops was possible only if those troops were fighting bloody battles in a noble cause, but the desperate fighting had ceased almost before the Australians had reached the field, and feeling against the Boers had subsided once they ceased to pose a threat to Imperial prestige, and once the press was obliged to drop the fiction of an evil, grasping foe in the face of contrary testimony from such correspondents as the widely read and highly respected Paterson. The work of the first and second contingents was not without merit, however, and was very significant in the development of Australian nationalism. Drawn predominantly from the part-time military forces of the colonies, they were able to make an immediate contribution to the war. Because their training had been along Imperial lines and their discipline fairly well developed, they had merged easily with British units. Contingent members had shown a keenness to fight and a dash in battle that had distinguished them from the more stolid Tommy. Their reputation for dash was partly a product of their excellent horsemanship, but fearlessness was also a factor. Australians did not throw up a fight readily and there is no parallel among them of the large-scale surrenders that plagued their British counterparts, the irregular Imperial Yeomanry.[206] Sunnyside, Pink Hill, Vet River, and Diamond Hill were minor engagements, but in them Australians had shown a competence and a reckless courage that heralded bigger things. Roberts, Kitchener, Hutton and other British generals could therefore praise them with confidence and the Australian people could justifiably believe that their representatives had brought added recognition to the new nation by their military prowess.

4 The Bushmen, the Draft Contingents, and the Australian Commonwealth Horse

The first and second contingents had not been easily raised from among the part-time military forces of the Australian colonies, but the six contingents that followed were drawn from applicants far in excess of the modest numbers needed. The main reason for the changed situation was that the later contingents were open to a much larger section of the population. Influenced by the success of irregular mounted forces in the early months of the war, British authorities began to encourage the recruitment of good horsemen who need not possess any military training. This suited the Australian colonies admirably. The bush was full of skilled horsemen, and there seems to have developed from the very outset of war a wide belief that the bushman, with his ability to ride, to endure, to improvise and to find his way, was the natural opponent for the unorthodox Boer. Therefore governments and, under their influence, military authorities, made the bushmen the core of the third and subsequent contingents.

These later, non-militia contingents[1] had something else in common. The decisions to raise them were made after strong external influences had been brought to bear upon governments. The clamour of the public was not one of those influences, however, for the exuberance shown over the novelty of the first two contingents marching off to war was not maintained. But before the voice of the street crowds died away to almost nothing, the departure of the two Bushmen contingents attracted a lot of interest because they were also a novelty: purely citizen soldiers who bore no taint of militarism as the militia did. They also carried about them the romanticism bestowed on bush dwellers by the literature of the nineties.

The public became completely undemonstrative in the last twelve months of the conflict. We have no idea of their attitude to the increasing ferocity of the war against the civil population of the Boer republics. They could have expressed any antagonism within the framework of an incipient peace movement which developed late in the war, but did not do so. Their silence could be taken to mean acquiescence in the dispatch of further contingents, or it could indicate the submission of the ordinary man to the power of the press, which continued to promote the Imperial cause in South Africa and scorn those who raised a voice in protest.

But public hubbub was not needed to keep the contingents sailing off to plunder farms. The impetus came from other quarters: a direct call from Kitchener or an implied call from the *Times*; an initiative taken by Canada or New Zealand; or agitation by a subordinate politician backed up by the press. Supporting factors were the enthusiasm of the military establishments, and the willingness of some young Australians to participate in a war that had long ceased to promise an atom of glory.

The history of the non-militia contingents is notable, then, for the circumstances of their raising. It is less notable for what they achieved in South Africa, although the limited action they saw added to the recently-won reputation of Australians as potentially fine soldiers. Several incidents in the field, however, brought our fighting men under critical scrutiny, and provided a test for the sincerity of public opinion which had been quick to make the Australians the equal of the best soldiers in the Empire.

Action to form a Bushmen's contingent emerged from a series of happenings which were reported in the press in the week beginning 21 December 1899. On that day was published the text of a cable from the Colonial Office which stated that volunteers for the second contingent 'must be good shots and competent riders, but need not be members of any regular trained force'.[2] The following morning the London cables reported that Canada had offered the services of 1000 experienced 'rough riders',[3] and that afternoon a member suggested to the New South Wales Legislative Assembly that the government send to South Africa a body of 'bushmen who were rough riders and good shots'.[4] Three days later it was reported that the Victorian government had suggested to Lyne the formation of a Bushmen's corps,[5] and after a further two days, the *Age* noted that Lyne had informed the Victorian premier that a corps of mounted bushmen was being raised privately in New South Wales.[6]

That colony quickly took the lead. A committee of citizens was formed with J. R. Carey as president and J. M. Atkinson as secretary. Its members included a number of the great pastoralists of the colony. The plan was to raise a force of five hundred bushmen for service as scouts in South Africa, to mount them on donated horses, and to raise enough funds to pay and equip them, in the manner of the first two contingents, for six months in the field (the anticipated duration of the war). It was considered that the recent British military calamities were the result of poor scouting. The original intention, therefore, was that the Bushmen be attached to British regiments in lots of twenty to fifty to be the eyes and ears of the regular forces.[7]

The committee set out to raise £30 000 and 500 horses. It raised the money, thanks to donations of £5000 each from S. McCaughey and W. R. Hall and £3000 from S. Hordern, but it ended up buying almost half the horses needed.[8] The government did not subsidize the contingent in New South Wales. Lyne assured the committee that he would not see the movement short of a few thousand pounds, but he hoped that it could maintain its voluntary nature so that the force could go forward as a truly Citizens' Bushmen's contingent.[9] French was instructed to work in with Carey and provide officers and N.C.O.'s to test and train the recruits.

Another unsuccessful effort was made to create a federal force after the Colonial Office accepted Lyne's offer of a Bushmen's contingent and undertook to send troopships. The New South Wales premier telegraphed his counterparts in the other colonies, and Carey communicated with the mayors of the colonial capitals, each wanting to know the number of men they could contribute to the contingent.[10] By this time, however, most colonies were going it alone in the accustomed fashion, making their individual offers to Chamberlain and regarding their contingents as independent units. But most of them encountered financial difficulties.

The movement lagged so badly in Victoria that the lieutenant-governor addressed a press letter to the people of the colony, promoting the Bushmen concept and asking for financial support.[11] This was not forthcoming in the amount required, and cabinet was obliged to take up the responsibility of sending a contingent of 250, after expressing regret at the poor response of the public.[12] The Western Australian government found it necessary to subsidize the movement pound for pound,[13] and the

131

Queensland government assumed full responsibility for the contingent; partly out of enthusiasm, it seemed, but mainly because the organizing committee had only raised £632 by 1 February.[14] The committee in South Australia reached its target without government assistance by making an appeal through the mayor of Adelaide for contributions to be sent to the Bushmen's Fund in preference to the Patriotic Fund, and by the successive sale without delivery of the horse, *Bugler*. This steed was paraded through town and country, and was responsible for raising £2500 of the £12 000 needed to send 100 Bushmen to war.[15]

The response of the Australian people to the various Bushmen's funds was average to poor. Contributions were certainly not proportional to the wild enthusiasm of the street crowds during the same period, and it is reasonable to regard the situation as evidence of the lack of depth in support for the war. Very modest support for the Patriotic funds corroborates this view.[16]

By the end of February all colonies had raised their contingents. The most interesting recruiting campaigns were in New South Wales, Victoria and South Australia. The New South Wales Bushmen's committee had no trouble in getting recruits. Its biggest problem was the physical difficulty of selecting 500 men from almost 2000 accredited bushmen volunteers, and having less than a month in which to do so. To make the task more difficult, there was friction between the committee and the military officers assigned to help in the preparation of the volunteers. The officers resented the intrusion of civilians into military matters, and the committee were keen to assert their ideas for organizing the contingent. The committee also had to cope with fraud on the part of incompetent volunteers who got friends to take riding and shooting tests for them, although the incidence was probably not high because fraudulent recruits were informed upon by disgruntled rejects.[17] There was also the problem of members of parliament who demanded that their recommendation of a bushman be accepted as an alternative to the recommendation of a pastoralist.[18]

The recruiting procedure was for a volunteer to complete an application form, which had to be signed by a member of the committee or a military or police officer in charge of a district as an endorsement of the applicant's ability to ride and shoot. A

Victorian Bushmen parading through Melbourne prior to embarkation

The Boer War Memorial at Goulburn, New South Wales. Similar memorials exist throughout Australia in silent tribute to otherwise forgotten men.

local medical officer's signature was also required as evidence of physical fitness. But even then the application was incomplete without a letter from a pastoralist commending the volunteer as an experienced bushman.[19] This procedure alone would have meant a decent standard of recruit, but quite stringent medical, riding, and shooting tests at the encampments at Randwick rifle range and Kensington racecourse ensured that the contingent was composed of fit men, at ease on a horse and handy with a rifle. What they were beyond that, the committee did not care, for as Atkinson said, 'We did not inquire into the morals or the morality of the men at all'.[20] But one newspaper was prepared to say that 'fully 60 percent' of the contingent were a fine stamp of intelligent manhood.[21]

An extant nominal roll of 'A' squadron of the New South Wales Citizens' Bushmen helps build up a picture of the contingent. They were bigger men than the general run of Australians, having an average height of five feet nine inches. With an average age of twenty-six years and ten months, they were old enough to have had extensive bush experience, but young enough to possess the dash and recklesness of youth. If it was the rural aristocracy who supplied the bulk of the equipment and other means of war, it was the rural proletariat who climbed lithely into the gift saddles. Only eighteen members of the squadron of 120 were men of property.[22] In order to control effectively 'the wild men', as French called them,[23] officers were appointed principally from the defence forces. Of the nineteen commissioned men, only five had not previously served as officers.[24]

The organization of the Victorian Bushmen's contingent was in the hands of a committee composed of D. McLeod, M.L.A., Rear-Admiral W. B. Bridges, pastoralist, and a Mr Pearson. McLeod admitted during discussion of the Victorian Military Contingent Bill (No. 3) that there had been grave shortcomings in selection procedures, for although 1700 men had volunteered only 400 were invited to attend for tests. And they had been invited solely on the basis of their letters seeking enrolment. In fact, 150 of these had originally been rejected by ballot, leaving 250 volunteers from which to select 200. But failure to report, along with rejections, made it necessary to call up the entire 400. McLeod acknowledged that under such a system many of the best men would not have been given a fair chance. In answer to members who questioned the genuineness of some bush applicants, he admitted that there were a number of city-dwellers in the contingent, but claimed that they had worked in the country.[25] As in New South Wales, officers were drawn from men with previous military leadership experience, and the ranks were filled predominantly from the lower order of rural society.[26]

Of all the colonies, South Australia came closest to making the raising of the Bushmen's contingent entirely a citizens' affair, and the title of Citizens' Bushmen, used only of the New South Wales contingent, could more validly have been applied to the South Australians. Committees did all the planning, referring occasionally to the military commandant for advice, and set about the task of recruiting 100 men on the basis of 'bush experience, general physique, intelligence and character'. Twelve hundred written applications were received in answer to press advertisements. Those volunteers under twenty-five were rejected first, as not of sufficient bush experience nor maturity. This left about 1000, who were reduced to the required number by a series of eliminations, including tests of fitness and horsemanship.

The position of commanding officer was eagerly sought by subalterns of the defence force, but the selection committee, advised by the commandant, considered that no officer of the rank of captain had the qualifications to lead such a unique body of men. It looked for 'some first-class civilian, used to authority', and the choice fell on S. G. Hubbe, the chief inspector of vermin destruction, and the man who led the South Australian stock route expedition from Oodnadatta to Fowler's Bay.[27]

The various colonial corps embarked mainly in the first days of March 1900 and if the size of the farewelling crowds was a barometer of public support for the war, there was a discernible waning. This was despite the fact that public holidays or half-holidays were invariably granted for the occasion. Only from South Australia were there reports of crowds in excess of those that farewelled the first two contingents. It was estimated that over 100 000 people thronged the streets of Adelaide.[28] Melbourne's farewell was without benefit of bands and military escort, but for the first time in Victoria the departing troops were mounted, and this provided new interest for the crowds. Most of the Bushmen carried flowers handed up to them by girls, while at the wharf many people wept and the lieutenant-governor said with pride, 'We have chosen you from among ourselves'.[29]

The Sydney crowds were reckoned to be smaller than for the departure of the second contingent, but nonetheless were estimated at 200 000. In contrast with the Melbourne ceremony, the Sydney farewell neglected none of the pomp and circumstance that had characterized the departure of the second contingent. There was a military escort of 1600 troops and the usual procession of official carriages. These were headed by the ministerial vehicles, one of which contained a Queensland guest, A. Dawson of the Labor opposition. Dawson had opposed the first contingent, supported the bill to send the second, and was now absorbing some of the reflected glory of the departure of the third. A carriage of ministers of religion followed their temporal brothers, and later in the procession came a waggonette of Roman Catholic clergy. But the centre of interest for the people were the 500 superbly mounted Bushmen. They sat their steeds with the ease and vanity of true bush horsemen, their 'flashness' enhanced by the uniform of the N.S.W.M.R. and a distinguishing 'A.B.C.' on the shoulder. There were speeches at the wharf. The lieutenant-governor, Sir Frederick Darley, warned them against impetuosity (possibly a result of Slingersfontein and Pink Hill), and Lyne spoke of courage and loyalty. Poor French could only express his own disappointment at again failing to get to South Africa.[30]

In the view of the press there was no doubt that a new and distinctive Australian product had emerged—the bushman soldier. A leading article in the *Sydney Morning Herald* proudly announced the event and hailed the Bushmen as possessors of 'all the mobility of the Boers, all their endurance, their knowledge of rough life, and their courage'.[31] The *Advertiser* saw the corps as representative of 'the only romantic figure left in colonial life'. The Bushmen would fill a disastrous scouting weakness in the British army, and develop into fine irregular troops, being 'tough and wiry, with abundant resource and self-confidence, steadfast and trustworthy'.[32] The *Argus* also idealized them.[33]

The final accolade came from the pen of Premier McLean, a versifier of some note among his friends, who now submitted his art to the public gaze in honour of the warriors mustered from the bush.

> . . . O'er Austral lands the bugles blow,
> And rolls the martial drum;
> Their warlike strains like magic flow,

> They reach the Bushman's home:
> From hills where snow-fed rivers flow,
> From forests deep, from mountains brow,
> From out each darksome vale below,
> The hardy Bushmen come . . . [34]

While the Bushmen were being selected and given their limited training, discussions concerning their eventual deployment in South Africa were proceeding in high places. The board of the British South African Company had become very concerned over the unprotected condition of Rhodesia, fearing a Kaffir rising as well as a Boer invasion. Approaches were made to the Imperial government for troops but it was reluctant to commit its forces any further. It did agree, however, to finance a force of 5000 men if the company took responsibility for raising them. The Home Government stipulated that the force be raised outside Britain. As only a limited number of recruits were available in Rhodesia, the company sent a confidential agent to initiate a recruiting campaign in Canada and the United States. At this point the Imperial government stepped in. Afraid of the repercussions of an unofficial scheme of obtaining volunteers in North America, it decided to send Imperial forces drawn from British Yeomanry and Australian volunteers. There were already 1300 Australian Bushmen about to embark, so why not direct them to Rhodesia and request a further 2000 from the same source?[35]

Chamberlain's cable to Lyne sought 2000 men 'of a similar kind to the Bushmen'. They would be paid 5s a day by the Imperial government, which would also meet other expenses involved in the raising of the force. Colonial governments were simply asked to act as agents for the Home authorities. Lyne wasted no time, again seeing himself in the role of co-ordinator of a federal force. He passed on the text of the Colonial Office cable on 28 February. Within four days all other colonial premiers had agreed to co-operate, Lyne had notified Chamberlain, and Chamberlain had expressed his pleasure at Australia's 'patriotic readiness'.[36]

The only difficulty arose when the New South Wales premier suggested representation in the contingent on the basis of population. Philp demanded a larger share of the contingent for Queensland, and was particularly indignant that Victoria was allotted 626 places, while Queensland was allotted only 270. He felt that this should not be, in view of the 'limited assistance previously rendered by Victorians' and the abundance of cheap horses and good bushmen in Queensland.[37] Unable to get anywhere with Lyne, Philp appealed to the Imperial authorities and was allowed an additional 120 places.[38]

Chamberlain's request for more troops seemed to set the final mark of approval on Australia's fighting men. The *Sydney Morning Herald* stated that the request was 'flattering to the newly-born military spirit of Australians' and believed that 'no greater compliment' could be paid to the people or the soldiers they had sent to the front.[39] The fourth contingent quite properly took the name of the Imperial Bushmen's Contingent. It was raised at Imperial request and was the responsibility of the Home government in all matters of pay, allowances and pensions.

The ranks of the Imperial Bushmen were filled with greater ease than those of the Australian Bushmen. More than 12 000 volunteers came forward for the 2000 available places. Victoria and South Australia had double the number that offered for the previous contingent, although applicants were given only a week in which to forward their names. Victoria had over 4000 volunteers from which to select 620.[40] South Australia had over 2000 from which to select 200.[41]

Greater efforts were also made to recruit none but real bushmen, for Chamberlain had specified that type. Recruiting officers in New South Wales and Victoria moved into the hinterland to get the genuine article. 'Go away out to the end of the railway track', French told his selection committee.[42] And that is where he enlisted most of his recruits. South Australian officers apparently did not go so far out along the tracks, because a detailed nominal role published in the *Advertiser* gives many urban occupations.[43] With ten volunteers seeking each place in the contingent, however, the men selected probably displayed those skills commonly associated with the bushman.

Colonel Tom Price had complained in the early months of the war of a lack of interest in the defence forces on the part of the wealthier classes in Victoria. His was a criticism that could validly have been applied to all colonies. The first three contingents were overwhelmingly proletarian. The Imperial contingent showed a decided increase in middle-class representation, however. Not only had more of this category come forward, but selection committees had clearly favoured them. The trend was probably the result of the increased status of the soldier, which had reached its peak in March with the general acceptance in Australia of the worth of the men of the first contingent and the Imperial call for more Australians. It was clearly discernible in South Australia and New South Wales. In the former colony there was little scope for a place in the commissioned ranks of the contingent, because the military commandant, who handled the recruiting, gave all but two places to officers of the defence forces.[44] But many men of substance gained selection as non-commissioned officers or troopers. Old boys of St Peter's and Prince Alfred colleges alone accounted for thirty-four places in the contingent.[45]

In New South Wales the emergence of an upper class element was most noticeable in the fight for thirty-three commissioned positions. A total of 222 persons applied, of whom 116 had previous military experience of varying significance. But of those selected ten had no military experience of any kind,[46] although they had high social standing. Three of them, John Oxley, Allan Gidley King, and Fitzwilliam Wentworth, came from old and revered families.[47]

The Imperial Bushmen were more fortunate than other contingents in that they had a month and more of basic training. This probably accounts for the praise they received for their military bearing during the progress to the docks, but perhaps they carried themselves so erect out of sheer pride at wearing the uniform of already proven soldiers. That is certainly what they were told on all sides as they left for South Africa. The *Advertiser* saw Australia henceforth as a recruiting ground for the War Office,[48] and the *Sydney Morning Herald* wondered how Australians could be done without in South Africa.[49]

Colonial governments were generally reluctant to declare public holidays for the departure of the fourth contingent. The omission may have owed something to custom having staled; but it could be attributed with greater certainty to an official attitude which regarded the Imperial Bushmen as a force for which Australian governments had little or no responsibility. Sydney was given a holiday on 23 April, St George's Day, but this was mainly to balance the public holiday granted on St Patrick's Day in recognition of the valour of the Irish regiments in the Natal campaign.

Despite the help of a public holiday, the Sydney send-off was not an enthusiastic affair. Decorations were sparse and the cheers sporadic. For the first time Lyne did not join his fellow ministers in the procession, but made a farewell speech at the docks in which he simply advised the troops to follow in the path of those who had already made a name for Australia.[50] The Adelaide farewell was the only one that was reported as equalling the earlier farewells in enthusiasm, despite the fact that there was no public holiday.[51]

With the Imperial Bushmen on the high seas, Australia's commitment to the war totalled 6600 men. This represented only 0.15 per cent of her total population, but the enlistment and dispatch of four contingents within six months had given public, press and parliaments plenty to divert themselves with. The excesses of statement and of ceremony which had surrounded the first contingents had moderated by the time of the departure of the Imperial Bushmen, however, and in the months that followed a self-satisfied quiescence fell upon the land. This feeling of well-being was sustained by the brief London cables which fed the local press, and which occasionally reported an action involving Australian units, or the praise of a British commander. Little more was needed and Australians got precious little more, for the correspondents covering the war for the major dailies of south-eastern Australia all ceased writing during 1900. W. J. Lambie of the *Age, Daily Telegraph* and *Advertiser* had been killed in February. W. T. Reay of the Melbourne *Herald* and South Australian *Register* had been forced home by illness when the army reached Bloemfontein. Donald Macdonald of the *Argus* and *Sydney Morning Herald* had returned to Australia a physical wreck after being besieged in Ladysmith. A. B. Paterson of the *Argus, Sydney Morning Herald,* and *Advertiser* had left the battlefield in July, two months before Roberts had reached Komati Poort. And Frank Wilkinson of the Sydney *Daily Telegraph,* the *Age* and the *Advertiser* also left South Africa before the end of 1900. Only Chaplain James Green of the Citizens' Bushmen continued to contribute newspaper articles into 1901. The Australian contingents thus disappeared for the most part into a communications vacuum, and that was to be the case for the rest of the war. Soldiers' letters to relatives appeared in the press in considerable numbers but they were rarely objective accounts. Most frequently they were tales of braggadocio and plunder that the radical press seized upon with glee as proof of the degeneracy of the conflict.

The home front came to life again in December 1900, however, with the return of the first contingent, and moves to send further troops to South Africa.

When Roberts handed over the South African command to Kitchener at the end of November 1900 the Boer armies had been fragmented but not beaten. They had formed into scores of highly mobile commandos which constantly harassed British troop movements and lines of supply. Only mounted troops were relevant against such a foe and there was an increasing dearth of these. Roberts had been reluctant to let the first colonial contingents return home and had refused to release the second Australian contingent before it had served twelve months in the field. Kitchener was so concerned that in late December he took action to obtain more mounted men from Britain and the colonies.

On 28 December it was revealed in the press that Chamberlain, on behalf of Kitchener, had suggested to the Australian colonies that they keep up the strength of their forces in South Africa by draft contingents. Pay would be at the rate of 5s a day and the Imperial government would also supply equipment.[52]

Although the colonies were within days of federating, there was still a marked desire among them to act individually. On 29 December it was reported that Tasmania was enlisting men.[53] On 3 January it was reported that South Australia was enrolling for a fifth contingent.[54] And on 4 January it was made public that Sir George Turner had approved the request of his minister for defence, the ultra-imperialist McCulloch, to raise a contingent of 400 men.[55]

Apparently some colony or colonies had notified British authorities of a willingness to send troops, for on 31 December Kitchener cabled the South Australian governor: 'I understand that Australia will send drafts to complete the contingents in the field. If so, when may I expect them? I wish to express my high appreciation of the most valuable services of the Aus-tralians . . .'[56] During all this activity, the colonial premiers were in Sydney for Commonwealth celebrations. On 7 January they met briefly to give joint approval for more troops. The tone of

Lyne's cable to Chamberlain was no longer that of a supplicant for Imperial favours; it was the rather imperious tone of a merchant who spoke for a product in high demand. The states would comply with the desire of the Imperial government for draft contingents, but British authorities must provide transport and equipment, and give New South Wales soldiers serving in South Africa the option of returning home.[57]

The reasoning behind individual state action was that the new contingents to be raised were actually drafts to replace men already sent by the separate colonies; in addition the Commonwealth department of defence was not yet functioning.

Recruiting began, and when more volunteers than were required came forward the infant states of the new federation fell back on old ways, and promptly began to compete in making troop offers beyond the numbers agreed to in Sydney. In succession, Victoria offered the War Office a sixth contingent of 500;[58] New South Wales offered to send 2000 instead of the 1000 which was her quota in the force of 2300 originally planned;[59] South Australia announced an offer of a sixth contigent; Queensland offered an additional 100 men,[60] and then undertook to fill another steamer if it were sent; and Western Australia and Tasmania each decided to send a sixth contingent.[61]

Just before this frenzy had begun, the prize-winning ode for Commonwealth Day, written by George Essex Evans, was announced. It is notable that the poem made neither reference nor allusion to Australia's military prowess, but it did contain two lines of supreme irony:

> Now are thy maidens linked in love
> Who erst have striven for pride of place.[62]

The initiative for the draft contingents had begun with Imperial authorities but it had soon passed to the premiers. Why had they pressed for the acceptance of additional troops when the war was generally regarded as being all but over? Admittedly there were stimulating factors such as the call from Kitchener, the enthusiastic public reception of the returning first contingent, and a rush of volunteers for the fifth contingent. But the pattern of activity of the parliamentary executives during January and February implied that state particularism was the prime motivating factor. And McCulloch was the man who started the bidding on this occasion. The Victorian minister for defence had served a term in the political wilderness after the dispatch of the first contingent, but he returned to resume the military portfolio with great enthusiasm, and much more was to be heard of him.

When recruiting began for the fifth contingent, the cry once more was for the bushman. Recruiting officials in Sydney were besieged by city men who made great efforts to prove they were bushmen, but only a few of the best were taken because 1500 applicants from the country were heading for Sydney on free rail warrants after rough local medicals. These were the men recognized by military authorities as 'most fitted to do credit to New South Wales'.[63] And when it was announced that the New South Wales contingent would be doubled, the first move was another call to the bush.[64] Queensland also sought the country man and Philp was able to announce proudly that 'fully 90 per cent' of the fifth contingent were bushmen.[65]

In all draft contingents there was a leavening of returned men and members of the defence forces. The latter category had gained few places in the Bushmen's contingents because of the peculiar nature of those corps, but they received preferential treatment in the draft contingents. This was particularly the case in the commissioned ranks. Of fifty-eight officers in the enlarged New South Wales fifth contingent, only five were listed as 'gentlemen'. The rest were from the defence forces and of these thirty-eight had seen service in South Africa, either as officers or in the ranks.[66] Victoria's forty-six officers all had previous military experience. Eleven of them were returned men.[67]

During February, March and April 1901 close to 5000 Australians left for South Africa. Some states sent their men separately as the fifth and sixth contingents. Others used the title of fifth contingent to cover the original force raised and the additional troops offered. Whatever the terminology used, the contingents sent represented an expeditionary force of good quality. Large numbers of volunteers had ensured high physical, riding, and shooting standards. Once again the men were overwhelmingly from the bush and therefore well endowed with the qualities of endurance and common sense. And there was a nucleus of experienced officers and men to lend stability to excellent raw material. J. See, the New South Wales premier, claimed that he had been told by 'competent judges' that the contingent from his state 'was equal, if not superior to any of its predecessors'.[68]

The farewell parades were relatively quiet affairs. But press editors and politicians still said complimentary things about what was widely regarded as another Imperial contingent, 'invited by one of the greatest commanders in the British army'.[69] Out of all the utterances emerged a common idea, however. The men of the fifth contingent had only to protect a military reputation that had already been won by the earlier contingents.

The keeness of Australians to serve in South Africa was evident in ways apart from the raising of the draft contingents. A representative of the Houlder Line, shippers of remounts to South Africa, revealed that the company had been 'besieged' by men wishing to work their passages to the Cape, and that 'upwards of 500 men' had been taken under those conditions already, with the object of joining South African irregular regiments on their arrival.[70] And at the same time as the fifth contingent was being raised in Victoria, agents of the Marquis of Tullibardine recruited 250 Victorians of Scottish descent to serve in the Scottish Horse, a regiment of irregular cavalry which the Marquis raised and led himself.

Direct recruiting within Australia for a British regiment created some resentment, however. The mayor of Melbourne, who was also president of the Caledonian Society, addressed a letter to the *Age* in which he dissociated himself from the Scottish Horse because he thought Australians should go in Australian regiments and preserve their identity.[71] And the Victorian commissioner for railways announced that only those employees who joined 'distinctly Victorian' contingents would have their positions kept for them.[72] Even sterner opposition resulted when Milner suggested that officers of Baden Powell's South African Constabulary might be allowed to recruit 1000 men in each state. The *Sydney Morning Herald* rejoiced that the request had received 'a point-blank negative' from Australian authorities. The paper drew a very uncertain distinction between sending volunteers to help fellow-subjects threatened with invasion, and transforming Australia into 'a happy hunting-ground for the recruiting sergeant'.[73] Australia had in fact long since become a reservoir of recruits for the War Office, with enlistment being greatly facilitated by 'recruiting sergeants' like Philp and

McCulloch. And the supply seemed inexhaustible within limits, as was to be shown when the Commonwealth contingents were raised early in 1902.

As 1901 progressed, the war in South Africa plunged further into the depths of inhumanity and agony. Kitchener stepped up his policy of laying waste to the land, and the women and children whom his soldiers took from ravaged farms died in increasing numbers in concentration camps. To these desperate strategies he added another, which aimed at destroying the marauding bands of Boers who continued to menace the 250 000-strong British army with waspish attacks. The block-house system was introduced. This initially entailed the construction of fortified posts at intervals along railway lines, but later the space between was closed with barbed wire to form great fences. Long lines of horsemen were then used to drive the enemy into the fences like fish into a net. For this operation and for generally chasing the enemy about the veldt, Kitchener wanted more and more mounted troops. And he wanted them quickly, for the protracted war was causing humiliation to the hero of Khartoum, and preventing him from succeeding to the coveted post of commander-in-chief in India.

The manner in which Australia was drawn further into the conflict demonstrates the power of a few individuals when backed by the press. The sequence of events, which ended in prime minister Edmund Barton's capitulation to a few voices, began on 9 December 1901 with the publication in the Australian press of a London account of German criticism of the colonial war effort. The German press was reported as saying that Australia's disinclination to send more troops to South Africa showed that England would find her colonies a broken reed to lean upon in times of trouble. It also considered that the military ardour of the British colonies had vanished as soon as they found that war was no nursery game.[74] On the same page the newspaper reported that a Canadian offer of nine hundred men had been accepted for service in South Africa.

On 10 December the *Age* and the *Argus* published a letter from McCulloch (who had lost his defence portfolio to the higher legislature), calling for a Commonwealth troop offer of 5000 men, as an answer to the 'broken reed' jibe.[75] On 12 December it was reported that See of New South Wales did not support McCulloch's call but two other premiers, A. Peacock of Victoria and Philp of Queensland, did. Barton was reported as saying that the state of affairs in South Africa did not warrant more troops, but if they were requested by the Imperial authorities the government would consider the matter.[76]

The case for further Australian commitment began to build up. The *Daily Telegraph* called for an offer of another contingent to silence German detractors, and noted that a New Zealand contingent of 1000 men was to go.[77] The following day it reported the warm praise of the English press for that colony's patriotic offer.[78] On 18 December the Victorian Legislative Assembly passed a motion, 'that this house expresses the hope that the Federal Government will offer, unasked, the services of an Australian contingent for South Africa'.[79]

Also on 18 December McCulloch wrote again to the press, mentioning the Canadian and New Zealand offers and wishing that 'we had at the head of our Commonwealth someone with sufficient backbone to rise to the occasion'.[80] But it was his next move that really brought results. Although the press did not get on to the story for some days, McCulloch breakfasted in Melbourne with Henniker Heaton of the House of Commons. Following their discussion the British M. P. cabled Chamberlain:

> Mr. McCulloch, Victorian Minister, asks me to inform you that he will undertake to equip and dispatch within one month a thousand good riders and shots (the majority of whom have already served in South Africa) with their horses, from Victoria, if you will wire Sir John Forrest to that effect.[81]

On 21 December Barton received a request from Chamberlain for 1000 men with the Imperial government meeting all costs.[82] Sections of the press were convinced that Heaton's cable, and Chamberlain's misconstruction of it as involving the Federal government, led to the request for troops.[83] Barton himself seemed to accept the awful truth when, in an interview with the *Advertiser*, he blamed 'intermeddling' persons for the request to Australia for only 1000 men when the people obviously wanted to send a larger contingent.[84]

Parliament was in recess when Barton received Chamberlain's request but cabinet promised compliance without delay. The prime minister obviously feared the wrath of the press more than he feared the Labor party which kept him in office and which had allegedly extracted a promise from him that he would take no action regarding more forces for South Africa without parliamentary sanction.[85]

Another pressure that had been constantly exerted upon Barton to commit Australia further was the attitude of the state premiers led by Peacock. The Victorian leader was happy to divulge to the press the details of a telegram to his fellow premiers which attacked Federal 'hesitation' and stressed the need for a show of Imperial loyalty for the benefit of continental powers. He asked each premier to bring pressure to bear on Barton, and sought support in raising a contingent should the prime minister not act. All states but New South Wales agreed, and each telegraphed Barton with a request for action, but the scheme was forestalled by Barton's response to Chamberlain's cable. There could be no doubt, however, that Peacock had gone 'within an ace of raising military forces in flat violation of the Federal Constitution'.[86]

Barton's eventual action on a contingent pleased none of his critics. The conservative press widely bemoaned the ignominy of Australia's having to be asked to help the Empire. The *Bulletin* was a little more understanding. A full-page cartoon depicted a miniature McCulloch dancing gleefully at the feet of a sombre Barton who scans a sheet listing the evils of militarism.[87] The same paper also referred to the new force to be raised as the 'Henniker Heaton Federal Cohentingent',[88] and printed a poem by Victor Daley which expressed a view of the war which none in the corridors of power could see or wanted to see. Entitled 'More Troops', its last verses ran:

> Australians, will ye falter? Are ye knaves?
> Cast off your foolish fear —
> The wind that blows across the children's graves
> Will soothe your dying ears.
> And ye shall, on the Day of Destiny,
> Lay claim to your reward:
> "We helped to choke in blood a people free —
> Look at our hands, O Lord![89]

On 14 January 1902 Barton brought before the House of

Representatives a two-part patriotic motion, and when he spoke in support it was obvious that his concern was to placate at one and the same time the powerful critics who had questioned his leadership and loyalty, and Labor parliamentarians who had wanted any decision on more troops to be a matter for debate in the legislature.[90] To excuse his earlier inaction Barton insisted that the Home government had created a clear precedent by asking the Australian colonies to raise the third, fourth and fifth contingents. Therefore it followed that when more troops were needed for South Africa the initiative would come from England. So Barton had waited and when the call from the motherland did come, that was sufficient reason for cabinet to decide on the dispatch of a Commonwealth contingent without reference to parliament, which was adjourned at the time.[91]

The remainder of this first and last federal debate on the war was Empire all the way. The only significant speech against the motion was made by H. B. Higgins and, although he still opposed Australian involvement on 'the simple old-fashioned ground of justice',[92] his love of Empire was as feelingly vouched for as his desire for justice for the Boers.[93]

The first part of the motion was resolved in the affirmative without division, and the second part carried by forty-five votes to five.[94] So after two years of a war which had lost most of its overt public support, and which had lapsed into a shabby affair begging for able critics, only five men in the parliament of the new federation stood up to be counted.

The second part of the resolution not only supported executive action in authorizing the first Commonwealth contingent; it also cleared the way for further military commitment. And Barton, smarting from the personal attacks of the previous weeks, was only too ready to implement the resolution; especially as the motherland called, and called again.

On 21 January he announced to the House that Chamberlain had asked for another 1000 men and that the Commonwealth government would cable compliance without delay.[95] And on 20 March he told the House that his government would meet as quickly as possible a request for a further 2000 Australians.[96] England had learned by this stage that to ask was to receive.

Within five months of receiving the first request for troops on 21 December 1901 the Commonwealth government raised and embarked 4273 men in three contingents. The federal forces were called the Australian Commonwealth Horse, and their members carried the initials 'A.C.' on their shoulder straps, hopefully to emphasize the unity and identity of battalions drawn from all states. Not that the Commonwealth authorities had originally envisaged an integrated federal army corps, however. When Barton met the military commandants on 30 December it was decided to raise nine units of 120 men for the first Commonwealth contingent.[97] And, captivated by the idea that small Australian units in South Africa had become the eyes and ears of the army, Barton inquired of the Home government whether the A.C.H. would be similarly employed. Chamberlain's wish, however, was that the Australians form two battalions.[98]

Recruiting for the Commonwealth contingents proceeded on lines laid down by the Imperial authorities. Volunteers were to be able to ride and shoot, with preference going to men with previous South African experience. Single men only were to be enlisted. Rates of pay were 1s 2d a day prior to embarkation and 5s thereafter. The Imperial government undertook to reimburse the Commonwealth for all equipment costs, and to provide arms and transport.[99]

The ranks were quickly filled. New South Wales, which with Queensland formed the first battalion, recruited her 350 troopers from 2000 volunteers. Of these 170 were returned men.[100] And thirteen of her fifteen subalterns had served in South Africa as officers or N.C.O's.[101] Victoria, which provided the bulk of the second battalion, raised a force of veterans. Of the 350 men attested, 230 had fought in South Africa, as had twenty-one out of twenty-four officers. Recruits were drawn principally from the lower socio-economic group.[102]

The number of veterans able and willing to return to South Africa was limited, however. They formed a minority of the third and fourth battalions, which made up the second Commonwealth contingent, and were even more poorly represented in the four battalions that formed the third contingent.[103]

The War Office had not stated any preference for bushmen in its call for more Australians, but the type was still favoured by local authorities,[104] and the organization of the third and largest Commonwealth contingent on a territorial basis directed recruiting activity entirely to the country. Each squadron was raised within boundaries that usually coincided with the area from which a mounted militia regiment was recruited. In New South Wales, for instance, the four squadrons that formed the fifth battalion were drawn from country districts associated with the New South Wales Lancers, the New South Wales Mounted Rifles and the Australian Horse.

The departure of the three Commonwealth contingents in February, March and May of 1902 indicated the negative attitude of the public towards the war in its final stages. Public demonstrations did not occur; and governments did nothing to promote them. For example, the first battalion embarked in Sydney at short notice and without benefit of a procession.[105] The Queensland members of the same battalion were farewelled from a Brisbane railway station at 6.45 a.m. on Sunday morning.[106] The South Australians marched to the docks at 8.00 a.m.[107] And the Victorian squadrons embarked without any show of pomp or ceremony.[108]

It is difficult to say whether the Commonwealth troops were victims of apathy or antipathy as they marched to the docks through undemonstrative streets. There is good reason why the latter emotion should have prevailed, because in the last months of the war the inhumanity and ferocity of the conflict were made quite evident. And the message did not come only from the radical press. The Brisbane *Worker* might publish details of Emily Hobhouse's investigation of the concentration camps,[109] and the *Bulletin* might thunder about 'the slaughter of the children',[110] but no less strident was the *Daily Telegraph*'s simple statement of the appalling concentration camp statistics.[111]

The publication of letters from the front also played a part in revealing to the Australian public the unheroic character that the war had assumed. Newspapers opposed to the war naturally printed the most lurid accounts of destruction and rapine, but the *Daily Telegraph*, demonstrating its growing disenchantment with the military adventure, published one of the most damning letters received from men in the field. Written by a sergeant of the fifth contingent, and featured under the heading of 'Looting and Burning of Farm Houses', it gave details of the worst aspects of the war.[112]

With the war proceeding in such a fashion, it was likely that the anti-war movement which developed late in 1901 would have gained considerable support, but this was not so.

The Anti-War League was formed in New South Wales in January 1902 under the influence of W. A. Holman and Professor G. A. Wood. At its first meeting it appointed Victor Daley and A. G. Stephens to head a literary committee aimed at combatting 'the dense ignorance' of the public, and prepared a petition calling on the House of Commons to discontinue the war, and to accord to the enemy an honourable peace with compensation.[113] The petition had little success, however. The New South Wales political Labor conference rejected by thirty-six votes to thirty-five a motion that the president sign on its behalf.[114] Many shire and municipal councils treated the petition with derision when its organizers asked that it be placed where it might receive signatures.[115] The Victorian Labor party declined to sign the petition, and just prior to its closure the appeal could only boast 1026 signatures in New South Wales.[116]

H. B. Higgin s petition to the Australian parliament on 21 January was also poorly supported. It sought the withdrawal of Australian troops and a just peace for 'a brave and gifted foe'.[117] According to one report, the petition carried about 800 signatures and was received by the House in complete silence, while Barton's announcement on the same day of the Imperial request for another 1000 troops was greeted with cheers.[118]

Another embryonic movement was the Peace and Humanity Society in Victoria. At a 'well attended' meeting in Melbourne, chaired by the Reverend Dr Rentoul, a Presbyterian minister and outspoken critic of the war, motions were passed condemning the Federal government for sending more troops, and denouncing the press for its support of the conflict.[119]

Despite the limited success of these intellectual peace movements, they did mark the beginning of a public reaction against the middle class view of the war. They would probably have gained in strength had the war continued, for there were signs that the ordinary people were prepared to take a stand. A public meeting at Goolagong passed a vote of confidence in W. A. Holman, the local member and the most active opponent of the war in Australia, and expressed sympathy with the objects of the

Anti-War League.[120] While the congregation of Kiama Catholic Church signed a petition calling for an end to hostilities.[121]

The most powerful voices in the land, however, were still espousing the Imperial cause, although they did this at the great patriotic demonstrations held to affirm Australia's faith in the British government's conduct of the war,[122] rather than at the farewells to the Commonwealth contingents. The Empire, after all, was a greater and more durable thing than Australia's citizen soldiers, whose sun was already setting.

Of the troops who followed the first and second contingents to South Africa it was the Bushmen who made a significant contribution to Australian military tradition. The third contingent, the Australian Bushmen, landed at Beira in Portuguese East Africa in April 1900, and made their way up through fever-ridden country to join Sir Frederick Carrington's Rhodesian Field Force at Bulawayo. Within two months the fourth contingent, the Imperial Bushmen, also joined Carrington, to make Australians the most numerous component of the R.F.F.

The objective of the force was to protect Rhodesia against the possibilities of Boer invasion and native uprisings, but with Roberts's capture of Pretoria the Transvaal commandos had chosen to disperse to east and west instead of across the Limpopo. And to assist in containing Boer activity in Western Transvaal, Carrington was ordered to the area. The greater part of the service of the Bushmen was in this locality, although sections of them came under British commanders other than Carrington. For the twelve months that the two contingents were in South Africa, the Bushmen threw themselves into the skirmishing of the guerrilla phase of the war with a dash and gusto which was so alien to the usual British methods that the Boers sat up and noted the advent of a new type of enemy. Military operations at the time were directed equally at the civilian population. There were farms to be burnt, crops to be destroyed, livestock to be confiscated, and families to be taken into custody; and there is every reason to believe that the Bushmen applied themselves to this aspect of the war with the same dash and gusto.

The first action involving the Bushmen was the relief of Mafeking. One hundred dismounted Queenslanders hurried out of Rhodesia by train and by forced march as an escort to a Canadian battery, but were denied a significant part in this glamour event because they arrived just as the siege was being lifted. In the brief time at their disposal, however, the Bushmen did reveal the brash fighting style that was to be their chief claim to fame. The Queenslanders had been given a subordinate position as support to a force of Fusiliers, but as the British regulars moved forward against the enemy they heard fiendish yells and found the Bushmen were with them, not behind them. A contemporary historian stated that the Fusiliers could have been forgiven for thinking that 'the Great White Queen had let loose upon the foe a battalion of Red Indian soldiers'; but he also considered that the Australians, who made no attempt to take cover, would have been killed to a man by a disciplined enemy.[123]

While the build-up of Australians in the Western Transvaal was still proceeding, two small and successful engagements fought by units of the Bushmen brought further recognition of their vigorous methods. A force under Colonel H. C. O. Plumer, an Imperial officer, took the town of Zeerust by employing what was said to be 'a highly novel and original method of warfare', namely, charging the Boers on horseback and dragging them off their horses.[124] And Rustenberg was captured by 900 Bushmen, again led by an Imperial officer, in a skirmish that won the praise of Colonel Baden Powell.[125]

Within a fortnight of these successes, however, disaster befell a force of three hundred Australian Bushmen from four colonies led by H. P. Airey, an old, ex-Imperial man who had been serving with the permanent artillery in New South Wales. Airey's command had been sent out from Rustenburg to help escort a large convoy from Elands River camp, but on 23 July they were attacked by a commando under General Lemmer at Koster's River. The Boer force was estimated at four hundred, but it increased during the day to about one thousand. The Australians were pinned down by rifle fire from a horseshoe of hills, and while they were able to take reasonable cover themselves, their horses were so exposed that over two hundred were killed or stampeded. In the heat of the engagement an isolated group of ten men hoisted a white flag; and a couple of hours later Colonel Airey decided to surrender as a matter of honour, for he considered that the white flag had compromised the entire position.

Major Vialls of Western Australia, who commanded part of the force, refused to comply, however, and the Bushmen held on until darkness fell and Lemmer's men withdrew before the approach of another British force. They had lost six killed and twenty-two wounded.[126] Vialls was eulogized in the Western Australian legislature for having disregarded the shameful order. A member even considered his action as 'parallel with that of Nelson both in its intent and its effect'.[127] But J C. Smuts, who was leading a commando in the area at the time, could only heap scorn on the Australians.[128]

Even as Airey's men made their way back to Rustenburg, the stage was being set for the most significant engagement fought by the Bushmen during the war. This was the siege of Elands River camp, and Smuts honoured it as the occasion on which the Boers were taught an appreciation of the fighting qualities of Australian soldiers.[129]

On 4 August a force of 2500-3000 Boers under Generals de la Rey and Lemmer attacked a stores depot guarded by fewer than 500 colonials. One hundred New South Wales Bushmen, 150 men of the Queensland Mounted Infantry, 75 Rhodesians and smaller numbers of Victorian and Western Australian Bushmen made up the British force. Anticipating an attack but hoping that a column under General Carrington would arrive before it eventuated, the colonials had improvised a defensive position out of ox waggons and boxes of stores. This precaution saved the camp, for in the first two days of the siege over 2500 shells from nine pieces of artillery were poured on to the compound, killing most of the 1500 horses, oxen and mules, scattering stores, and taking toll of the defenders.

On the second day of the investment, Carrington came into view with a mounted force of 1000 men, made up equally of the New South Wales Imperial Bushmen and South African irregulars. But the cheers of the defenders were short-lived, for Carrington, employing no scouts, rode into an ambush and was soon in headlong retreat towards Zeerust.

By this time the garrison had completed its defences, burrowing into the rocky ridge on which the camp was situated with nothing but picks and shovels. The mining experience of some of the men helped greatly, but the main reasons for success were a determination not to surrender and a capacity to labor long and hard. The situation for the defenders was also improved after the second day by a considerable reduction in the rate of bombardment, possibly because of the damage to stores that de la Rey needed badly. But the fight was kept going at a hot pace by small arms fire by day and by night, when small parties of Australians and Rhodesians ran the gauntlet to fetch water from the river half a mile away.

On the seventh day of the siege de la Rey invited the camp to surrender. In recognition of 'the gallant defence' that had been made he was prepared to allow the officers to retain their arms, and he guaranteed a safe passage for the entire force to the nearest British position. Colonel C. O. Hore, the Imperial officer commanding at Elands River, declined the offer (although later rumours attributed the refusal to surrender to the attitude of some of Hore's subordinate officers).

In the meantime Colonel Baden Powell had moved towards the besieged position with a force of 2000 men, including a large number of Bushmen; but when within twenty miles of the camp, he turned away on orders from Roberts, who had been advised by Carrington that the garrison had capitulated. A lone rider whose name is lost to history got through the Boer lines, however, and alerted Mafeking to the true state of affairs. On 15 August the Boer forces withdrew as Kitchener's column of 10 000 men approached, and early next morning the commander-in-chief rode into camp to praise the colonials for 'a wonderful defence'. Imperial and colonial officers walked around the carcase-strewn ridge and marvelled at the extent and efficiency of the improvised fortifications.[130] The twelve-day defence had cost the colonials twelve dead and thirty-eight wounded, and seven Kaffirs had also been killed.[131]

The action at Elands River won wide praise for the defenders. An assessment of the action by J. C. Smuts is the most significant.

Never in the course of this war did a besieged force endure worse sufferings, but they stood their ground with magnificent courage. All honour to these heroes who in the hour of trial rose nobly to the occasion, and amid retreats and flights and capitulations, shed a glory all their own on the brief comic page of Baden-Powell's occupation of the Western Transvaal.[132]

Strangely enough, the Australians were not widely acclaimed in their own land despite the comprehensive reports of the action by the Reverend James Green. Perhaps this was because editorial comment failed to emphasize the event. Perhaps it was because war-fever had subsided. Or perhaps it was because Australians had already accepted their soldiers as heroes. The noted balladist, George Essex Evans, did see something significant in the engagement, however, and he honoured it in verse.

We saw the guns of Carrington come on and fall away;
We saw the ranks of Kitchener across the kopje gray,
For the sun was shining then
Upon twenty thousand men
And we laughed, because we knew, in spite of hell-fire and delay,
On Australia's page for ever
We had written Eland's River—
We had written it for ever and a day.[133]

The reverse side of the Elands River coin was the retreat of Carrington's force. There was nothing shameful about the British general's withdrawal of his untried column from an ambush executed by a force of Boers superior in number and commanded by the most competent Transvaal soldier. What was shameful was that Carrington kept on running, and without good reason. When he extricated himself from the ambush, having suffered seventeen minor casualties, he made for Zeerust by a series of forced marches, firmly believing that a formidable portion of the Boer army was in pursuit. The Boer force that was tailing him, in fact, amounted to fewer than one hundred men. This, of course, was a further indictment of the poor scouting of the colonial force.

Carrington only stopped long enough in Zeerust to attempt to burn all British stores, before continuing his flight towards Mafeking. He was soon ordered back to Zeerust by Roberts, however, who was not amused by the series of blunders in Western Transvaal. From there he was sent back to Rhodesia, leaving the Australians of his command in the hands of more capable leaders.

The Reverend James Green came across a number of Carrington's Imperial Bushmen after the retreat and found them in a state of some shame, although they claimed that they had known little of what was really going on.[134] But the damage had been done, and contemporary reports from both sides were highly critical of the inglorious retreat.[135]

The London cables, however, which supplied exaggerated and partisan reports of the most routine engagements, were able to turn the debacle into a dogged withdrawal, in which the Imperial bushmen distinguished themselves by admirable scouting and skirmishing.[136]

The Bushmen of the third and fourth contingents were only involved in three other skirmishes of any significance before they returned home. The first of these was at Rhenoster Kop, north of Pretoria. Late in November 1900, Plumer led a force of 1000 regular infantry and 1000 Australians and New Zealanders against a comparable Boer force. A brisk one-day fight followed in which the British side lost 100 men killed or wounded. The Boers withdrew at night because a larger British force was approaching. Plumer's men put up a good showing, but it was the New Zealanders who so distinguished themselves that Lord Milner was prompted to cable his congratulations to the New Zealand premier.[137]

The Bushmen were not to be subordinated in their next fight, however. In February 1901 a number of Australian units of the second, third and fourth contingents joined with British regiments in the greatest of the three 'hunts' after de Wet. But it was Plumer's column of Imperial Bushmen, Queensland Mounted Infantry, and King's Dragoon Guards that put up the best show of endurance and dogged pursuit.

De Wet had moved into Cape Colony in a desperate attempt to secure advantage for the sorely-pressed Boer forces by stirring up disaffection among Dutch settlers. Two other Boer columns had preceded him, but so formidable was the reputation of the Free State general that all British forces available in the area were directed to halt him and turn him back across the Orange River.

On 13 February Plumer's column engaged de Wet on a line of kopjes and turned him, 'the Australian Bushmen with great dash carrying the central kopje'. De Wet then made to the north-west but could not shake off Plumer. For a week, in rain and hail, 'the two sodden, sleepless, mud-splashed little armies swept onward over the Karoo', until the Free Staters were halted by the flooded Orange River. Plumer hit again and took 100 prisoners, but de Wet slipped along the river looking for a crossing. He had acquired fresh horses from another commando, while Plumer's men were riding the same mounts, which were dropping dead under their riders. The Boer force eventually found a ford and crossed into the Orange Free State, minus its guns, its convoy, about one thousand horses and three hundred men.[138]

After the de Wet hunt, virtually all the third contingent Bushmen fit for action came under the command of Plumer, and were utilized in an advance from Pretoria north to Pietersburg. But this force of six hundred seasoned men encountered little resistance. Even Pietersburg was taken with ease, although three Bushmen, two officers and a trooper were killed by a Boer concealed in long grass before he was riddled with bullets by angry Australians.[139]

Further proof of the dash of the Australian horsemen was given at Hartebeestefontein in Western Transvaal on 21 March, when a force of New Zealanders and Imperial Bushmen under Colonel Raleigh Evans of the Inniskilling Dragoons carried out an old-fashioned cavalry charge against Boer positions. According to one historian, the attack was foolhardy but proved 'that a charge of mounted troops in open order was one of the best methods of demoralising the enemy'.[140] Another writer described the event: 'With wild cheers the New Zealanders and Bushmen raced down on their foes . . . and the whole force fled terrified before the furious charge'.[141]

The episodes described above formed a minor part of the work of the Bushmen, however. Most of their time was spent in implementing the scorched-earth policy of first Roberts, and then Kitchener. Some of the men involved gave blunt accounts of the operations.

We arrived here yesterday after an eight days' march, on which I don't believe more than six shots were fired. We burn all the wheat and take all the oaten hay and mealies. In the eight days we collected eight prisoners of war, 62 men, 930 women and children, 354 horses, 28 mules, 5,688 cattle, 14,834 sheep, 133 waggons, and 108 Cape carts. We burnt most of the waggons and carts. We cannot get the Boers to stand and fight, so we are going to starve them out.[142]

Burnt the mill in passing—have burnt altogether about 60 farms during the past 4 days.[143]

We cleared the country by burning all farm-houses; and the poultry fell to the victors.[144]

Like their compatriots of the first and second contingents, the Bushmen were keen to return home when they had completed twelve months service in South Africa. Plumer's biographer tells of 'signs of incipient mutiny' when the Australians were ordered out on trek just before their time was up. General Paget spoke to them without effect, but Plumer, who had won their affection and respect with his competence and quiet personality, was greeted with cheers when he told them that both he and they would parade next morning.[145]

Some of the Bushmen stayed on in South Africa and, supported by reinforcements from the draft contingents, carried the name of the corps through to the end of hostilities. The achievements of the Bushmen were so uneven that it is difficult to generalize on their worth. But most people who observed them in the field, if asked to describe the corps in a phrase, would have agreed with General G. A. French that they were 'wild men' of the Australian contingents.

The fifth contingent was in the field by the middle of 1901, but by that time the conflict did not merit the name of war. The Australians found themselves part of a mere police function, although they could hardly have expected anything more when they volunteered.

Private Otto Techow of the 6th W.A.M.I. kept a detailed diary of his experiences. It tells of a campaign that would have contributed little to the Australian military image. Certainly the men had to endure great hardship. It was common to ride for the greater part of the night, frequently in bitter cold, in order to attack a laager or farmhouse at dawn.[146] But usually the engagement was a trivial affair. On one occasion a column of seven hundred men, West Australians and regulars, found that they were surrounding a laager of nineteen men when dawn broke.[147] Another all-night march culminated in a dawn attack on a farmhouse which sheltered one sleeping Boer.[148] Sometimes the phantoms materialized, however, and Techow tells of an engagement over four days against a Boer force reported to be 2000 strong. Yet even this protracted action cost the British column only five killed and eleven wounded.[149]

Fights against Boer commandos might have been rare, but the destruction of the resources of the two republics was a continuing process. Techow's observations, as unfeeling as they are laconic, reveal a grim situation.

> Told off to escort waggon to kraal for mealies, kaffirs howled badly while we were taking them . . . Up at 4.30 ordered to burn 3 farms—get geese and pigs with Boers watching from hill, get firewood from a grave . . . Ermilo being burnt every house and store being set on fire . . . amused myself by going to the farms and kraals for loot . . . reached Amsterdam a nice little town which we burnt . . . into Paullpietersburg which we destroyed and burnt . . . broke up pulpit of church to boil dixie.[150]

Very few Australians who left any sort of record of their experiences in South Africa made any reference to sexual matters, but Techow was one who implied that there was something to be had down at the kraals in addition to mealies. '[We] had a great bit of fun down at a kraal after dinner', he wrote 'the girls being full of life'.[151] But this would have been an isolated episode in twelve months of uninspiring and unrewarding warfare. Techow apparently yearned for more heroic things, and his diary, in common with many others that came out of the campaign, includes transcripts of exaggerated war verse.

Accounts of the work of the fifth New South Wales contingent, known as the 3rd N.S.W.M.R., indicate that Techow's version of the mode of warfare in 1901 was accurate. The potential of the New South Wales regiment as a military strike force was considerable. With a strength of two thousand men, it was a sizeable unit. It was commanded by Colonel C. Cox of the New South Wales Lancers, and many of its officers and N.C.O.'s were Lancers who had seen service in South Africa under Cox. It was brigaded with the Inniskilling Dragoons (as the New South Wales Lancers had been), and the column of which it formed an equal part was led by General M. F. Rimington, one of the most competent and dashing cavalry leaders of the war. But there was no real fighting to be had, and a return of operations for the last five months of 1901 shows how the column was expending its energies. In 153 days it trekked 1814 miles in pursuit of elusive bands of Boers or on convoy duty. It had thirteen skirmishes in which five men were killed and nineteen wounded. It killed 27 Boers, wounded 15 and captured 196. In so doing, it expended

64 563 rounds of .303 ammunition and 1761 horses. During the period 114 mules, 388 horses, 17 989 cattle, 272 waggons and 214 carts were captured. No figure was given for the number of farms burned.[152]

The disinclination of Australians to serve longer than twelve months in the field was evident among the men of the 3rd N.S.W.M.R., and a spokesman made his appeal to go home direct to the top. During an address to the Australians by the commander-in-chief, a trooper asked, 'Mr. Kitchener when are you going to let us blokes go home? You know we only signed on for twelve months'. One could imagine the great man turning apoplectic had a British soldier asked such a question, but he had no doubt learned to accept Australian brashness. Just one more job, he promised, then you shall go.[153] On 28 April 1902 the Australians withdrew from the column, leaving the Inniskillings to fight on alone. Rimington praised them highly, paying tribute to their dash, their steadiness in action, their alertness, and their ability to endure privation cheerfully.[154] These compliments recognized the best qualities of the Australian soldier, but with the conflict about to end he still had not been tried in the true crucible of war. He had not faced any Colensos or Magersfonteins.

There was one occasion, however, when an Australian unit of the fifth contingent was subjected to the full blast of war, but it was under conditions of great disadvantage and the result was humiliation rather than honour.

On 12 June 1901 350 men of the 5th V.M.R., led by an Imperial officer, Major Morris, with the unit's O.C., Major W. McKnight, second in command, camped at Wilmansrust near Middelburg in Eastern Transvaal. The force was making its way back to a column commanded by General F. C. Beatson, after failing to engage a small commando that was known to be in the area. At 7.30 p.m., as the men were settling down to sleep or to read mail that had just arrived from Australia, a force of 140 Boers, taking advantage of a poorly secured camp, launched an attack from point-blank range.

Within five minutes eighteen Australians had been killed, and forty-two wounded and the fight was over. Of the remainder some fifty evaded capture by fleeing into the darkness. Those taken prisoner were released almost immediately, for the Boers had long since ceased to detain their captives because of lack of facilities. Over one hundred horses were killed and about the same number taken as prizes of war. The remainder broke loose to die from their wounds on the veldt or to fall into the gleeful hands of some passing commando or column.[155]

Lord Kitchener's report to the Australian government on Wilmansrust was merciful in its brevity. It merely gave the statistics of Australian losses and claimed that the V.M.R. had been surprised by a superior force.[156] Barton acknowledged the rout as 'a most regrettable disaster' but drew comfort from the fact that whatever the cause of the surprise the men acted with 'heroic valour',[157] and the Duke of York cabled his admiration for the Victorians who had 'so gallantly given their lives in the service of the Empire'.[158]

However, others were more critical of the conduct of the Australians in what was the most serious mishap to befall any overseas colonial force. Kitchener was reported to have 'flushed with anger' when advised of the reverse, for it represented to him a blunder in the midst of success.[159] His biographer was particularly severe on the men who, he claimed, had 'failed alike in vigilance and discipline', for in addition to their failure to secure the bivouac, they had not responded to the Imperial officer's attempts to rally them.[160]

The accusation that the force showed little vigilance was not unfounded. The V.M.R. knew there were Boers in the area, and in fact they had been followed all day by a section of General Ben Viljoen's commando. Yet security arrangements for the night were nonchalant to say the least. The pickets, it appears, were too few and too casual, and the attacking force slipped past them with ease. Within the camp there was no measure of alertness, either, as men lounged around camp fires or read by candlelight, their rifles anywhere but at their sides. Such laxness on the part of both officers and men was understandable, however, and was a measure of the state of the war at the time. British columns could hardly be expected to maintain maximum security precautions when enemy activity was generally confined to daylight sniping by small bands of Boers.

Less excusable was the panic that possessed the Australians when they were attacked. A member of the Boer raiding force has left a detailed account of the affair which places the Australians in a very poor light. R. H. Schikkerling's narrative of Wilmansrust begins with the meeting of the war council of a commando of 150 men, and the council's unanimous decision to attack and loot the camp of the Australians. In the view of Schikkerling the Boers exposed themselves to observation when it was still light and when within two miles of the camp. From there 150 horsemen moved past the pickets and halted about 800 yards out. Thirty men remained with the horses and the rest advanced on foot until within 100 yards of the Australians, when a shot signalled the beginning of the attack. A line of about eighty horses standing between the two forces took the first fire and within seconds were all killed or maimed. Then the Boers rushed the camp, halting about twenty-five yards out to fire into a confused enemy. Had they stayed at that distance and continued the attack, the Victorians would have been annihilated, but the readiness of the men of the V.M.R. to surrender and the desire of individual Boers to get their hands on loot brought the engagement to a halt after no more than ten minutes fighting. In Schikkerling's words,

> The enemy was taken quite by surprise and was terribly panicky, firing far too high even at close quarters . . . They now surrendered in big batches, and near the cattle kraal seven in a body surrendered to me alone. Some lay flat on the ground, afraid to even lift their heads . . . Deeper in the camp I encountered three behind an ox wagon . . .

For many a night after, the taking of the Australian camp was the sole topic of conversation among the elated Boers.[161]

It was generally held that the victory at Wilmansrust raised Boer morale out of all proportion to the magnitude of the engagement. The two Boer governments met on 20 June to decide whether to continue the war, and although an exhortation from Kruger abroad to keep on fighting was a major factor in deciding the issue, any remaining disinclination was dispelled by the elation over the Australian disaster.[162]

Australians generally and Victorians in particular would have been pleased to let Wilmansrust slip quietly into history, but the affair had an unfortunate sequel which served to bring the whole matter before the public gaze. On 28 September 1901 the *Age* published a personal letter written by an un-named member of the 5th V.M.R. In it the soldier described an attempt by three Australians to incite their comrades to mutiny because General

Beatson had described the defenders of Wilmansrust camp as 'white-livered curs'. A photographic copy of a court martial schedule included with the letter showed that a Private J. Steele had received the death penalty for his part in the attempted mutiny, but that this had been commuted to ten years imprisonment by Lord Kitchener.[163]

As incomplete as it was, this account understandably caused great concern and soul-searching in Australia. Hitherto little had been said publicly of the humiliation of Wilmansrust, but Beatson's accusation of cowardice brought the matter under wider scrutiny. There was also concern over Australian soldiers being involved in mutiny, and consternation that Australians could be court martialled, convicted, and incarcerated in British gaols without the Australian government having any knowledge of the proceedings.

The press was quick to react. Victorian newspapers in particular endeavoured to explain the misfortunes of the 5th V.M.R., although the exercise was usually an attempt to find a scapegoat. The *Argus* published a lengthy and surprisingly knowledgeable account of the tribulations of the Victorian unit in South Africa, which must have been based on communications from men in the field, and which the paper had obviously not seen fit to publish before. The article lamented the fact that the fifth contingent of Victorians had seriously damaged the reputation of the Australian soldier in South Africa, for previously no large body of Australians had ever thrown down their arms to the enemy. It blamed the fifth also for tarnishing the image of the Australian in Cape Town by misconduct. Indiscipline was regarded as the main cause of all the contingent's trouble. This was attributed to the poorer type of recruit who had come forward towards the end of the war, and officers who were either inexperienced or, having come from the ranks, too familiar with the men. To climax these shortcomings, according to the *Argus*, the regiment had the misfortune to be placed under a regular officer who adopted a 'hostile and offensive attitude' towards them. This manifested itself in strict disciplinary measures and disparaging remarks. Apart from his reference to the Australians as 'a lot of white-livered curs', Beatson chanced to ride by when a group of them were engaged in bayoneting pigs at a farmhouse and he told the men that was all they were good for. 'When the Dutchmen came along the other night you didn't fix bayonets and charge them', he was alleged to have said, 'but you go for something that can't hit back'. It was a few days after this incident that Private Steele suggested to his comrades that they should not again go into the field with such a man.[164]

The *Age* made a contribution to elucidating the troubles of the 5th V.M.R. when it published an interview with a returned officer of the regiment. He admitted that the regiment had become almost uncontrollable by its officers, but claimed that this was because of the strict discipline imposed by General Beatson who, for example, would make the entire regiment walk for a day as punishment for some men having sore-backed horses.[165]

The Melbourne *Punch* accepted the failure of the fifth contingent, but attributed much of the blame to Imperial officers who were 'no more fit to handle a body of irregulars than a mule is fit to command eagles'.[166] A week later it again attacked the leadership of British officers in a page of satirical cartoons.[167]

The interstate press left Victoria pretty well to deal with her own shame, but an exception was the *Daily Telegraph*. In an editorial following the release from English prisons of 'the so-called mutineers' of the 5th V.M.R., it attacked 'the foul and infamous language of the Imperial officer commanding' and suggested that if the death penalties had been carried out public outcry would have led to the recall of every Australian soldier in South Africa.[168]

In Federal parliament questions were asked of the prime minister after the disclosure by the *Age* of the mutiny, but Barton would say nothing until he received an authoritative report although he clearly showed that he had no sympathy for mutinous soldiers who had taken an oath of allegiance and become subject to the British Army Act.[169] A month later Major McKnight's report was tabled and Barton was able to announce that a matter which 'had agitated Australia very considerably' had been brought to a 'happy termination'. The sentenced men had been released and an Imperial officer superseded in his command.[170]

It was not until 7 November, however, that Barton received a reply to a telegram of 3 October to the Colonial Office. It disclosed that Privates J. Steele, A. Richards and H. Parry had been tried by general court martial for inciting to mutiny and sentenced to death. The sentences were commuted to ten years imprisonment in the case of Steele, and one year imprisonment with hard labour in each of the other cases. When the Judge Advocate General reviewed the proceedings of the court martial, he had declared that there were legal flaws in the convictions for the men had been tried under the wrong section of the Army Act. The immediate release of the troopers was therefore ordered.[171]

Parliament had demonstrated a minimum of concern over Wilmansrust and its aftermath. And when, three months later, the House of Representatives was in high dudgeon over the libels of the continental press, a member made a pertinent observation. A British officer had called Victorians 'white-livered curs', a more abusive expression than anything uttered by the continental press, yet the House had 'never attempted in any shape or form to take exception to it'.[172]

Australian pride had undoubtedly been hurt by the events involving the 5th V.M.R., but very little sympathy had been generated for the soldiers who had brought Australian fighting men into disrepute. In fact, there was a tendency to disown them. More marked, though, was the desire to make Imperial officers the scapegoats for Australian errors.

One outcome of the trial and imprisonment of the three Australians was a request by Barton to Kitchener for a record of punishments by courts martial of members of Australian contingents.[173]

Australia had a chance to regain lost prestige with the dispatch of 4000 members of the Australian Commonwealth Horse in 1902. These went in three contingents totalling eight battalions. But the war was over before half the A.C.H. got to South Africa. The first and second battalions did see some service in the great drives that were to end the war, but the third and fourth never heard a shot fired, and the fifth, sixth, seventh and eighth were still on the high seas when peace came on 31 May.[174] There were no A.C.H. casualties in action, but twenty-eight men died from illness.[175]

The first and second battalions landed in Natal in March and formed an Australian brigade for the great Eastern drive aimed at encircling de Wet and Louis Botha. But the mists and storms of the Drakensburg range allowed the Boers to make an easy escape, and all the Australians caught were severe colds which were treated by the A.A.M.C. unit which formed part of the brigade.

The Australians were then sent to Western Transvaal to join Colonel Thornycroft's Field Force, composed of the New Zealand brigade, New South Wales Bushmen, Haslee's Scouts (an irregular corps consisting of 'mostly Australians') and Thornycroft's own regular mounted infantry. The field hospital for the force was provided by the A.A.M.C. This predominantly Australian column moved forward as part of General Ian Hamilton's force of 20 000 men. The advance was known as the great Western drive and it was the last of the war. The object was to drive de la Rey and his commandos back against a chain of blockhouses. This was accomplished almost without incident, and the untried Australians for weeks had then nothing to do but sit and wait for the inevitable peace.[176]

The Australian Commonwealth Horse did not get an opportunity to contribute much to Australian military history, but its conduct in the field was almost beyond reproach, despite the monotony of operations and weeks of inactivity. The regiment did a lot to allay the fears of those to whom Australian discipline had so recently become suspect. A major factor in the improved state of affairs was the evident determination of Australian commanders to see that a good standard of discipline was maintained. The battle orders of the second battalion (predominantly a Victorian unit) indicated a high standard of discipline, with peremptory punishment for offenders.[177] British commanders were warm in their praise for Australian discipline at this time,[178] and the return of courts martial for the period 1 April to 30 June shows only twenty-seven cases, with the crimes mainly being disobedience, drunkenness, and insubordination.[179]

The good standard of discipline enforced in South Africa was not maintained aboard at least one transport that brought troops back to Australia, however, and the slackness which followed was a contributing factor in the greatest misfortune to befall the Australian contingents at sea. S.S. *Drayton Grange*, out of Durban on 11 July 1902 with 2043 troops aboard, dropped anchor in Melbourne on 7 August with five men already dead and twelve more to die within a fortnight of landing.[180] The main killers were measles and influenza, both of which had been brought aboard in the incubation stage, and a Royal Commission found that the presence of these illnesses had been aggravated by overcrowding, deficient hospital accommodation, and neglect of the discipline of mere routine which would have meant a more sanitary ship.[181]

This account of Australians in South Africa has only followed the fortunes of those who served with Australian units, but thousands more fought with irregular regiments raised at the seat of war. These men drifted into the various corps in small numbers on their own initiative, and ceased to exist as far as the Australian government and public were concerned. There was one group of Australians, however, who succeeded in maintaining their identity in an irregular unit. They were men who were recruited in Australia specifically as Australian squadrons of a South African corps.

In December 1900 the Marquis of Tullibardine, who had served with the Royal Dragoons in Natal earlier in the war, began raising a force known as the Scottish Horse. He split it into what he called two regiments, and it was to help fill the ranks of the 2nd Scottish Horse that he obtained permission from Kitchener to wire to the Caledonian Society in Melbourne for assistance. This he did on 1 January 1901, and on 8 March three hundred Victorians, mainly Scots by birth or descent, joined the corps in South Africa.[182]

The Marquis did not receive the fullest co-operation of Victorian authorities, however. In addition to Malcolm McEachern, the president of the Caledonian Society and mayor of Melbourne, declining to assist in any way,[183] military authorities were also cool towards the idea. Eventually a retired army officer got the recruiting movement going, with the Victorian government accepting responsibility for riding, shooting and medical tests. Uniforms, equipment, and pay were matters to be cared for by the Marquis when the men reached the Cape.[184]

Tullibardine found things much more difficult when he sought to recruit another three hundred Australians to replace the first draft, which had been enlisted for six months only. Perturbed by the British desire to recruit in Australia for Baden Powell's South African Constabulary, the Federal government declared against

Australia being used as a recruiting ground for non-Australian regiments. The Marquis was obliged, therefore, to send his recruiting officers aboard ships that were carrying indulgence passengers to the Cape. Lieutenant Alured Kelly, formerly a private in the 2nd V.M.R., was such an officer. On one occasion he competed with another recruiter for the services of 150 indulgence passengers and enlisted 106 of them after the ship had cleared Australian waters.[185]

The indulgence scheme was a subtle form of Imperial recruiting whereby, in return for providing a free berth on an otherwise empty troop-ship (with the person paying for his own messing at 1s 6d a day), the British authorities secured an experienced soldier at a time when the demand for horsemen for the irregular corps seemed insatiable. And the Army made sure it got its man, for military officers boarded the ship at the Cape and obliged the Australians to sign on with a corps or take the next boat home.[186] The potential of indulgence passages as a recruiting method was considerable, for there was extensive unemployment in Australia at the time and the Federal government had ruled out more overt recruiting.[187] But the scheme yielded only about four hundred men. This poor response was partly due to the opposition of the New South Wales and Victorian governments. See, the premier of New South Wales, refused to provide free transport for volunteers to the embarkation point (a condition agreed upon by the Imperial and Federal governments), and made a strong protest to the Home government over the continuance of recruiting in New South Wales.[188] Peacock, the Victorian premier, refused to pay the fares of Victorians to pick up ship in Sydney for he considered the men to be going 'for their own personal benefit'.[189]

For the Scottish Horse draft 544 men were recruited either within Australia or from among indulgence passengers. Tullibardine spoke glowingly of these troops. There were also 'many Australians' among the 1458 men recruited at ports and elsewhere in South Africa for the Scottish Horse, but he was inclined to rate them as inferior to those recruited in Australia.[190] The Scottish Horse fought under conditions that were typical of the period, and Sergeant Robert Hodgson's excellent diary testifies that its Australian component served conscientiously and efficiently, although not as well, according to Tullibardine, as the men recruited from the yeomanry and volunteer militia of Scotland.[191]

It is difficult even to estimate the number of Australians who served in irregular South African corps, but it must have been several thousands, although most of these would have served originally with Australian units. Press lists of men returning from South Africa late in the war often included a sprinkling of names of men who had served with South African regiments. The Houlder Line alone had carried to the theatre of war by the end of 1900 over five hundred seeking to enlist.[192] And then, of course, there were the indulgence passengers.

Australian political leaders were not the only persons opposed to returned soldiers going back to South Africa to join non-Australian regiments. The veterans themselves displayed an obvious reluctance. When the *Britannic* sailed from Sydney in August 1901 she had about two hundred men on board, and these were mainly ex-Bushmen who had been rallied by newspaper notices inserted by Major J. F. Thomas, a former officer of the Citizens' Bushmen.[193] The *Britannic* was scheduled to pick up at only one other port, Albany, so it is extremely doubtful whether the captain of the vessel took to South Africa the 400-500 men he was told he would be transporting.[194] When the *Harlech Castle* sailed from Sydney at the end of September, only 49 out of 111 New South Wales men granted indulgence passages were on board, and there were only 18 from Victoria, Queensland and Tasmania. With only Albany to call at, the total complement of indulgence passengers could not have been more than 100.[195]

Many other Australians joined South African regiments in preference to returning home at the end of their year's service with Australian units. Others stayed to make a new life in South Africa. Some of these had been enticed by land offers from the Chartered Company. All colonies were aware of the situation. South Australia considered, however, that if the Imperial government made an offer to soldiers to stay in South Africa, it was hardly the duty of the colonial government to protest.[196] Queensland did not seem to care at all.[197] New South Wales was the only colony to take steps to prevent her soldiers being discharged in South Africa. One action that Lyne took was to see that the troops were not paid off until they returned.[198] Another was to ask Chamberlain to ensure that New South Wales troops were not disbanded in South Africa.[198] A year later See was unable to say how many New South Wales men had stayed in South Africa but he was confident it was not a large number.[200] But with the colonies generally making no effort to ensure that their troops returned, many would have found their way into the scores of irregular regiments which constantly sought recruits.

With thousands of Australians of an adventurous inclination scattered through numerous irregular units that were often poorly officered and dubiously motivated, there was a good chance that somewhere, sometime, a few of them would get into trouble. And they did.

The story of the Bushveldt Carbineers and H. Morant and P. Handcock, the two Australian lieutenants who died before a British firing squad, is the best known episode of Australian involvement in the war. Lieutenant G. R. Witton, who was court martialled along with Morant and Handcock, and who had access to the papers of Major J. F. Thomas, the defence counsel, wrote fully and authoritatively on the subject.[201] 'Frank Renar' (pseudonym of Frank Fox of the *Bulletin*), gave another reliable account based on conversations with the executed men's commanding officer, Major R. W. Lenehan.[202] F M. Cutlack later wrote a book which relied mainly on the work of Witton and Fox, but which raised unwarranted doubts by claiming that the records of the courts martial available to Witton were incomplete, and by noting the disappearance from the War Office of the trial documents.[203] All three writers accepted the contention of the defence counsel that the verdicts were influenced by the representations of the German government, which demanded justice for the murder of Hesse, a German missionary. Morant and Handcock were acquitted of this charge, however, so it is hardly logical to suggest that the death sentence was carried out because of German pressures. There was also a strong inclination among the authors to suspect Kitchener of something devious in failing to act on the court's recommendations for clemency, and in ordering hasty executions. Kitchener may have wanted to see the men face the firing squad, and without delay, as a deterrent to the disregard for military law which was increasing among the irregular corps. Or he may have wanted the thing done before Australian opinion could influence the outcome. But it is difficult to see how the firing squad would cover up any irregularities on Kitchener's part.

The facts are plain enough. Early in 1901 an irregular regiment called the Bushveldt Carbineers was formed for service in the wild country of north-eastern Transvaal. At the time of the outrages it was commanded by an Australian, Major R. W. Lenehan. It had several Australians among its subalterns, and a large number of Australians in its strength of 350 men. The corps was engaged in the usual type of police work, but was left mainly to its own resources because of the remoteness of the area. It was operating with considerable effect on the roving bands of Boers in the district when a series of murders took place involving a section of the corps commanded by Morant. A wounded Boer prisoner, Visser, was shot on Morant's orders after a farcical 'drumhead' court martial, and groups of three, eight, and six prisoners were also shot. The German missionary was shot while on his way to Pietersburg, allegedly to report the activities of the corps.

In a series of courts martial which began at Pietersburg on 16 January 1902 Morant, Handcock and Witton, and an English irregular, Lieutenant Picton, were each found guilty on one or all of the charges involving Visser and the groups of three and eight Boers. Captain A. Taylor, a colonial intelligence officer, was acquitted of the charge of inciting to murder in the case of six Boers. Handcock and Morant were acquitted of the murder of Hesse, although it is very likely that they were guilty. They were the prime suspects, and their other actions indicated that they would have had no scruples about killing the missionary. 'Renar' hinted at their guilt in his book.[204] And in a letter to J. F. Thomas, written on 21 October 1929, Witton claimed that after the trial Handcock admitted to him that he followed and shot Hesse at Morant's command.[205] Despite the court's recommendations of mercy (strong in respect of Handcock and Witton who were acting on orders from Morant), Handcock and Morant were shot by a squad of Cameron Highlanders at dawn on 27 February 1902. Witton's sentence of death was commuted to life imprisonment, and Picton was cashiered.

Justice does not appear to have been done, mainly because the cases were argued at two different levels of justice. The prosecution argued on the basis of King's Regulations and the Manual of Military Law, while the defence argued on the basis of the realities of Kitchener's degenerate type of warfare. Of the men court martialled, Morant was the most deserving of punishment as the instigator of the killings, and at the trial he took full responsibility for his subordinates' actions. But in his favour it can be said that he was acting under orders from his superior, Captain Hunt, to take no prisoners, and that he was fighting an unorthodox war with little or no direction from headquarters. Morant also believed, rightly or wrongly, that his friend Hunt met his death in particularly brutal circumstances.

Morant gained stature at his trial and execution. He would not defer to the court in any way, claiming that he fought the war in the only manner it could be fought, by 'rule 303', and promising to have Kitchener brought to trial for his war crimes. And at the end of his reckless life he asked that the blindfold be taken from his eyes, and advised the firing squad to shoot straight and not mess the job up. Of such deeds are folk-heroes made, but the Australian people fell too quickly on the defensive to take the opportunity.

Handcock's sentence stands out as the most unjust of the whole affair. Poor, simple, sincere Handock was obsessed with the idea of duty, and never questioned any orders from his superior. He did not initiate any crimes himself, but he faced the same penalty as Morant, the architect of several crimes. A letter written to his sister just before his execution suggests a man who killed out of a blind sense of duty.

> I have but one hour longer to exist, and although my brain has been harassed for four long months, I can't refrain from writing you a few last lines. I am going to find out the Grand Secret. I will face my God with the firm belief I am innocent of murder. I obeyed my orders and served my King as I thought best.
>
> If I overstepped my duty I can only ask my people and country for forgiveness . . . [206]

One man who got off lightly was Captain Taylor. He was acquitted of inciting others to murder the six Boers, although those who carried out the act claimed it was on Taylor's orders. The testimony of other witnesses during the trials also indicated that Taylor freely subscribed to the policy of no prisoners.

In Australia the reaction to the affair was no less reprehensible than the bloody deeds themselves, or the callousness of Kitchener.

It took the forms of a supine attitude on the part of the government towards Imperial authorities, an unseemly haste on the part of the press to disown the wrong-doers, and apparent public acquiescence in the executions.

As with Wilmansrust, no official notification of the matter was received in Australia. It was said that Barton heard the news from a returned trooper.[207] A month after the executions Isaac Isaacs sought in parliament information on a matter he claimed was 'agitating the minds of people . . . in an almost unprecedented degree'. Barton's reply showed a strong desire to disclaim all responsibility for the men. Australia could expect no official information, he said, because the soldiers concerned 'were not in any way employed by Australia, nor were they in a corps that was raised in Australia or was distinctly Australian'.[208] A little later, in reply to a question whether the government would obtain the court martial depositions, Alfred Deakin said that it was 'not entitled to demand the depositions as a right', but they had been asked for 'as a matter of courtesy'.[209] Kitchener's response to the request was a terse telegraphic report of the findings of the courts martial which apparently satisfied the Federal government.

Press reports and editorial opinion were completely antagonistic. The *Daily Telegraph* published an item from the London *Daily Mail* which identified the executed men as Australian members of 'a mixed scallywag body' and stated that 'the atrocious murder and looting of surrendered Dutchmen and natives required, for the credit of England, exemplary punishment'.[210] The Sydney paper's own opinion was that the public should regard the men as breakers of the laws of war.[211] It also printed interviews with an Australian and a New Zealander who had served with the Bushveldt Carbineers. Both of them regarded the shootings as cold-blooded murders.[212] The *Brisbane Courier* took comfort from the fact that Morant, 'the chief offender', was an Englishman and that the regiment was not an Australian corps.[213] The *Advertiser* expressed its confidence in Kitchener and military justice and considered the death penalty richly deserved. It was also of the opinion that although the officers involved had been spoken of as Australians 'they were not so in the true sense of the word'.[214] The Brisbane *Worker* deplored the 'wholesale cold-blooded butchery of defenceless men'.[215] The most thoughtful comment came from the *Bulletin*. In an article on Morant, a former contributor to its literary pages, it branded him an 'accomplished good-for-naught' who had carried out the 'callous or revengeful shooting of surrendered Boers in cold blood',[216] but it also saw the Australian officers as victims of their own ignorance of military law and of Kitchener's carelessness 'in appointing blacksmiths, drovers and what-nots, as responsible military officers in disturbed districts'.[217] In a further issue, 'Frank Renar' predicted that Morant would become a bush hero along with Ned Kelly and Starlight, and suggested that his death might lead to the regeneration of jingoistic Australia. 'Is it to be the fate of "the Breaker", wearing his blood-smeared halo, to lead Australians back to the path of Right?' he asked.[218] And the answer must be a partial affirmative, for the episode of the Bushveldt Carbineers did more than anything else to foster Australian disenchantment with the war.

The Handcock-Morant affair had a sequel some sixty years later. For more than fifty years relatives and friends of Handock had campaigned to have the officer's name placed on the Boer War Memorial in Bathurst, his home town, but without success. Then in 1963, on receipt of a suggestion from a Western Australian veteran of the war, the Bathurst branch of the Returned Servicemen's League satisfied itself, by reading such accounts as that of Witton, that Handcock had been too harshly dealt with. The branch put its case successfully to the Bathurst City Council and Handcock's name was added to the monument.[219]

It has been widely accepted over the years that the name of Handcock was removed from the original list of names on the memorial at the command of Kitchener, who unveiled the monument on 10 January 1910. But this is almost certainly untrue. There is no trace of a name having been removed, and Mrs N. Rutherford, the Archives Officer of the Bathurst Historical Society, states that so far as she can determine Handcock's name was never placed on the monument. Press lists of names to be honoured on the memorial never included that of Handcock, nor did the press at the time of Kitchener's visit make any reference to its alleged removal.[220]

When 'Frank Renar' suggested that the tragedy of Harry Morant might lead Australians to look more critically at their role in the war, he was predicting a process of national introspection that had already begun. The affair of the Bushveldt Carbineers represented the greatest shock of the war to Australian complacency over the nation's military image in South Africa, but a number of events preceding and following it also contributed to disenchantment with the cult of the warrior. Some of these events involved public displays of military indiscipline; others indicated a readiness on the part of soldiers to demand more than they perhaps deserved.

There is evidence that some Australians put up their best South African fighting performances in the streets of Cape Town. These episodes were never given any prominence in the Australian press, but an occasional newspaper reference to them, helped along no doubt by the tall tales of returning soldiers, would have made Australians aware of the disturbing behaviour of the bearers of the national honour. One of the first incidents occurred when drunken members of the second Victorian contingent became involved in a minor battle with military and civil police in Cape Town.[221] Then there was the hauling down and burning of the Transvaal flag flying over the offices of the Dutch paper, *Ons Lands*,[222] and other damage allegedly done in the city by men of the fifth New South Wales contingent.[223] But the most serious incident was the attack by Australians on the offices of the *South African News*, a paper which favoured the Boer cause. It seems that a number of Bushmen of the third contingent took umbrage at an article on 14 February 1901, which described the reception in Melbourne to troops aboard the *Harlech Castle* as 'a disgusting debauch'.[224] Under the heading of 'Mob Rule in Cape Town', the *South African News* gave its version of the attack.[225] It reported that on the night of 28 March about two hundred Australian troopers took over a number of the main streets and 'defied and utterly disregarded the military and civil police'. Cafe proprietors and publicans were reported as suffering at their hands; and the manager of the National Sporting Club 'was severely handled' because his establishment had been the venue for a boxing match in which the decision had gone against an Australian named McKell. From there the troopers went to the offices of the newspaper and did extensive damage.

The transport *Morayshire*, carrying New South Wales and Queensland Bushmen mainly, was the scene of another ugly incident. Serious consequences were avoided, however, by the courage of an officer and the restraint of the majority of the men. On the voyage back from the Cape ten troopers were given forty-two days cells for refusing to holystone the decks.[226] However, they were soon freed by twenty of their fellows, although the released men immediately reported to Major W. Tunbridge. This officer called all the troops together, read the Mutiny Act and defied any man to make a move to harm him. The soldiers dispersed and the released men returned voluntarily to their cells.[227]

Other incidents stemmed from pay grievances. The men of the first contingent claimed that they had been promised Imperial pay of 1s 2d a day in addition to 4s 6d a day colonial pay, whereas it had been the intention of the military commandants who had met in Melbourne in September 1899 that the Imperial cavalry rate of 1s 2d should be made up to a total of 4s 6d by colonial authorities. Because of lack of liaison between the New South Wales military commandant and his pay staff, the first contingent went to South Africa thinking they were being paid at the rate of 5s 8d a day. The second and third New South Wales contingents claimed the higher amount, also, on the grounds that they had been promised first contingent pay rates.

The misunderstanding was first realized in May 1900 by returning invalids, and from then until 1907 there was agitation by returned men for the 1s 2d a day which had been paid them by Imperial authorities in South Africa and which had been deducted from their total earnings by New South Wales authorities. In 1901 the New South Wales government undertook to reimburse the 1s 2d to the first contingent, mainly as an act of grace, and the Royal Commission of 1905-06 found in favour of the second contingent, although the commissioners contended that some men undoubtedly knew the true position before they sailed for the Cape. The Commission disallowed the claims of the third contingent.[228]

In the interim some of the men made life uncomfortable for political leaders. J. See was heckled over the pay issue when he farewelled the first battalion of the Australian Commonwealth Horse.[229] And at a luncheon at Clontarf to mark the first South Africa Day (a reunion of veterans), men crowded around the official marquee and 'bawled out their grievances' about back pay while the premier and other dignitaries were making speeches.[230]

The *Daily Telegraph*, which had solidly supported the war throughout, appeared to lose patience with the returned soldiers at this point. 'Some of these returned men', it claimed, 'have been grumbling since they first set foot on the outward bound transport, and they will probably continue until they all get into fat government billets'.[231]

The paper was even more caustic about soldiers when men returning aboard the *Aurania* gave Albany a sample of what they had earlier handed out to Cape Town. Following upon reports of damage and theft, and holding compensation claims for £900 from Cape Town and Albany, Sir William Lyne, acting federal minister for defence, went aboard to investigate when the ship docked at Melbourne. The O.C. troops disclaimed any responsibility for looting in Cape Town and argued that 'no great excesses were committed in Albany'. Lyne accepted this view, but the *Daily Telegraph* passed contrary judgement. In a leading article titled 'The Sacking of Albany' it castigated the behaviour of the troops. Their actions 'realised the worst of the evils to be locally expected of militarism, that of forcible domination of citizens by swaggering soldiers'.[232] The wheel had turned full circle. The 'swashbuckling' militiaman of pre-war had passed through two years of adulation to become again an object of contempt. And to his destruction as hero he had made a major contribution himself.

Australian troops had little to grumble about, for they had been well treated by their governments and the public. And they had not had to suffer greatly for the benefits brought by being a member of a contingent. The casualty rate was low, and the men had only to spend twelve months in the field. In line with a recommendation of the commandants' conference, most colonies took out £250 death policies on members of the first three contingents.[233] The Victorian government was one exception, preferring to stand by the dependants of deceased soldiers itself.

All Australian soldiers were eligible for Imperial pensions and compassionate allowances, but these were usually inadequate because they were geared to the poor Imperial pay rates. Needy cases, however, could get additional assistance from the Imperial Patriotic Fund, to which Australians had contributed £100 000 by 30 March 1900.[234] Colonial governments also stepped in with financial assistance and medical care where it was considered a special need existed. Pensions and compassionate allowances were not a big factor in rehabilitation, however, for few married men had been enlisted, and the dead and wounded represented small percentages of the contingents. Soldiers invalided through disease were the most numerous category and they were usually taken care of by periods of leave that covered their convalescence.

A far greater worry to Australian governments was the problem of unemployment among the thousands of returning troops. This was met partly by giving returned soldiers preference in government employment, and thus a precedent was set for subsequent wars in which Australians were involved.[235] However, a suggestion that Australian colonies should follow the lead of the government of Ontario in granting 160 acres to returned soldiers was flatly rejected in the two parliaments in which the matter was raised.[236]

Many years after the war ended federal governments showed some compassion for the veterans. In 1941, when the majority of them would have been receiving, or were about to receive, the old age pension, they were declared eligible for the service pensions that World War I men had been granted in 1936. To qualify for the service pension, the monetary equivalent of the old age pension, a returned soldier had to be aged sixty, or permanently unemployable, or a victim of pulmonary tuberculosis. In 1973, along with World War I veterans, they were granted free medical attention without a means test. As service pensioners they would already have been eligible for free medical care, although with a means test which would have excluded very few of them. So the nonagenarian survivors of the war on the veldt would have gained little or nothing from the 1973 gesture. South African veterans were never made eligible for war service home loans or soldier settlement blocks.

After thirty-one months of war peace came to South Africa on 31 May 1902. The Boers went back to their devastated farms to begin the long and heart-breaking process of rebuilding. The British went home to inquire into the poor showing of their cumbersome military machine. The Australians went home to find their nation bent on forgetting the whole thing. Peace came as a blessing to the Australian people, not because it ended a period of national bloodshed and grief, but because it closed an episode in their history which in their enthusiasm and ignorance they had elevated into a great national trial and triumph; only to find, as their enthusiasm dulled and their ignorance lifted, that they were embroiled in a war that brought no national honour. Understandably then, the end of the war was celebrated with restraint in Australia. Commonwealth offices closed immediately the news came through on 2 June, but the Federal government took no other initiative in celebrating the end of hostilities. According to one report, the declaration of peace had absolutely no effect in Sydney.[237] On the following Sunday thanksgiving services were held throughout the nation, but those reported in New South Wales stressed humility rather than military glory.[238]

Press comment was anything but chauvinistic. The *Age* observed that the conflict had not been 'a great or bloody war', and gave a summary of the event in terms of Imperial triumph and tragedy.[239] The *Daily Telegraph* gave a full-page summary of the war, also from the Imperial viewpoint, although it did mention Diamond Hill as a spot 'famous in the annals of Australian military history'.[240] The *Advertiser* said nothing about the Australian contribution, but appraised the conflict as a British affair.[241] And the *Brisbane Courier* was full of praise for 'a conquered and brave enemy'.[242] Much more could have been said of Australian participation and achievement, but it would have been anti-climactic after the earlier excessive praise of the Australian contingents.

5 *Opinions of the Australian Soldier*

Letters, diaries and reports of soldiers indicate that the men of the contingents were keen to win golden opinions for themselves and their country in Australia's very first war. And because they were a new and colourful force on the world's battlefields they prompted appraisal on many sides. Opinions of them were not always golden, but they were seldom unfavourable. And out of the total there emerges a well-defined contemporary image of the Australian soldier.

Contribution to the image from within Australia was limited, for Australians never regarded their military representatives with any degree of certainty, moving from a highly exaggerated view of their prowess early in the war to disillusionment later in the conflict.

The enemy's conception of the Australian soldier was also influenced by emotionalism, for to the Boers the overseas colonials had come voluntarily and thoughtlessly into a fight that was none of their concern. They could make allowances for the British regular who went where he was told, but the Australians, New Zealanders, and Canadians appeared to them as callous soldiers of fortune.[1]

A foremost, modern South African historian, Johannes Meintjes, has summarized impressions of the Australian soldier that he gained through wide research into the war. He sees him as 'a man very much like a Boer, lean and tough, brave and resourceful'. Australians, he considered were 'instinctive guerillas' and 'on the whole . . . were gallant, full of guts and at times ingenious', but Meintjes feels that they lost their enthusiasm for fighting when they came to appreciate the true situation in South Africa. He can recall no record of offensive behaviour towards civilians or natives, although their conduct was at times exuberant in the manner of all soldiers on foreign soil.[2]

Meintjes' conclusions regarding the conduct of the Australians towards civilians and natives may be a little gracious, but if we exclude their harassment of some Cape Town citizens, there was very little that was seriously reprehensible about Australian behaviour elsewhere in South Africa. They were certainly no worse than other British troops, and their conduct was natural in the circumstances.

The Australians' dealings with Boer farm women in the early part of the war were quite proper, although they would have been helped in their propriety by the high moral character of the women. There are numerous reports of soldiers, usually officers, being treated to cups of tea, but very little evidence suggesting deeper relationships. When farm burning began, any social intercourse would have been out of the question, and the soldiers' attitude towards the women could only be judged by the compassion they showed in carrying out their duties. And there is more evidence of compassion than of callousness, and no evidence of brutality.

In their treatment of the native population, the Australians could rely on the attitudes of their homeland. The Kaffirs were merely 'niggers' who were there to be exploited as servants or subjects of practical jokes, and who had been rightfully relegated to the dirtiest non-combatant duties by both sides in this 'white man's war'. Many Australians wrote disapprovingly, however, of the often brutal treatment of natives by their Boer masters. As a source of food when supplies were low, the native kraal was as much a target as the Boer farmhouse, and there is evidence that the Australians (and no doubt other troops) were not averse to threatening violence to obtain food from the natives. As virtually the only sex objects available to the Australians outside Cape Town, the native girls came in for some attention, the extent of which cannot be estimated on the evidence. However, a few guarded references in soldiers' diaries and some incidence of venereal disease point to the existence of fraternization.

The record of the proceedings of the Elgin Commission is a rich source of opinion on all colonial and regular troops who fought in South Africa, and it gives a clear and consistent picture of the Australian soldier as he was seen by senior British officers. Unfortunately Kitchener was not prepared to draw any comparisons among the troops of his command,[3] and Roberts

181

and many of the column commanders were almost as non-committal when it came to making distinctions among the colonials. Roberts said that 'all the colonials did extremely well', and especially the first contingents which he equated in value with the first battalions of Imperial Yeomanry.[4]

General Ian Hamilton spoke of 'the instinct of Colonials for country, their greater touch with nature and individual initiative',[5] and it was generally accepted by the commissioners that the colonials were more intelligent than British soldiers.[6]

The word 'dashing' was commonly used of the Australians, and to exploit this quality the Marquis of Tullibardine armed his '50 best Australians' with short lances and used them with great effect against pockets of Boer resistance.[7] General Rimington also cast the Australians of his command into the role of shock troops when he directed them on several occasions to make mounted charges with fixed bayonets.[8]

All colonials were regarded as being more deficient in horsemastership or care of horses than British mounted men.[9] But Tullibardine put the matter in perspective when he said of the Australians that 'had they been less good horsemen they would have been better horsemasters'. By this he meant that their great ability to ride led them to push their horses to the utmost. On the other hand, the Scots in Tullibardine's regiment were never inclined to gallop their horses because they were less competent riders.[10]

Australians won no plaudits for their marksmanship,[11] and this was in keeping with the very ordinary standard of musketry displayed by the generality of volunteers in shooting tests prior to enlistment.

It was widely held by witnesses that colonial officers were inadequately trained, and that colonial units did better when commanded by Imperial officers.[12] However, Tullibardine spoke highly of Australian subalterns as troop leaders,[13] and Colonel Plumer was happy to accept them in that capacity, but no higher.[14] As commander of a group of twenty men, a troop leader was of course perilously close to a non-commissioned officer in function. And the Australian officer's training fitted him for little more than that. Duntroon was still a decade away, and officer training for the part-time defence forces was extremely limited in time and content. A minimum of training was sufficient to turn a bushman with his ready-made military attributes into a passable soldier, but much more training was needed to produce a leader. Even Rimington in his praise of Australian officers was obliged to exclude their performances in matters of discipline and organization.[15]

There was very little criticism of Australian discipline by witnesses and when it was brought up in respect of the Bushmen corps, General Knox said, without rancour, that the state of indiscipline which prevailed was just what you would expect from a group of bushmen.[16]

The views of the Imperial officers before the Elgin Commission are corroborated by views expressed elsewhere,[17] and the Australian was accepted as a soldier of some achievement and very great potential. His dash and courage, his fearless and skilled horsemanship, his ability to endure and to find his way, and his independence and initiative, all promised the emergence of a soldier without superior if he were given good leadership, and so thoroughly trained that his tendency to indiscipline and impetuosity were eliminated.

Seventy years on, some of the surviving veterans of the war were given an opportunity to comment on themselves. Twenty good responses to a questionnaire were received from old soldiers in New South Wales and Victoria. In general terms, they saw themselves as men who had gone to war either out of loyalty to the Empire or a desire for adventure. Two described themselves as economic conscripts. They believed they were at least equal to the British regular soldier, although they regarded their own strength as being in guerrilla style warfare in which initiative and resourcefulness were paramount, whereas the Tommy was supreme where disciplined courage was called for. The Imperial Yeomanry they looked upon as being quite as useless as the 'new-chum' Englishman in the Australian bush. They had profound respect for the ability and humanity of the Boer soldier, and saw themselves as the equal of the Boer in his type of warfare. While they realized their own officers were untrained in higher military strategy, they considered them at least equal to the British in most things and far superior as men. They regarded them as being more democratic and more practical than the British, whose pomposity was the butt of many Australian jokes. And the Australian soldier regarded himself as quite a practical joker and teller of tall stories.

Ex-Corporal Fred Moore of the N.S.W.M.R. recounted the

story of an English major whose legs were so small that he used to draw from Australians cries of 'Look at the leg on him!' The major complained to Colonel Cox but got no help there. 'They call me Charlie the Bastard and I can do nothing about that', said Cox. Ex-Trooper Alfred Cattanach of the Australian Commonwealth Horse told a similar story of a 'bombastic' British captain 'with a plum in his mouth' and a big black moustache which earned him the title of 'Monkey Bill'. On occasions when the captain inspected Australian lines, several voices in turn would call out, 'Monkey Bill, there he goes!', and the poor chap would put on a crazy turn trying to locate the culprits, but always without the effective help of the Australian officers and N.C.O.s who would never give the jokers away. Ex-Trooper Matthew French of the N.S.W. Imperial Bushmen wrote of an Imperial officer who came to inspect an Australian unit. Putting his eyeglass to his eye, he asked, 'Are you the Orstralians?' Whereupon a wag put a stirrup iron up to his eye and replied, 'Yers, we are the bloody Orstralians'.

All the veterans recalled their distaste at having to evict Boer families and burn their houses, but the majority of them saw the practice as the only way to end the war, so integrated were the Boer citizens and citizen soldiers. Most veterans considered they had done a good job for Australia, and a few thought they should have been treated better on their return to civilian life. The main complaint was the slowness of the Australian authorities in according to the veterans some of the benefits bestowed on the returned men of World War I.

The flattering estimate of the young nation's first soldiers by renowned British generals is all the more commendable because it was achieved amid some difficulty. When the Australians took the field their equipment was frequently inadequate, inappropriate or superfluous. The men of the first contingent had to be re-equipped with numerous items from Imperial stores. The second contingent fared even worse, for much of their equipment had been hurriedly manufactured by unscrupulous contractors. The New South Wales and Victorian contingents were the main sufferers,[18] and R. Sleath hurried back from his tour of the battle area to head a parliamentary select committee on the equipment and organization of the New South Wales contingents.[19] A poet had already been at work, however, and expressed the situation rather more succinctly than Sleath's committee was to do.

On the night before the battle, as I snatch a wink, perhaps,
I'll be dreaming of my country, also of my stirrup straps.
I'll be thinking in my slumbers of the glory that I'll gain
If my shoddy cardboard leathers only stand the
blooming rain . . .[20]

The equipment situation was watched more closely in subsequent contingents, but hundreds of sore-backed horses were a legacy of earlier inefficiency.

There were numerous other problems to contend with. The Australians' horses were given no time to acclimatize, and most fell early victims to exhaustion and an influenza-type sickness. And the re-mounts they got in place of expended horses were usually inferior types. All too frequently colonial contingents were fragmented almost to the point of losing their identity, and the relatively short time that they spent in the field meant that they left the theatre of war just when they were becoming experienced troops. They were also opposed to an elusive enemy who was reluctant to provide them with significant engagements, and they were subject to the dual command of their own and Imperial officers.

The small numbers of casualties suffered also made it difficult for contingents to appear as having been through the heat of battle. Australia lost 518 dead, or about three per cent of the 16 000 troops sent. These were divided almost equally between deaths in action and deaths through disease. Total deaths from disease among the Imperial armies were double the deaths sustained in action. Therefore Australian deaths were considerably fewer because of greater resistance to disease, and one could also say that deaths in action were fewer than they might have been because as a mounted man, and a superior horseman with it, the Australian would have got himself out of many dangerous situations (see Appendix D for casualties).

But if the casualty list was short, the list of decorations was long (see Appendix E). Members of Australian contingents won five Victoria Crosses by rescuing de-horsed or wounded comrades from the field of battle,[21] and while perhaps none of these acts was comparable with the conduct that won Victoria Cross citations in the two world wars, they indicated reckless courage, good horsemanship, and a desire to stick to one's mate in the legendary Australian tradition. The award of a C.B. to Colonel Ricardo raised serious doubts about the genuineness of decorations, however, and the commander of the Q.M.I. was the subject of a derisive attack in the *Evening Observer* of 23 April 1901. This led to a lengthy libel suit which earned Ricardo £500 damages, but which revealed his grave inadequacies as a leader.[22]

When the veterans of the war returned to the more ordinary pursuits of field and factory, many were suffering from the ravages of enteric fever or from sores or wounds that were unusually slow to heal because of an infection common to the battlefield. But a greater hurt they had to endure was the fact that the cause for which they had fought had been discredited and they were discredited in turn. They were not immediately forgotten, however, and officialdom busied itself with its last gesture to the war—the erection of monuments throughout the country in memory of the 518 men who lay wrapped in their blankets six feet down on the veldt, and the 16 000 men who had done their duty and survived. Otherwise the nation turned its back on the war, although it clearly marked the beginnings of the Anzac legend and the tentative emergence of the soldier as folk hero in place of the bushman. With the advent of the greater conflict of 1914-18, relegation of the war to a minor place in our history was made complete.

But for those who cared to look there was a lot to be seen in the young Australian soldier. Two contemporary poets perhaps made the most discerning judgement. Rudyard Kipling recognized his practical qualities, his democratic view of life, his superior physique, his carelessness regarding a cause, and his trace of larrikinism in 'The Parting of the Columns':

> . . . You had no special call to come,
> and so you doubled out,
> And learned us how to camp
> and cook an' steal a horse and
> scout . . .
> 'Twas how you talked and
> looked at things which made
> us like you so.
> All independent, queer an' odd, but
> most amazin' new,
> My word! You shook us
> up to rights.
> . . . Good-bye you bloomin' Atlases![23]

Walter Murdoch, an Australian man of letters, saw more heroic qualities in the Australian soldier, and envied him for having experienced an exhilaration denied those who stayed at home.

> . . . Be sure, for one great hour he felt
> The rapture of imperious joy . . .
> He felt it as he stormed the hill,
> And touched the topmost crest of Life.
> . . . How shall we mourn him — we, whose days
> Creep on in sluggish, level stream . . . [24]

And that was something no one could deny the volunteer. He had experienced moments of exultation denied the ordinary citizen. But he had also experienced hardship and death in a war to which he had gone willingly and in good faith. For those things his life is not without a smatch of honour at a time when very little honour rested elsewhere in the land, for the war had revealed grave deficiencies in the national character.

Appendix A

Report of the Commandants' Conference[1]

It was decided, ad interim, that the following recommendations should be made:—

1. That, in the opinion of this conference, the necessary Acts be passed without delay by each of the several colonies to enable their respective military contingents to act, either as a combined force or otherwise, for service outside Australia, and this proposal be communicated at once to the Premier, with a view to his taking the necessary action to carry out the recommendations of the conference.

2. That, in the opinion of this conference, it is desirable that information be obtained by cable as to whether the Imperial Government will defray cost of sea transport in the event of any contingents sent from Australia.

RATES OF PAY AND ALLOWANCES

The following rates of pay and allowances are recommended:—

	per day	Deferred pay per day	Total
Gunners and privates	2/3	2/3	4/6
Acting bombardiers	2/9	2/3	5/
Bombardiers	4/3	2/3	6/6
Corporals	4/9	2/3	7/
Sergeants	5/9	2/3	8/
Company sergeant-majors	6/3	2/9	9/
Staff sergeants	6/6	3/6	10/
Warrant-officers	7/6	4/	11/6
		Field All'nce	
Lieutenants	16/	3/	19/
Captains	20/	3/6	23/6
Majors	25/	4/6	29/6
Lieutenant-colonels	30/	6/6	36/6

Adjutants, 5s per day, in addition to pay of their rank.

189

Report of the Commandants' Conference

COMPOSITION OF FORCE

Resolved that — 'Apart from all other considerations, the Military Conference is met to consider what united force should be sent to represent Australia, and that it should be representative of all arms, and that the details should be arranged by units.

CAVALRY: A squadron—120 to 160 of all ranks.

ARTILLERY: A battery of Horse Artillery (4 to 6 guns); 120 of all ranks (4 guns).

INFANTRY: A Company—50 of all ranks. A Battalion—Six Companies, with regimental staff.

MOUNTED RIFLES: A Company—60 of all ranks. A Battalion—Four companies, with regimental staff.

Machine Gun Section (Mounted): Two machine guns and 17 of all ranks.

Machine Gun Section (Dismounted): Two machine guns, with one officer and 20 N.C.O.'s and men (including escort).

Bearer Company: 61 of all ranks, based on N.S.W. distribution.'

STRENGTH OF FORCE

The conference submits the following numbers as suitable for a limited Australian contingent in South Africa. In making this recommendation the members have considered the desirability of furnishing a large proportion of mounted men, while yet representing all branches of the forces, and are of opinion that if a sufficiently large force representing all arms be sent it will always remain intact, as an Australian contingent, capable of acting alone or in concert with the regular troops, but if a small force be sent there is the probability of its being scattered amongst other corps of the regular service, or being tacked on to some other colonial contingents, and thus have its identity destroyed.

The formation of the force proposed has received very careful consideration, and due attention has been given to the question of 'units'. Any increase or reduction in these numbers should be made by 'units' so as not to dislocate the organisation proposed.

NEW SOUTH WALES: Horse Artillery, 120; Cavalry and Mounted Rifles, 300; Infantry, 265; Departmental Corps and Engineers, 60; total, 745.

VICTORIA: Cavalry and Mounted Rifles, 198; Infantry, 345; total, 543.

QUEENSLAND: Cavalry and Mounted Rifles, 275; total, 275.

SOUTH AUSTRALIA: Cavalry and Mounted Infantry, 60; Infantry, 80; total, 140.

TASMANIA: Infantry, 160.

WEST AUSTRALIA: Infantry, 160.

The detail for general staff is put down at 30, giving a grand total of 2,053 officers, N.C.O's and men.

PENSIONS AND COMPASSIONATE ALLOWANCES

Recommended that pensions and compassionate allowances on the Imperial military scale should be paid by the colonies concerned to the wives and children of married officers and warrant officers killed on service or dying from wounds inflicted on service, on the terms and conditions prescribed by Imperial regulations; and that it is desirable that colonies concerned should in the case of all married N.C.O.'s and men of the contingents sent on service take out policies for life assurance, and for such amounts that reasonable income will be provided for widows and for children under 18 years of age.

SELECTION OF N.C.O.'s AND MEN

The following conditions should be kept in view in selecting N.C.O.'s and men for service:—

(a) The preference should be given to single men.

(b) Age to be from 20 to 40 years.

(c) The preference should be given to good rifle shots, and present and past efficient members of the defence forces.

(d) Pass strict medical examination.

OFFICER IN COMMAND AND STAFF

Recommended that the positions of officer commanding, second in command, and principal staff officers be filled so as to represent fairly the three larger colonies, representation on the staff or in minor commands being afforded by those colonies to the other contributing colonies.

It is also recommended that when the strength and composition of the combined force has been agreed upon by the several Governments, and the appointment of the General officer commanding and second in command is decided upon, a further meeting of those commandants who can conveniently attend be held in Sydney to select the officers of the staff.

Appendix B

Colonial Office Despatch of 3 October 1899[2]

Secretary of State for War and Commander-in-Chief desire to express high appreciation of Her Majesty's Government for the patriotic spirit exhibited by the people of Australia in offering to serve in South Africa and to furnish following information to assist organisation of forces offered into units suitable for military requirements:—

Firstly. Units should consist of about 125 men.

Secondly. May be infantry, mounted infantry, or cavalry. In view of numbers already available, infantry most, cavalry least, serviceable.

Thirdly. All should be armed with .303 rifles or carbines, which can be supplied by Imperial Government if necessary.

Fourthly. All must provide own equipment, and mounted troops their own horses.

Fifthly. Not more than one captain and three subalterns to each unit. Where more than one from single colony force may be commanded by officer not higher than Major.

In considering number which can be employed, the Secretary of State for War, guided by nature of officers, desires that each colony should be fairly represented and limits are necessary if force is to be fully utilised.

Available staff is integral portion of Imperial forces.

Would gladly accept two units each from New South Wales and Victoria, and one from South Australia.

Conditions as follows:—

Troops to be disembarked at port of landing in South Africa, fully equipped, at cost of colonial Governments or volunteers.

From date of disembarkation, Imperial Government will provide pay at Imperial rates, supplies and ammunition, and will defray expenses of transport back to the colony, and pay wound expenses and compassionate allowances at Imperial rates.

Troops to embark not later than 31st of October, proceeding direct to Capetown for orders.

Appendix C

Details of Colonial Contingents[3]

NEW SOUTH WALES

Contingent	Number		Arrived in S.A.	Left S.A.
	Off.	Men.		
1st Contingent				
N.S.W. Lancers	9	163	Nov. 1899 and Mar. 1900	Oct. 1900
1 co. N.S.W. Army Med. Corps (Field Hospital and Bearer Co.)	10	105	2 Dec. 1899	Dec. 1900
"A" Battery N.S.W. Arty.	5	174	5 Feb. 1900	July 1901
Draft for do.	1	43	Apr. 1901	do.
2nd Contingent				
1st Regt. N.S.W. Mtd. Rifles	6	124	7 Dec. 1899 and 19 Feb. 1900	Apr. 1901
	4	121		
	20	381		
1 co. N.S.W. Army Med. Corps (Field Hospital, Bearer Co. and Mtd. Bearer Co.)	10	105	17 Feb. 1900	Dec. 1900
1st Australian Horse (1 sq.)	8	130	23 Feb. 1900	Nov. 1900
3rd Contingent Citizen's Bushmen (1st Regt. Australian Bushmen)	33	498	Apr. 1900	May 1901
4th Contingent 6th Regt. N.S.W. Imp. Bushmen	40	722	17 May 1900	18 June 1901
5th Contingent 2nd Regt. Imp. N.S.W. Mtd. Rifles	36	673	13 Apr. 1901	3 May 1902
3rd do. do. do.	40	1,046	do.	do.
3rd N.S.W. Imperial Bushmen (formed May 1901, from drafts sent out for the Citizen's and 6th Regt. Imperial Bushmen).	13	479	From end of 1901 to Mar. 1902	June 1902
6th Contingent 1st Bn. Aust. Com. Horse	21	351	Mar. 1902	
2nd do. do.	22	351	Apr. 1902	
5th do. do.	26	467	June 1902	
Army Medical Corps	3	36	Apr. 1902	
Total	305 [307]	5,969		

Colonial Contingents

VICTORIA*

Contingent	Number		Arrived in S.A.	Left S.A.
	Off.	Men.		
1st Contingent	12	240	Nov. 1899	Dec. 1900
2nd do.	15	250	6 Feb. 1900	May 1901
3rd do. (Aust. Bushmen)	15	261	12 Apr. 1900	June 1901
4th do. (Imp. Bushmen)	31	598	May 1900	26 June 1901
5th do.	[1]46	971	Mar. 1902 [1901]	8 Apr. 1902
2nd Bn. Aust. Commonwealth ⎱ Horse ⎰	20	371	Mar. 1902	July 1902
4th do. do. (2nd Commonwealth Contingent ⎰	17	235	Apr. 1902	do.
6th Bn. Aust. Commonwealth ⎱ Horse ⎰	22	467	{ beg. June 1902 }	do.
Total	248 [178]	3,393		

*The additions in square brackets indicate the author's amendments.

QUEENSLAND

	Off.	Men.	Arrived	Left
1st Queensland Contingent (M.I.)	14	250	13 Dec. 1899	13 Dec. 1900
2nd do. do.	10	150	Jan. 1900	3 May 1901
3rd do. (Bushmen)	16	298	Mar. 1900	13 June 1901
4th Queensland Imperial ⎱ Bushmen ⎰	25	372	June 1900	6 Aug. 1901
5th do. do.	23	517	Mar. 1901	30 Apr. 1902
6th do. do.	17	422	Apr. 1901	20 June 1902
Aust. Commonwealth Horse	6	122	Mar. 1902	
do. do.	5	116	19 May 1902	
do. do.	23	466	22 June 1902	
Total	139	2,713		

194

SOUTH AUSTRALIA

Contingent	Number		Arrived in S.A.	Left S.A.
	Off.	Men.		
1st Contingent ("S. Aust. Infy")	6	121	26 Nov. 1899	3 Nov. 1900
2nd Cont. (with 1st Cont. known as S.Aust. M.R.)	8	113	25 Feb. 1900	26 Mar. 1901
3rd S.A. Bushmen Cont. (1st Bushmen's Corps)	6	94	11 Apr. 1900	Apr. 1901
4th S. Aust. Imp. B. Corps	12	218	29 May 1900	7 July 1901
5th do. do.	22	303	25 Mar. 1901	Apr. 1902
6th do. do.	11	127	29 Apr. 1901	do.
1st Aust. Com. Horse, D. Co. 2nd Bn.	5	116	17 Mar. 1902	5 July 1902
2nd Aust. Com. Horse, C. Co. 4th Bn.	5	116	29 May 1902	
3rd Aust. Com. Horse, 8th Bn.	10	231	21 June 1902	
Total	85	1,439		

WESTERN AUSTRALIA

Contingent	Off.	Men	Arrived	Left
1st Contingent	5	125	Nov. 1899	Nov. 1900
2nd do. (called 3rd Bushmen)	6	97	Feb. 1900	Mar. 1901
3rd do. (W.A.M.I.— Bushmen's Cont.)	7	109	Apr. 1900	Apr. 1901
4th do. (Bushmen)	7	119	June 1900	July 1901
5th do.	13	207	Mar. 1901	Apr. 1902
6th do.	13	214	Apr. 1901	do.
E sq. 2nd Bn. Aust. Com. Horse	2	58	Mar. 1902	5 July 1902
Aust. Army Med. Corps (W. Aust. Section)	—	7	do.	do.
D sq. 4th Bn. Aust. Com. Horse	5	115	Apr. 1902	11 July 1902
D sq. 8th Bn. Aust. Com. Horse	4	116	June 1902	27 June 1902
Total	62	1,167		

Colonial Contingents

TASMANIA

Contingent	Number		Arrived in S.A.	Left S.A.
	Off.	Men.		
1st Contingent	4	72	Nov. 1899	3 Nov. 1900
Draft for above	1	47	18 Feb. 1900	3 Nov. 1900
2nd Contingent (Tasmanian Bushmen's Cont.)	3	49	31 Mar. 1900	19 May 1901
3rd Contingent (1st Tasmanian Imperial Bushmen)	5	119	May 1900	7 July 1901
4th Contingent (2nd Tasmanian Imperial Bushmen)	11	243	24 Apr. 1901	22 May 1902 (8 and 159)
E sq. 1st Aust. Com. Horse	3	60	14 Mar. 1902	11 July 1902
E sq. 3rd Aust. Com. Horse	5	115	10 May 1902	do.
C sq. 8th Aust. Com. Horse	5	116	21 May 1902	
Total	37	821		

CANADA

Contingent	Number		Arrived in S.A.	Left S.A.
	Off.	Men.		
1st Contingent				
2nd Bn. R. Can. Regt.	44	995	30 Nov. 1899	Oct. 1900
Draft for do.	3	100	Early Apr. 1900	
2nd Contingent				
1st Bn. Canadian Mtd. Rifles (Royal Canadian Dragoons from Aug. 1, 1900)	19	360	21 Mar. 1900	Nov. 1900
2nd Bn. Canadian Mtd. Rifles (Canadian Mtd. Rifles from Aug. 1, 1900)	21	357	26 Feb. 1900	13 Dec. 1900
Brigade Div. R. Canadian Artillery	19	520	16 Feb. 1900	13 Dec. 1900
Strathcona's Horse	29	562	10 Apr. 1900	Jan. 1901
3rd Contingent				
2nd Regt. Canadian Mounted Rifles, with draft	45	880	Feb. 1902	27 June 1902
10th Canadian Field Hospital Co. A.M.C.	5	56	Feb. 1902	do.
4th Contingent				
3rd Regt. Canadian Mounted Rifles	26	483	30 May 1902	2 July 1902
4th Regt. Canadian Mounted Rifles	26	483	June 1902	do.
5th do. do.	26	483	do.	do.
6th do. do.	26	483	do.	do.
Total	289	5,762		

N.B.—Canada contributed 30 officers and 1,208 N.C.O.'s and men to the South African Constabulary—not included in the above figures.

Colonial Contingents

NEW ZEALAND

Contingent	Numbers		Arrived in S.A.	Left S.A.
	Off.	Men		
1st Contingent N.Z. M. Rifles	9	206	Nov. 1899	Nov. 1900
2nd do.	11	247	Feb. 1900	31 Mar. 1901
3rd do.	12	252	Mar. 1900	do.
4th do.	20	446	Apr. 1900	May 1901
5th do. (Imp. Bushmen)	24	500	do.	do.
(Reserves)	3	68	do.	
6th Contingent	27	551	Feb. 1901	
7th do.	28	572	May 1901	22 May 1902 (larger part) July 1902 (part)
8th do.	45	951	Mar. 1902	July 1902
(Details)	8	192	do.	
9th Contingent	48	1,028	Apr. 1902	do.
10th do.	45	961	beg. May, 1902	do.
(Details)	7	155	do.	
Total	287	6,129		

INDIA AND CEYLON

Lumsden's Horse	15	292	25 Mar 1900	Dec. 1900
1st Ceylon Contingent (M.I.)	6	119	18 Feb. 1900	About 12 mths. later
2nd do. do.	5	98	May 1900	
Total	26	509		
GRAND TOTAL	Officers, 1,478; [1,410]		Men, 27,902	

Appendix D

Selected Casualties[4]

Corps	Killed or Died of Wounds		Died of Disease		Wounded		Captured by the Enemy		Missing		Total	
	Offs.	Men	Offs.	Men	Offs.	Men	Offs.	Men	Offs.	Men	Offs.	Men
Imperial Yeomanry	67	470	25	839	131	1,236	42	899	8	54	273	3,498
City Imperial Volunteers	1	10	—	51	1	58	—	6	—	6	2	131
Volunteers	2	29	11	527	12	117	1	47	—	9	26	729
Australian Contingent	29	222	9	258	77	658	5	99	—	43	120	1,280
Canadian	7	87	3	76	23	255	1	20	—	35	34	473
New Zealand	7	78	4	87	26	176	2	35	—	6	39	382
South African	119	1,354	69	1,538	328	3,005	53	1,177	14	530	583	7,604
Other Contingents	2	6	—	5	—	14	1	8	—	—	3	33
Total Empire Casualties	719	6,863	406	12,733	1,758	19,399	290	8,135	36	1,817	3,209	48,947

Appendix E

Australian Decorations[5]

	V.C.	C.B.	C.M.G.	D.S.O.	D.C.M.	M.I.D.	R.R.C.	Total
N.S.W.	1	8	1	24	16	96	1	141
Vic.	1	3	2	12	13	75	1	107
Qld.		5	3	8	13	60		89
S.A.		3		8	10	42	1	64
W.A.	1	1		6	8	59		75
Tas.	2	3		4	5	34		48
Total	5	23	6	62	65	366	3	524

This table excludes awards to men not serving with Australian units, e.g. Sgt. J. Rogers, V.C., of the South African Constabulary.

Abbreviations

A.A.M.C.	Australian Army Medical Corps
A.C.H.	Australian Commonwealth Horse
A.W.M.L.	Australian War Memorial Library
C. of A.P.D.	*Commonwealth of Australia Parliamentary Debates*
C.O.	Colonial Office
G.O.C.	General Officer Commanding
M.L.	Mitchell Library
N.L.A.	National Library of Australia
N.S.W.A.M.C.	New South Wales Army Medical Corps
N.S.W.M.R.	New South Wales Mounted Rifles
N.S.W.P.D.	*New South Wales Parliamentary Debates*
N.S.W. V. & P.	*New South Wales Votes and Proceedings*
Q.M.I.	Queensland Mounted Infantry
Q.P.D.	*Queensland Parliamentary Debates*
R.A.A.	Royal Australian Artillery
S.A.P.D.	*South Australia Parliamentary Debates*
V.M.R.	Victorian Mounted Rifles
V.P.D.	*Victoria Parliamentary Debates*
W.A.M.I.	West Australian Mounted Infantry
W.A.P.D.	*Western Australia Parliamentary Debates*

Notes

1 The Australian Commitment to the South African War

1 The New South Wales contingent to the Soudan had arrived too late for any combat.
2 Hutchinson and Myers, *The Australian Contingent*, p. 3.
3 Wilkinson, *Australian Cavalry*, p. 18. The offer was from the O.C., N.S.W. Lancers, but other units were interested.
4 *ibid.*, p. 13.
5 *ibid.*, p. 16.
6 Wilkinson, *op.cit.*, p. 16; Hutton Papers, vol. 6; *Daily Mail*, 22 April 1897.
7 *N.S.W.P.D.*, vol. XCVII, p. 411.
8 Hutton Papers, vol. 6; *Sydney Morning Herald*, 10 July 1893.
9 Hutton Papers, vol. 9; *Hawke's Bay Herald*, 20 February 1897.
10 All figures on strength and attendances are derived from contemporary reports of military commandants to colonial parliaments, and from the Western Australian Year Book for 1900. The reports are available in the appropriate collections of parliamentary papers and, more conveniently, in the library of the Australian War Memorial, where they are collected by colony in single volumes covering several years.
11 Correspondence of N.S.W. Governor with Colonial Office, C.O. 201/625, Mackay's letter to Beauchamp/French, 18 July 1899. The Colonial Defence Committee put the idea aside until completion of federation and the end of the war in South Africa.
12 The three Imperial major-generals commanding in the eastern colonies were particularly active.
13 Hutton Papers, vol. 6; *Daily Telegraph*, 17 October 1893.
14 A. B. Paterson, *Rio Grande and Other Verses*, p. 145.
15 *Age*, 12 May 1899, p. 5.
16 *ibid.*, 17 May 1899, p. 5.
17 *ibid.*, 23 May 1899, p. 5.
18 *ibid.*, 6 June 1899, p. 5.
19 *ibid.*, 16 September 1899, p. 9.
20 *ibid.*, 19 September 1899, p. 5.
21 Correspondence of Victorian Governor with Colonial Office, C.O. 309/148, Notation on a cable from Lord Brassey, 19 May 1899, reporting Melbourne meeting on Uitlanders.
22 22 June 1899, p. 5.
23 16 May 1899, p. 4.
24 5 July 1899, p. 4.
25 *Brisbane Courier*, 7 July 1899, p. 5.
26 5 July 1899, p. 6.
27 22 July 1899, p. 8.
28 15 July 1899, p. 6.
29 p. 5.

[30] *ibid.*

[31] *ibid.*

[32] *N.S.W. V. & P.* of Leg. Ass., 1900, vol. 4, p. 874. A Labor member of the Parliamentary Select Committee on the Administration of the Military Department claimed that French had used these words.

[33] '. . . jingoism is the breath of his nostrils, and every officer naturally desires to end up his career amidst military glory'. 30 September 1899, p. 15.

[34] More than half the company of 100 were reported to have volunteered. *Daily Telegraph*, p. 9.

[35] *ibid.*, 11 July 1899, p. 5.

[36] *ibid.*, 17 July 1899, p. 5.

[37] *ibid.*, 14 July 1899, p. 5.

[38] The preface to the reply to Chamberlain's telegram from the N.S.W. governor indicates that Canada was approached as well as N.S.W. and Victoria. See C.O. 201/625, telegram of 9 July 1899.

[39] The actual cable is not included in the relevant Colonial Office correspondence in the National Library of Australia. The above is a reported version appended by the Colonial Office to the reply of 5 July 1899 of the Governor of N.S.W. See C.O. 201/625. Chamberlain's approach was kept a close secret, no mention of it appearing in the press. Reid made a passing reference to it in the October debate, but he did not elaborate and the matter remained secret. No secondary accounts of the war indicate a knowledge of the request.

[40] Two months later Chamberlain recognized Beauchamp's efforts in a note: 'I had already realized before I received your letter that you had done all that was possible to persuade Mr Reid'. But Mr Reid was not to be persuaded. Letters to Lord Beauchamp, 1899-1901; from J. Chamberlain, 31 August 1899, p. 53. Collection A 3012, ML.

[41] C.O. 309/148, telegram from Brassey, 5 July 1899.

[42] *ibid.*, telegram from Brassey, 12 July 1899.

[43] C.O. 309/148, noted in telegram from Brassey, 5 July 1899.

[44] C.O. 201/625, Beauchamp to Colonial Office, 9 July 1899.

[45] C.O. 201/625, telegram to Beauchamp.

[46] C.O. 201/625, Beauchamp to Colonial Office, 14 July 1899.

[47] C.O. 201/625, notation on a Colonial Office memo of 15 July 1899 which, incidentally, indicated that there was no thought at all of utilizing Australian volunteers. Wingfield was the Permanent Under-Secretary.

[48] C.O. 309/148, minute from Colonial Office to War Office, 14 July 1899.

[49] Amery (ed.), *The Times History of the War in South Africa*, vol. II, p. 306; Conan Doyle, *The Great Boer War*, p. 62; Harding, *War in South Africa*, p. 565: '. . . the offer of Queensland was like a spark to gunpowder and the patriotism of all Australia was at once aflame'; Creswicke, *South Africa and the Transvaal War*, vol. 3, p. 152: '. . . the honour of being the first of Great Britain's children to come forward to her assistance . . . our warlike brothers across the ocean . . . speedily [Dickson's] action was imitated all over the world'.

[50] *Q.P.D.*, vol. LXXXII, p. 350. The letter was read in parliament during the October debate.

[51] *ibid.*, p. 440.

[52] *ibid.*, p. 474.

[53] *ibid.*, p. 341.

[54] Correspondence of Queensland Governor with Colonial Office, C.O. 234/68.

[55] C.O. 201/625. 'Wait and see whether the action of Queensland will change

their attitude'—Wingfield's notation on a telegram from Beauchamp, 12 July 1899.
56 *Argus*, 14 July 1899, p. 5.
57 C.O. 201/625.
58 Letters to Lord Beauchamp, p. 52, letter of 31 August 1899.
59 *Argus*, 31 July 1899, p. 5.
60 From a volume of N.S.W. Government papers in the Australian War Memorial Library entitled *N.S.W. Soudan and South Africa Contingents 1885-1907*, p. 38. Hereafter N.S.W. Government Papers. The cable was sent on 25 July and received in Sydney the following day.
61 *N.S.W.P.D.*, vol. C, pp. 1394-5. The Lyne ministry assumed office on 14 September.
62 N.S.W. Government Papers, p. 38. It is interesting to note that Reid's telegram to Turner and Turner's cable to the Colonial Office were both dispatched on 1 August. The practice of 'one-up-manship' was so prevalent among colonial premiers at the time that one cannot easily dismiss the suspicion that Turner may not have been completely truthful in his reply to Reid.
63 *N.S.W.P.D.*, vol. C, p. 1395; from Wise's account.
64 N.S.W. Government Papers, p. 38. No date shown.
65 *S.A.P.D.*, 1899, p. 595.
66 4 September 1899, p. 4.
67 *Argus*, 14 September 1899, p. 5.
68 p. 5.
69 Dalley committed N.S.W. troops to the Soudan campaign on executive authority only. He was subjected to much parliamentary criticism as a result.
70 *Argus*, p. 5.
71 *ibid.*, 20 September 1899, p. 7.
72 *ibid.*, 21 September 1899, p. 5. The *Age* of the same date, p. 5, reported that the suggestion for a military commandant's conference was made by McCulloch.
73 C.O. 309/148.
74 *ibid.*
75 N.S.W. Government Papers, p. 39.
76 *ibid.*
77 *Age*, 22 September 1899, p. 5.
78 C.O. 234/68.
79 *Age*, 30 September 1899, p. 9.
80 N.S.W. Government Papers, p. 50.
81 *ibid.*, p. 51.
82 *Daily Telegraph*, 6 October 1899, p. 5.
83 The Queensland offer was accepted by a similar but separate telegram, much to the delight of Dickson and Gunter one would think. Tasmania and Western Australia were not included in the common telegram to the other colonies because neither had made any sort of offer, but it was generally assumed that they would form part of any contingent sent from Australia.
84 Vol. II, p. 117.
85 *ibid.*, p. 116.
86 'Report of His Majesty's Commissioners Appointed to Inquire into the Military Preparations and Other Matters Connected with the War in South Africa', being vols 40-42 of *Reports from Commissioners, Inspectors and Others* , vol. 40, p. 349. Hereafter Elgin Commission.

[87] *ibid.*, p. 78. He might also have had in mind another body of 'irregular cavalry' — the New South Wales Lancers.

[88] The Lancers had just completed six months of exercises and tournaments with British regular cavalry units.

[89] The words are those of Robb.

[90] C. F. Cox Papers; also *C. of A.P.D.*, vol. 141, pp. 3752-3.

[91] N.S.W. Government Papers, p. 41.

[92] *ibid.*, p. 44; telegram to Lyne of 5 October.

[93] N.S.W. Government Papers, p. 41.

[94] *ibid.*, pp. 42-3.

[94] p. 4.

[96] *W.A.P.D.*, vol. XV, p. 1556. Forrest's motion, the terms of which he telegraphed to the other colonial premiers on 4 October, was probably prepared before he received news of the Colonial Office cables to New South Wales, South Australia, Victoria and Queensland.

[97] *ibid.*, p. 1558.

[98] On 28 September the New Zealand Assembly voted 51 to 5 to send 200 mounted riflemen at the colony's expense should they be needed.

[99] *S.A.P.D.*, 1899, pp. 608-9.

[100] *ibid.*, p. 609, H. A. Grainger.

[101] *ibid.*, p. 621, E. L. Batchelor.

[102] *ibid.*, p. 652, E. A. Roberts. Many politicians underwent drastic changes under pressure of public opinion, but none went so far as Roberts. Despite his opposition to the war and his denigration of the military forces, he volunteered for service with the Imperial Bushmen's Corps and went to South Africa as a lieutenant.

[103] *ibid.*, pp. 630-1.

[104] *ibid.*, p. 657, F. W. Conybear.

[105] *ibid.*, p. 620.

[106] *ibid.*, p. 659.

[107] *ibid.*

[108] *ibid.*, p. 628.

[109] *S.A.P.D.*, Leg. Council, 1899, p. 146.

[110] *ibid.*, p. 147.

[111] *ibid.*, p. 155.

[112] 11 October 1899, p. 4. The *Age* reported that two members voted against the motion—13 October 1899, p. 6.

[113] Turner's information on Boer 'brutality' would have come from that morning's *Age*, which carried as headlines: 'Atrocious Boer Brutalities —Women and Children Maltreated—Spitting in Ladies Faces— Children Dying in Cattle Trucks'. The reference was to an incident in the general exodus from the Rand of Uitlander families. According to the London cable, a train carrying 70 women and children was shunted into a siding and left for a considerable period, during which time two children were said to have died. It was also claimed that 'several women gave birth to children during the terrible journey' (*Age*, 10 October 1899, p. 5). Undoubtedly the exodus meant hardship for many families, but it would have been difficult to sustain a charge of Boer brutality in relation to it. The London report was given prominence by a big section of the Australian press, and it played a significant part in the parliamentary debates on the first contingent.

[114] *V.P.D.*, vol. 92, pp. 1727-8.

[115] *ibid.*, pp. 1731-4.

[116] *ibid.*, pp. 1777-9.

[117] *Q.P.D.*, vol. LXXXII, p. 348.

[118] *ibid.*, p. 344.

[119] Another person influenced by Dickson was the governor of Lagos, who wrote to the premier saying he had followed his example and offered 300 men to the Home government. They would probably have been too dusky to participate in this white man's war—*Age*, 14 October 1899, p. 10. Dickson's offer also had an echo in the Canadian House of Commons when a Colonel Hughes commended the Queensland offer and urged that Canada, whose defence forces were already volunteering, should send a regiment—*Argus*, 15 July 1899, p. 9. Colonel Hughes, in the face of government inaction, set about raising a contingent in case of war. On 3 October the Canadian Military Institute came out openly in support of a contingent. (Hutton was Canadian military commandant at the time)—Creswicke, *op. cit.*, vol. 3, pp. 138-9. In July the Canadian government had expressed its sympathy with the Uitlanders and its faith in Imperial policy, but it was reluctant to do much else. On 13 October, in view of public clamour which was highlighted by telegrams from the mayors of 300 towns and cities urging the government to action, Sir Wilfred Laurier waived constitutional principles (parliament was not in session) and issued an order-in-council which allowed for the raising of 1000 volunteers—*The Times History*, vol. III, pp. 38-40.

[120] See note 113.

[121] *Q.P.D.*, vol. LXXXII. See pp. 339-43 for Dickson's speech.

[122] *ibid.*, p. 347.

[123] 17 October 1899, p. 4.

[124] 28 October 1899, p. 3.

[125] *Q.P.D.*, vol. LXXXII, p. 505. Another version of the finale was rather different: 'Stephenson called for three cheers for the Queen, and Dunsford did ditto for 'Liberty'. The response to each was not enthusiastic'—*Worker*, 21 October 1899, p. 11.

[126] *N.S.W.P.D.*, vol. C, p. 1379.

[127] 23 September 1899, p. 8.

[128] *N.S.W.P.D.*, vol. C, p. 1379.

[129] *ibid.*, pp. 1380-93.

[130] *ibid.*, pp. 1428-36.

[131] *ibid.*, p. 1466.

[132] *Grenfell Record*, 27 January 1900, p. 2.

[133] *ibid.*, 26 May 1900, p. 2.

[134] *N.S.W.P.D.*, vol. C, pp. 1573-4.

[135] *ibid.*, p. 1553.

[136] Although several Labor members were reported to have wanted to support the motion before the South Australian Assembly, a majority decision taken by the party held all members to the negative—Sydney *Daily Telegraph*, 13 October 1899, p. 6. Such was not the case in New South Wales where R. Sleath and A. Griffith clashed over the contingent issue and both expressed a willingness to take up the matter outside. Sleath charged Griffith and Holman with having ignored their pledge of allegiance to party majority opinion—*Age* 21 October 1899, p. 9.

[137] p. 2.

[138] 19 October 1899, p. 3.

[139] 29 September 1899, p. 7.

[140] *Bulletin*, 21 October 1899, p. 8.

2 Preparations for War

1 *Daily Telegraph*, 6 October 1899, p. 5.
2 Coghlan, *The Wealth and Progress of New South Wales, 1898-9*, p. 209.
3 New South Wales Government Papers, pp. 39, 41, 46.
4 C.O. 201/625, Cable to Colonial Office, 11 October 1899.
5 *ibid.*, Cable to Colonial Office, 13 October 1899. Lyne had no intention of doing a 'Dalley'.
6 *N.S.W.P.D.*, vol. C, p. 1376.
7 *ibid.*, p. 1381.
8 *Daily Telegraph*, 21 October 1899, p. 5.
9 *ibid.*, 25 October 1899, p. 5.
10 J. M.Antill, 'Record of N.S.W. Mounted Rifles', Macarthur Papers. Preference in recruiting was for single men over 20.
11 C.O. 201/625, Lieut- Colonel K. Mackay to Earl Beauchamp, 18 July 1899.
12 List of officers, Non-Commissioned Officers, and Men of New South Wales Military Contingents Serving in the Boer War, 1899, 1900, ML.
13 *Daily Telegraph*, 1 November 1899, p. 5.
14 In military terms, cavalry were horsemen trained to fight mounted. Their weapons were the carbine (short rifle) and the sword or lance, and their main tactic was the charge. Mounted infantry were soldiers who were trained to ride for reasons of mobility, but who did their fighting dismounted. The terms mounted infantry and mounted rifles were used indiscriminately in the Australian colonies, but British commanders came to apply the term mounted rifles exclusively to colonial irregulars.
15 Cox Papers, Colonel J. Burns to French, n.d.
16 *Daily Telegraph*, 14 October 1899, p. 9. The paper was promoting its 'Lancer Insurance Fund' so it may have exaggerated.
17 *ibid.*, 28 October 1899, p. 9. The only statistic available for draft put the average age at twenty-eight.
18 *ibid.*, 25 October 1899, p. 5 and 28 October 1899, p. 10. The government had generally barred the colony's few permanent troops from joining the contingent, but an exception was made for the A.M.C.
19 Coghlan, *op. cit.*, p. 209.
20 *Daily Telegraph*, 26 October 1899, p. 5. Medical rejections were highest among the volunteer infantry, who did not undergo a medical test on entering the service. Medical standards were not high.
21 *Argus*, 21 October 1899, p. 14. Lyne's attitude reflected a wider opinion that colonial officers and men should have preference over Imperial men. Nationalism would have been a factor in this outlook but there was a desire to have the maximum possible number of colonial troops experience war conditions.
22 *ibid.*, 20 September 1899, p. 7.
23 *ibid.*, 28 September 1899, p. 5.
24 *ibid.*, 12 October 1899, p. 5.
25 *ibid.*
26 *Age*, 17 October 1899, p. 5.
27 *ibid.*, 14 October 1899, p. 9, and 16 October 1899, p. 5.
28 *Argus*, 20 October 1899, p. 5.
29 *V.P.D.*, vol. 92, p. 1993.
30 13 October 1899, p. 5.
31 *Argus*, 19 October 1899, pp. 5-6.
32 Brisbane *Worker*, 16 September 1899, p. 5. The Q.M.I. was a part-time force with an excellent attendance record for parades and camps.

[33] *Q.P.D.*, vol. LXXXII, p. 440.
[34] *ibid.*, p. 776.
[35] *ibid.*, p. 350.
[36] *Brisbane Courier*, 11 October 1899, p. 5.
[37] *Q.P.D.*, vol. LXXXII, p. 460. The Brisbane *Worker* took up the cause of the 'pumpkin grower' and by cartoon and comment set out to promote him as a symbol of humanity and goodness.
[38] *ibid.*, p. 718.
[39] *Daily Telegraph*, 13 October 1899, p. 6.
[40] *Age*, 13 October 1899, p.5.
[41] *Daily Telegraph*, 9 October 1899, p. 5.
[42] *Argus*, 11 October 1899, p. 8.
[43] Nominal Roll of South Australian First Contingent, Australian War Memorial Library; and Haydon, 'South Australia's First War' in *Historical Studies of Australia and New Zealand*, vol. 11, no. 42, p. 227.
[44] *Argus*, 11 October 1899, p. 8.
[45] *ibid.*, 13 October 1899, p. 5.
[46] *Western Argus*, 9 November 1899, p. 19.
[47] These figures are based on statistics available for the Aldershot detachment of Lancers and the 1st N.S.W.M.R.; and recruit averages for more than 1000 entrants into part-time forces of N.S.W. in 1899-1900. For the recruit averages see *N.S.W.V. & P.*, 1900, Appendix No. 2 to Appendix C, Annual Report of N.S.W. Medical Services, p. 27.
[48] These statistics were gleaned from reports of military commandants, as published in parliamentary papers and colonial year books.
[49] The only difference between the Lee-Metford and the Lee-Enfield was in the rifling.
[50] South Australia still had the Martini-Henry.
[51] 27 October 1899, p. 6.
[52] *Western Argus*, 26 October 1899, p. 18.
[53] 6 November 1899, p. 6.
[54] 28 October 1899, p. 12. The qualification is significant.
[55] Haydon, *op. cit.*, p. 226.
[56] 3 October 1899.
[57] 16 October 1899, p. 2.
[58] 26 October 1899, p. 18.
[59] 19 October 1899, p. 4.
[60] 17 October 1899, p. 6. The rate of privates, as recommended by the commandants' conference, was 4s 6d a day, made up of the Imperial cavalry rate of 1s 2d and 3s 4d deferred pay met by the colonies.
[61] p. 4.
[62] 14 October 1899, p. 22.
[63] 30 September 1899, p. 2.
[64] 28 October 1899, p. 2.
[65] 25 November 1899, p. 6.
[66] *Daily Telegraph*, 29 September 1899, p. 5.
[67] *ibid.*, 13 October 1899, p. 6.
[68] *ibid.*, 28 October 1899, p. 8.
[69] *Age*, 15 November 1899, p. 8.
[70] *ibid.*, 25 November 1899, p. 8.
[71] A Prayer for Her Majesty's Force in South Africa, (Sydney, n.d.), leaflet in M.L.
[72] *Age*, 7 November 1899, p. 5.
[73] *Daily Telegraph*, 17 October 1899, p. 5.

[74] *ibid.*, 17 October 1899, p. 5.
[75] *ibid.*
[76] *Age*, 23 October 1899, p. 6.
[77] *Daily Telegraph*, 14 November 1899, p. 5.
[78] *Argus*, 23 October 1899, p. 6.
[79] *Age*, 7 November 1899, p. 5. Moran added that W. B. Dalley had done better than that in 1885.
[80] *Daily Telegraph*, 30 October 1899, p. 7.
[81] *Age*, 26 October 1899, p. 5.
[82] *Daily Telegraph*, 27 October 1899, p. 5.
[83] C.O. 309/148, letter of 18 October 1899.
[84] *Age*, 30 October 1899, p. 5.
[85] *Argus*, 9 November 1899, p. 5.
[86] *Age*, 20 October 1899, p. 5.
[87] *Argus*, 10 November 1899, p. 4.
[88] C.O. 201/625.
[89] Creswicke, *South Africa and the Transvaal War*, vol. 3, p. 154.
[90] A steamer carried other M.P.s and their wives. On board toasts were drunk to Colonial Secretary See who was seriously designated 'the Minister for War'—*Daily Telegraph*, 30 October 1899, p. 6.
[91] *Daily Telegraph*, 3 November 1899, p. 5.
[92] Hutton Papers, vol. 9, pp. 90-1.
[93] *Daily Telegraph*, 25 October 1899, p. 6.
[94] *Argus*, 27 October 1899, p. 5.
[95] *Age*, 23 October 1899, p. 6.
[96] V.P.D., vol. 92, pp. 2240-2.
[97] *Argus*, 28 October 1899, p. 13.
[98] Birch, *History of the War in South Africa*, p. 11.
[99] *Bulletin*, 25 November 1899, p. 6.
[100] 23 December 1899, p. 7.
[101] Abbott, *Plain and Veldt*, p. 19.
[102] Vol. 3, p. 27.
[103] Abbott, *op. cit.*, pp. 29-30.
[104] 1 January 1900, p. 4.
[105] 30 October 1899, p. 4.
[106] Gordon, *The Dominion Partnership in Imperial Defense 1870-1914*, p. 152.
[107] *V.P.D.*, vol. 92, pp. 1919, 1993. The relatives' passes were intended also as mementos. They set out 'with picturesque effect the unity of the empire and Australian devotion to the mother country'—*Argus*, 29 October 1899, p. 5.
[108] *Daily Telegraph*, 30 October 1899, p. 5.
[109] *ibid.*, 4 November 1899, p. 9.
[110] *ibid.*, 14 November 1899, p. 5.
[111] *Argus*, 28 October 1899, p. 13.
[112] *Age*, 30 October 1899, p. 13.
[113] Tremearne, *Some Austral-African Notes and Anecdotes*, pp. 5-6.
[114] *ibid.*, p. 8.
[115] *Daily Telegraph*, 25 November 1899, pp. 9-10.
[116] *Age*, 12 October 1899, p. 5.
[117] *Daily Telegraph*, 25 November 1899, p. 10.
[118] *ibid.*, p. 9.
[119] Cox Papers, letter from Cox to Burns, n.d.
[120] *Daily Telegraph*, 29 November 1899, p. 7.
[121] *ibid.*, 28 November 1899, p. 6.
[122] *ibid.*, 2 December 1899, p. 10.

[123] *Singleton Argus*, 2 December 1899, p. 4.
[124] *Age*, 8 December 1899, p. 5.
[125] *N.S.W.P.D.*, vol. CI, pp. 2090-1.
[126] *ibid.*, p. 2093.
[127] *ibid.*, pp. 2093-4.
[128] *Daily Telegraph*, 13 December 1899, p. 7. Burns was not considering the nine sick men.
[129] *ibid.*, 18 December 1899, p. 6.
[130] *ibid.*, 8 December 1899, p. 7.
[131] 26 May 1900, p. 7.
[132] *C. of A.P.D.*, vol. 141, p. 3753.
[133] *Age*, 6 November 1899, p. 5. Lyne's action owed nothing to Sir Wilfred Laurier's offer of a second Canadian contingent which was reported in the *Argus* of 10 November.
[134] *Argus*, 6 November 1899, p. 5.
[135] *Age*, 7 November 1899, p. 5.
[136] Conan Doyle, *The Great Boer War*, p. 152.
[137] Quoted in the *Age*, 15 December 1899, p. 5.
[138] *ibid.*
[139] *ibid.*, 16 December 1899, p. 9.
[140] *ibid.*, 18 December 1899, p. 6.
[141] *ibid.*, 21 December 1899, p. 6.
[142] *N.S.W.P.D.*, vol. CII, p. 3521.
[143] *Q.P.D.*, vol. LXXXIII, pp. 1473-4.
[144] *V.P.D.*, vol. 93, p. 2867.
[145] *ibid.*, p. 2865. Murray was later the subject of a most undemocratically conducted censure meeting at Warrnambool—*Age*, 20 January 1900, p. 9.
[146] *ibid.*, p. 2870.
[147] *ibid.*, p. 2880.
[148] *S.A.P.D.*, 1899, p. 1075.
[149] *ibid.*, p. 1077.
[150] *Age*, 20 December 1899, p. 8.
[151] *ibid.*, 19 December 1899, p. 6.
[152] *ibid.*, 21 December 1899, p. 5.
[153] *ibid.*, 22 December 1899, p. 5.
[154] *ibid.*, 1 January 1900, p. 6. The New South Wales mounted infantry uniform for the second contingent was a khaki tweed field service jacket with coloured facings, bedford cord breeches and putties, and a helmet.
[155] *ibid.*
[156] *ibid.*, 20 December 1899, p. 7.
[157] *ibid.*, 29 December 1899, p. 6.
[158] *Daily Telegraph*, 27 December 1899, p. 6.
[159] As Colonel Hoad had gone to South Africa as a Special Service officer, the British restriction on maximum rank of major for the colonial units did not apply. Special Service officers were attached to British units for experience.
[160] *Daily Telegraph*, 27 December 1899, p. 6.
[161] *ibid.*
[162] *N.S.W.P.D.*, vol. CII, p. 3058.
[163] *Age*, 20 December 1899, p. 7.
[164] *ibid.*, 29 December 1899, p. 6.
[165] *ibid.*, 10 January 1900, p. 8.
[166] *ibid.*, 30 December 1899, p. 7.
[167] *ibid.*, 1 January 1900, p. 5.
[168] *ibid.*, 2 January 1900, p. 6. Religions of the Victorian unit were given as:

Church of England, 159; Presbyterian, 45; Wesleyan, 30; Roman Catholic, 25; and other Denominations, 5—*Age*, 8 January 1900, p. 6.

[169] *ibid.*, 10 January 1900, p. 8.
[170] *Sydney Morning Herald*, 4 January 1900, p. 7.
[171] *Daily Telegraph*, 18 December 1899, p. 6.
[172] General Forrestier-Walker had inspected the half field hospital which had gone with the first contingent, and was so impressed that he requested the remainder of the corps.
[173] *Daily Telegraph*, 18 December 1899, p. 6.
[174] *Sydney Morning Herald*, 11 January 1900, p. 7.
[175] *ibid.*, 5 January 1900, p. 5.
[176] *Daily Telegraph*, 25 December 1899, p. 5. Eventually a half-squadron of Lancers, raised and equipped at no cost to the government, was allowed to embark on 16 February 1900—*Sydney Morning Herald*, 16 February 1900, p. 8.
[177] *Sydney Morning Herald*, 11 January 1900, p. 7.
[178] *ibid.*, 5 January 1900, p. 6.
[179] *ibid.*, 15 January 1900, p. 7.
[180] *ibid.*, 19 January 1900, p. 8, and 20 January 1900, p. 9.
[181] *ibid.*, 15 January 1900, p. 7.
[182] *Age*, 28 December 1899, p. 6.
[183] *Advertiser*, 5 January 1900, p. 4.
[184] Nominal Roll of Second Contingent South Australian Mounted Rifles, Australian War Memorial Library.
[185] 30 December 1899, p. 15.
[186] 13 January 1900, p. 19.
[187] 3 February 1900, p. 16.
[188] 6 January 1900, p. 7.
[189] 6 January 1900, p. 6.
[190] *Bulletin*, 27 January 1900, p. 32. In this poem Lawson correctly forecast the emergence of the soldier image at the expense of the bush ethos.

> Both in letters and in art he will play the paying part
> (And 'tis farewell to the swagman and his mate).

[191] See *Bulletin*, 3 March 1900, p. 7, and 16 June 1900, p. 32.
[192] *Age*, 7 November 1899, p. 5.
[193] *Daily Telegraph*, 27 December 1899, p. 5.
[194] *Grenfell Record*, 27 January 1900, p. 2.
[195] *Catholic Press*, 20 January 1900, p. 11.
[196] *Advertiser*, 26 February 1900, p. 5.
[197] *Argus*, 8 January 1900, p. 6.
[198] *ibid.*
[199] *Age*, 15 January 1900, p. 6.
[200] *ibid.*, p. 5.
[201] *Sydney Morning Herald*, 15 January 1900, p. 7.
[202] *ibid.*, 29 January 1900, p. 8.
[203] *Age*, 15 January 1900, p. 6.
[204] *ibid.*
[205] *Sydney Morning Herald*, 18 January 1900, pp. 6-8.
[206] *Bulletin*, 27 January 1900, p. 8.
[207] *Sydney Morning Herald*, 18 January 1900, p. 6.
[208] Creswicke, *op. cit.*, vol. 3, p. 149.
[209] *Sydney Morning Herald*, 27 January 100, p. 9.
[210] *Advertiser*, 27 January 100, p. 7.
[211] *How Westralia's Sons Served the Empire*, (Melbourne, n.d.), p. 11.

212 14 October 1899, p. 2.
213 20 December 1899, p. 8.
214 18 January 100, p. 9.
215 *Daily Telegraph*, 24 October 1899, p. 6.
216 *Age*, 13 November 1899, p. 5.
217 The *Argus* listed seven members of the Victorian Legislative Assembly who opposed the sending of the first contingent and who were defeated in the November elections—2 November 1900, p. 5.
218 *Daily Telegraph*, 28 July 1898, p. 6.
219 *ibid.*, 5 July 1901, p. 6.
220 The result for Geelong (two members returned): Gurr 2070, Andrews 1880, Higgins 1642, Brownbill 682, Leon 642—*Argus*, 2 November 1899, p. 6.
221 *C. of A.P.D.*, vol. 7, p. 8753.
222 *Argus*, 15 October 1899, p. 7.
223 *ibid.*, 2 November 1899, p. 7.
224 10 February 1900, p. 8.
225 *Age*, 18 January 1900, p. 6.
226 *Sydney Morning Herald*, 5 February 1900, p. 8.
227 *ibid.*, 17 March 1900, p.10.
228 *ibid.*, 13 January 1900, p. 10.
229 *Advertiser*, 12 January 1900, p. 4.
230 *ibid.*, 23 February 1900, p. 5.
231 *Age*, 24 January 1900, p. 5.
232 *ibid.*, 23 January 1900, p. 6.
233 *Argus*, 31 January 1900, p. 8.
234 *Age*, 4 January 1900, p. 6.
235 *Argus*, 18 January 1900, p.6.
236 *Age*, 17 January 1900, p. 8.
237 *Argus*, 30 January 1900, p. 6.
238 *Age*, 18 January 1900, p. 6.
239 *Argus*, 13 February 1900, p. 5.
240 *Age*, 8 January 1900, p. 6.
241 *Sydney Morning Herald*, 22 January 1900, p. 8; *Age*, 13 January 1900, p. 10.
242 *Age*, 18 January 1900, p. 6.
243 *Sydney Morning Herald*, 30 January 1900, p. 5.
244 *Age*, 18 January 1900, p. 6.
245 *Argus*, 11 January 1900, p. 6.
246 *Age*, 18 January 1900, p. 6.
247 *Sydney Morning Herald*, 22 January 1900, p. 8.
248 *Age*, 8 January 1900, p. 6.

3   The First and Second Contingents in the Field

1 Maurice (ed.), *History of the War in South Africa, 1899-1902*, vol. IV, Appendices 13 and 20. Hereafter *Official History*.
2 *ibid.*, vol. IV, Preface.
3 Vol. II, pp. 26-40.
4 *Official History*, vol. IV, Appendix 13.
5 C. B. Holme, letter of 14 February 1900.
6 See Kelly, 'Personal Account of Service with 2nd Victorian Contingent', p. 3; A. Paterson, *Happy Dispatches*, p. 3; W. A. Steel, Diary, pp. 7-9.
7 *Argus*, 31 October 1899, p. 5.
8 *ibid.*, 1 November 1899, p. 7.
9 This neglects expatriate Australians who fought in Natal with the Imperial

Light Horse, and other Uitlander Corps. Australians formed up to 10 per cent of the original I.L.H. regiment, and one of their number, Major Karri Davies, helped found it and was its second-in-command—Gibson, *The Story of the Imperial Light Horse in the South African War*, pp. 16, 20.

10 *Official History*, vol. I, pp. 211, 227-51, 311-29.
11 Report of Major G. L. Lee to N.S.W. Military Commandant, 4 May 1900.
12 Vernon (ed.), *The Royal New South Wales Lancers*, 1885-1960, p. 43.
13 Barton and others, *The Story of South Africa*, p. 49.
14 *The Times History*, vol. III., p. 115.
15 Barton, *op. cit.*, p. 87.
16 *ibid.*, p. 88.
17 Creswicke, *South Africa and the Transvaal War*, vol. III., p. 65.
18 Vol. III, P. 117.
19 5 January 1900, p. 5.
20 Creswicke, *op. cit.*, vol. III, p. 63; *Cassell's History of the Boer War*, vol. I, p. 371; Harding, *War in South Africa*, p. 590.
21 6 January 1900, p. 17.
22 *Sydney Morning Herald*, 12 May 1900, p. 9.
23 A. B. Paterson noted this as a general tendency a little later—*Sydney Morning Herald*, 9 March 1900, p. 5.
24 *Official History*, vol. III, p. 3.
25 Wilkinson, *Australia at the Front*, pp. 57-60.
26 Reay, *Australians in War*, p. 35.
27 *ibid.*
28 *ibid.*, pp. 35-6.
29 Report, 7 January 1900.
30 *ibid.*, 6 December 1899.
31 *ibid.*, 28 December 1899.
32 *Sydney Morning Herald*, 29 January 1900, p. 8, and 31 January 1900, pp. 7, 8, Letters.
33 Reay, *op. cit.*, p. 83.
34 *Sydney Morning Herald*, 28 February 1900, p. 7, letter of Private E.E. Hines.
35 Reay, *op. cit.*, p. 102.
36 Tremearne, *Some Austral-African Notes and Anecdotes*, p. 19.
37 *Sydney Morning Herald*, 16 February 1900, p. 7.
38 *ibid.*, 16 February 1900, pp. 7, 8.
39 *Cassell's History*, Vol. I, p. 550.
40 Wilkinson, *op. cit.*, p. 46.
41 *Sydney Morning Herald*, 7 March 1900, p. 7.
42 *ibid.*, 19 February 1900, p. 8.
43 Report of Major G. L. Lee, January 1900.
44 Vol. III, p. 143.
45 Hales, *Campaign Pictures of the War in South Africa*, pp. 30-6.
46 *Sydney Morning Herald*, 9 May 1900, p. 7.
47 11 May 1900, p. 4. This editorial view would also have owed something to the reports of A. B. Paterson who, like Dowling, had come to accept the Boer as an honourable foe.
48 *Sydney Morning Herald*, 6 February 1900, p. 6.
49 *Official History*, vol. II, p. 593.
50 *The Times History*, vol. III, p. 460.
51 Hales, *op. cit.*, p. 21.
52 Reay, *op. cit.*, p. 159.
53 *ibid.*, pp. 163-5.
54 *ibid.*, p. 166.
55 *ibid.*, pp. 169-73.

[56] *ibid.*, p. 169.
[57] *ibid.*, p. 181.
[58] 21 February 1900, p. 6.
[59] 21 February 1900, p. 4.
[60] Vol. III, p. 466.
[61] *The Great Boer War*, p. 188.
[62] Reay, *op. cit.*, p. 178.
[63] *ibid.*, p. 185.
[64] *ibid.*, p. 178.
[65] *Argus*, 17 February 1900, p. 13.
[66] Reay, *op. cit.*, p. 246.
[67] Lieut-Colonel Tom Price, 'Services of Victorian Troops in the Boer Campaign'.
[68] *The Times History*, vol. III, pp. 375-7.
[69] Forrest, *Life of Lord Roberts*, p. 201.
[70] *ibid.*, p. 202.
[71] Jackson, *A Soldier's Diary*, p. 11.
[72] Ricardo Papers, letter to Arthur Ricardo, 28 February 1900.
[73] Diary of W. H. Barham, a news clip of letter to his wife, 26 February 1900.
[74] Williams and Perkins, 'The N.S.W. Army Medical Corps' in Barton, *The Story of South Africa*, p. 375.
[75] 'With French to Kimberley', in *Rio Grande and Other Verses*, p. 6.
[76] Vol. III, p. 402.
[77] Vol. III, p. 406.
[78] *ibid.*, p. 407.
[79] *Official History*, vol. II, p. 96.
[80] Ricardo Papers, letter to Arthur Ricardo, 28 February 1900.
[81] Stacey, 'Canada and the South African War' in *Canadian Army Journal*, vol. 4, no. 4, 1950-51, p. 38.
[82] Williams and Perkins, *op. cit.*, p. 378.
[83] Paterson, *op. cit.*, p. 36. Fiaschi got his D.S.O.
[84] *Sydney Morning Herald*, 2 April 1900, p. 8.
[85] James, *Lord Roberts*, p. 294.
[86] *Sydney Morning Herald*, 1 March 1900, p. 8.
[87] *ibid.*, 2 March 1900, p. 6.
[88] p. 8.
[89] *op. cit.*, p. 259.
[90] Letters of Charles B. Holme, letter of 8 April 1900; Abbott, *Tommy Cornstalk*, p. 194.
[91] *The Times History*, vol. III, pp. 494-5; *Official History*, vol. II, p. 180.
[92] *Sydney Morning Herald*, 20 March 1900, p. 5.
[93] Vol. II, pp. 221, 224.
[94] *Sydney Morning Herald*, 13 March 1900, p. 7.
[95] Vol. II p. 239.
[96] The 1st N.S.W.M.R., for example, lost only one man killed and 12 wounded—McLean, *Letters*, p. 31.
[97] Ricardo Papers, letter to Arthur Ricardo, 6 February 1900.
[98] W. A. Steel, Diary, p. 27.
[99] Letters of Charles B. Holme, letter of 22 March 1900.
[100] *Rio Grande and Other Verses*, p. 156.
[101] Equine losses in the South African campaign were appalling. A total of 518 794 horses went into the service with the British forces, and of these 347 007 were expended during the war—Elgin Commission, vol. 42, p. 258. The Boers were superior horsemasters and their ponies were more durable

than imported horseflesh, but it would be reasonable to estimate that the fully mounted armies of the two republics lost enough horses to bring the total of expended animals to about half a million.

[102] *Sydney Morning Herald*, 21 April 1900, p. 10.

[103] Enteric was endemic to South Africa and it reached epidemic proportions through concentrations of men in conditions of poor sanitation. Flies carried the germ from open latrines; faeces deposited near river banks were washed into the stream; and pulverized excreta and dried urine became wind-borne. Boiling of water was essential but impracticable because of the time factor and scarcity of fuel.

[104] *op. cit.*, p. 279.

[105] Abbott, *op. cit.*, p. 140.

[106] Williams and Perkins *op. cit.*, pp. 371-4.

[107] Scot Skirving, 'Our Army in South Africa', National Library Pamphlets, vol. 185, no. 3589, p. 24.

[108] Wilkinson, *op. cit.*, p. 100.

[109] *ibid.*, p. 98.

[110] Barton, *op. cit.*, p. 159.

[111] See Steel Diary, p. 114; Report of Lieut-Colonel M. W. Bayley.

[112] Wilkinson, *op. cit.*, p. 140.

[113] Vol. 42, p. 158.

[114] *Sydney Morning Herald*, 7 January 1901, p. 7.

[115] *ibid.*

[116] When Colonel Hoad was commanding the Australian Regiment at Enslin, Williams approached him with a suggestion that the men wear an 'Australia' badge on the shoulder strap. The idea was taken up—see Report of Colonel W. D. C. Williams, January, 1900.

[117] Report of 4 April, 1900.

[118] *Sydney Morning Herald*, 9 May 1900, p. 7.

[119] *ibid.*, 10 May 1900, p. 8.

[120] Ricardo Papers, letter to Ralph Ricardo, 5 May 1900.

[121] Wilkinson, *op. cit.*, p. 106. The same writer also stated that the lack of an Australian officer of sufficiently high rank to command was another reason for no Australian brigade being formed—p. 241.

[122] *Sydney Morning Herald*, 11 May 1900, p. 6.

[123] *Official History*, vol. III, p. 528.

[124] Hutton Letters, vol. I, letter VI.

[125] *ibid.*, letter VII.

[126] *The Times History*, vol. IV, pp. 86, 95.

[127] *op. cit.*, p. 321.

[128] Donald Macdonald, 'A History of the Australian Contingents in the South African War' in Harding, *op. cit.*, p. 634.

[129] Wilkinson, *op. cit.*, p. 156.

[130] On one occasion, Hutton sent his Canadians across a bridge over the Klip River to take a ridge and thus secure the crossing for the rest of the brigade, but French came up and made the Canadians wait twenty minutes while the cavalry moved ahead of them—Hutton Letters, vol. II, letter XXI.

[131] Rapid-firing artillery which used one-pound shells.

[132] Barton, *op. cit.*, pp. 249-52.

[133] *ibid.*, p. 249.

[134] Satchwell, *On Active Service*, p. 67.

[135] The Boers generally were loath to fight on the Sabbath.

[136] Vol. III, p. 48.

[137] *ibid.*, p. 49.

138 W. A. Steel, Diary, p. 83.
139 *Sydney Morning Herald*, 21 June 1900, p. 8.
140 Hutton Letters, vol. I, letter XVI.
141 *ibid.*, letter XV.
142 *The Times History*, vol. IV, p. 118; Letters of Trooper H. L. Harnett, letter to father, 13 June 1900.
143 Watkins Yardley, *With the Inniskillings Dragoons*, p. 88. After Bloemfontein the Lancers formed a distinct squadron of the Inniskillings. They were commanded by Allenby of the Inniskillings, who was to become one of the great leaders of World War I.
144 *The Times History* compared the progress of Roberts's army with the progress of a man-of-war, the Boer forces parting like the waves of the seas but gathering again as the enemy moved on—vol. IV, p.159.
145 Hutton Letters, vol. II, letter XXIII.
146 *The Times History*, vol. IV, p. 162.
147 Ricardo Papers, letter to Ralph Ricardo, 20 June 1900.
148 Letters of Charles B. Holme, letter of 12 June 1900.
149 *Q.P.D.*, vol. LXXXIV, p. 386.
150 Queensland Defence Force: Reports of Commandant, 1877-1900, Report of 1900, p. 9.
151 McLean, *op. cit.*, p. 50. The scattering was invariably caused by troopers being de-horsed and falling behind their units.
152 Elgin Commission, vol. 41, p. 43.
153 *ibid.*, p. 301.
154 Diary, pp. 96, 105.
155 Kelly, 'Personal Account', p. 6. It was claimed that Madam Melba's brother was sent home as 'unsuitable' because he lost heart as soon as he found he was lousy—Hodgson, Diary, no page or date identification.
156 The biscuits were highly nutritious but extremely hard. They were called 'forty-niners' after the number of perforations in them. 'Forty-niners' were sometimes fed to the starving horses of the Australian Regiment as it advanced to Bloemfontein. The noise was deafening,—Reay, *op. cit.*, p. 319.
157 Diary, pp. 83, 92.
158 *op. cit.*, p. 325.
159 *Sydney Morning Herald*, 20 April 1900, p. 5.
160 'What a multitude of sins that word commandeering covers!' wrote one of them. 'What we call at home thieving, looting, burglary, and horse-stealing, is all called commandeering here, and is very much in fashion'—Diary, Barham, letter to wife, 19 May 1900.
161 *ibid.*, entry of 12 July 1900.
162 Diary, p. 105.
163 Hancock and Van Der Poel (eds), *Selections from the Smuts Papers*, vol. I, p. 557.
164 *Sydney Morning Herald*, 28 July 1900, p. 11. This was not the first occasion when Australians were mistaken for Boers. Paterson reported that it was a common occurrence in the Colesburg area, where the Lancers were once fired on by the 6th Dragoons—*Sydney Morning Herald*, 29 January 1900, p.8. But it was a London report that the Q.M.I. had been about to fire on the V.M.R. that led the New South Wales commandant to issue the second contingent with hastily and poorly manufactured helmets instead of slouch hats. French soon regretted his haste and the fourth and subsequent New South Wales contingents reverted to hats—*N.S.W.V. & P.*, vol. 4, Select Committee on the Administration of the Military Department, Minutes of Evidence, p.40.
165 *The Times History*, vol. IV, 289, 292.

[166] *Sydney Morning Herald*, 28 July 1900, p. 11.

[167] Wilkinson, *op. cit.*, p. 199.

[168] Barham, Diary, entry of 14 June 1900.

[169] *The Times History*, vol. IV, p. 484.

[170] James, *op. cit.*, pp. 356-7.

[171] *The Times History*, vol. V, pp. 76-7.

[172] *ibid.*, p. 67; Conan Doyle, *op. cit.*, pp. 387-8.

[173] Hutton Letters, vol. II., letter XXXVII. The blood-lust seemed to be upon Hutton. 'We must kill and slay if our superiority as a race is to be established over that of the Dutch in South Africa'—letter XXXIII.

[174] *Sydney Morning Herald*, 1 August 1900, p. 7.

[175] McLean *op cit.*, pp. 51-61.

[176] Ricardo Papers, letter to Ralph Ricardo, 29 August 1900.

[177] Letters of Charles B. Holme, letter of 8 November 1900.

[178] *Sydney Morning Herald*, 9 August 1900, a report dated 30th June 1900. Paterson got himself home quickly enough, arriving in early September.

[179] Murray Papers, Series 2, letters to wife, letter of 22 July 1900.

[180] *ibid.*, letter of 1 September 1900.

[181] *ibid.*, letter of 19 September 1900.

[182] *ibid.*, letter of 6 October 1900.

[183] Report of Major G. L. Lee, 27 October 1900.

[184] Vol. V, p. 71.

[185] Headlam (ed.), *The Milner Papers*, vol II, pp. 166-7.

[186] Reports from Officers.

[187] *N.S.W.P.D.*, vol. CIII, p. 578, and vol. CIV, p. 2020. Further parliamentary concern was shown by two M.P.s, R. Sleath and B. O'Conor, who, during a fact-finding trip to South Africa in mid-1900, extracted a promise from Roberts at Bloemfontein that he would send the R.A.A. to the front.

[188] See *Sydney Morning Herald*, 5 March 1900, p. 8.

[189] There were wild scenes when the news of the relief on 17 May broke, and even wilder ones on 23 May, a public holiday throughout Australia known as Mafeking Relief Day. Pride of Empire and pride of race were the dominant themes in the celebrations, but larrikanism was a souring factor in Sydney and Melbourne—See the *Age*, 21 May 1900, pp. 3, 5, 6, and 24 May 1900, p. 7.

[190] Among the presents to B.P. were a cabbage-tree hat, a gold sword and two chargers, and while colonial parliaments were still discussing the raising of memorials to Australians, a twelve-foot monument to B.P. was unveiled at Murray Bridge—*Sydney Morning Herald*, 2 October 1900, p. 5, 21 December 1900, p. 7, and 18 January 1901, p. 7.

[191] The invalid rate was high. Of the 130 officers and men of the 1st N.S.W.M.R., for instance, 50 were invalided. A minority of these were sent to England for treatment and convalescence—Antill 'Record of N.S.W. Mounted Rifles'.

[192] *Age*, 26 May 1900, p. 9.

[193] *Sydney Morning Herald*, 30 May 1900, p. 5.

[194] *ibid.*, p. 6.

[195] *ibid.*, 2 July 1900, p. 8.

[196] *ibid.*, 9 June 1900, p. 9.

[197] For this reason, Roberts's evidence before the Elgin Commission was not very meaningful.

[198] *Sydney Morning Herald*, 6 November 1900, p. 5.

[199] *Age*, 3 December 1900, p. 5.

[200] 6 December 1900, p. 4.

[201] *Age*, 5 December 1900, pp. 6, 8.

202 *Sydney Morning Herald,* 7 December 1900, p. 5.
203 *ibid.,* 9 January 1901, p. 5.
204 *S.A.P.D.,* 1900, pp. 1014-15.
205 *W.A.P.D.,* vol. XVIII, pp. 2080-8.
206 The corps was referred to in South Africa as 'I Yield' and 'De Wet's Remounts'.

4 The Bushmen, the Draft Contingents, and the Australian Commonwealth Horse

1 The fifth to eighth included some militia members, but the distinction is convenient and valid enough.
2 *Age,* p. 6. This left the way open for the bushman with no military training and a number of them sailed with the second contingent.
3 *ibid.,* 22 December 1899, p. 5.
4 *ibid.,* 23 December 1899, p. 8.
5 *ibid.,* 26 September 1899, p. 6.
6 28 September 1899, p. 6. The Victorian minister for defence claimed later that he had waited a week for Lyne's reply—*Age,* 10 January 1900, p. 8. Having regard to the antipathy that existed between the two governments, it is easy to suspect Lyne of taking steps in that week to foil the Victorian initiative, which could have been prompted by the Colonial Office cable or the Canadian offer.
7 *Report of the Royal Commission of Inquiry into Claims of Members of New South Wales Contingents in South Africa . . .,* p. 173. Hereafter *Royal Commission on Pay.*
8 *Sydney Morning Herald,* 28 February 1900, p. 7.
9 *ibid.,* 27 January 1900, p. 10.
10 *ibid.,* 22 January 1900, p. 8.
11 *ibid.,* 19 January 1900, p. 8.
12 *ibid.,* 30 January 1900, p. 6.
13 *ibid.,* 25 January 1900, p. 8.
14 *ibid.,* 1 February 1900, p. 8.
15 Blackmore, *The Story of the South Australian Bushmen's Corps, 1900,* p. 19.
16 By 30 March 1900 contributions to the funds had fallen to a trickle, and the total Australian subscription amounted to sixpence per head of population —*Argus,* 30 March 1900, p. 6.
17 *Royal Commission on Pay,* evidence of J. M. Atkinson, pp. 47, 278.
18 'Select Committee on the Administration of the Military Department', evidence of J. R. Carey, p. 226.
19 *Sydney Morning Herald,* 29 January 1900, p. 8.
20 'Select Committee on the Administration of the Military Department', p. 216.
21 *Sydney Morning Herald,* 28 February 1900, p. 7.
22 Uncatalogued MSS., Set 267, M.L.
23 *Royal Commission on Pay,* p. 140.
24 Supplement to New South Wales Government Gazette, 12 April 1900. The officers were selected by French from lists submitted by the committee.
25 *V.P.D.,* vol. 93, pp. 320-1.
26 *Argus,* 12 February 1900, p. 6, and 14 February 1900, p. 14.
27 Blackmore, *op. cit.,* pp. 8-11. Although Hubbe was Australian-born, his German parentage brought anonymous complaints to the selection committee—*Advertiser,* 3 March 1900, p. 8.

[28] *Advertiser*, 7 March 1900, p. 4.
[29] *Argus*, 12 March 1900, p. 4.
[30] *Sydney Morning Herald*, 1 March 1900, p. 7.
[31] 28 February 1900, p. 6.
[32] 18 January 1900, p. 4.
[33] 3 February 1900, p. 12.
[34] *Argus*, 20 March 1900, p. 5.
[35] *The Times History*, vol. IV, pp. 363-8.
[36] *Sydney Morning Herald*, 6 March 1900, p. 7.
[37] *ibid.*, 30 March 1900, p. 5.
[38] *ibid.*, 2 April 1900, p. 8. Philp's case was helped by the presence in London of Dickson as a federal delegate.
[39] 5 March 1900, p. 6. See also *Argus*, 6 March 1900, p. 4, and *Advertiser*, 7 March 1900, p. 4.
[40] *Argus*, 16 March 1900, p. 6.
[41] *Advertiser*, 13 March 1900, p. 6.
[42] 'Select Committee on the Administration of the Military Department', p. 56.
[43] 25 April 1900, p. 6.
[44] One of these two appointments went to E. A. Roberts, a Labor M.L.A., who had strongly opposed the sending of the first contingent.
[45] *Advertiser*, 12 April 1900, p. 6.
[46] 'Select Committee on the Administration of the Military Department', p. 332.
[47] For personal details of the officers selected see *Sydney Morning Herald*, 13, 14, 17, 18, 19, 21, 23 April 1900; and Supplement to the New South Wales Government Gazette, 12 April 1900.
[48] 1 May 1900, p. 4.
[49] 23 April 1900, p. 6.
[50] *Sydney Morning Herald*, 24 April 1900, p. 6.
[51] *Advertiser*, 1 May 1900, p. 4. Imperial loyalty flourished strongest in this most British of the Australian colonies.
[52] *Sydney Morning Herald*, p. 5.
[53] *ibid.*, p. 9.
[54] *ibid.*, p. 7.
[55] *ibid.*, p. 5.
[56] *ibid.*, 4 January 1901, p. 5. Cables were sometimes sent to the South Australian governor for transmission to the other colonies because South Australia was at the end of the British cable route.
[57] *ibid.*, 8 January 1901, p. 5. He was referring to the second contingent.
[58] *ibid.*, 19 January 1901, p. 9.
[59] *ibid.*, 5 February 1901, p. 6.
[60] *ibid.*, 7 February 1901, p. 7.
[61] *ibid.*, 14 February 1901, p. 7.
[62] *ibid.*, 27 December 1900, p. 5.
[63] *ibid.*, 18 January 1901, p. 7.
[64] *ibid.*, 6 February 1901, p. 7.
[65] *ibid.*, 9 February 1901, p. 7.
[66] *ibid.*, 27 February 1901, p. 7, and 28 February 1901, p. 7; Cox Papers, Chart of War Service of Officers of 3rd N.S.W.M.R.
[67] *Sydney Morning Herald*, 19 January 1901, p. 9 and 30 January 1901, p. 7.
[68] *ibid.*, 7 March 1901, p. 7.
[69] *ibid.*, 18 March 1901, p. 5.
[70] *ibid.*, 2 February 1901, p. 9.
[71] 19 January 1900, p. 9.

72 *Sydney Morning Herald*, 6 March 1901, p. 7. The Federal and Victorian governments went along with the Scottish Horse recruitment, with the Victorian government prepared to take responsibility for medical, riding and shooting tests only—*Age*, 2 February 1901, p. 10.

73 19 February 1901, p. 4. South Australia was the one state inclined to co-operate, but only to the extent of 100 recruits—*Sydney Morning Herald*, 21 February 1901, p. 7.

74 *Daily Telegraph*, p. 5. For a far less provocative translation see *C. of A.P.D.*, vol. 7, p. 8740.

75 Mentioned in the House of Representatives by Barton—*ibid.*, p. 8741.

76 *Daily Telegraph*, p. 5. Philp said that Barton should have offered men long ago because 'What they want to end the war is a lot of Australians', —*Brisbane Courier*, 12 December 1901, p. 5.

77 16 December 1901, p. 4.

78 p. 5.

79 *V.P.D.*, vol. 99, pp. 3680 ff. John Murray opposed on the grounds that the war was now being conducted against Boer women and children, but received a tirade of abuse from interjectors who regarded his statement as 'shameful' and 'terrible' and called on him to withdraw it—p. 3688.

80 *Daily Telegraph*, p. 7. An *Age* editorial also castigated Barton—19 December 1901, p. 4.

81 *Daily Telegraph*, 25 December 1901, p. 5. Forrest was the Federal minister for defence.

82 *C. of A.P.D.*, vol. 7, p. 8740.

83 *Daily Telegraph*, 25 December 1901, p. 5.

84 28 December 1901, p. 8.

85 See *Brisbane Courier*, 1 January 1902, p. 4.; *Age*, 25 December 1901, p. 4.; *Daily Telegraph*, 15 January 1902, p. 6.

86 *Daily Telegraph*, 25 December 1901, p. 4.

87 28 December 1901, p. 17.

88 11 January 1902, p. 7.

89 28 December 1901, p. 7.

90 The first part of the motion expressed 'indignation at the baseless charges made abroad against the honour of the people and the humanity and the valour of soldiers of the Empire'; the second part affirmed 'the readiness of Australia to give all requisite aid to the mother country in order to bring the present war to an end',—*C. of A.P.D.*, vol. 7, p. 8739.

91 *ibid.*, pp. 8739-47.

92 *ibid.*, p. 8753.

93 *ibid.*, p. 8759.

94 *ibid.*, p. 8799.

95 *ibid.*, p. 8954.

96 *ibid.*, vol. 8, p. 11099.

97 *Daily Telegraph*, 31 December 1901, p. 5.

98 *ibid.*, 4 January 1902, p. 11.

99 *C. of A.P.D.*, vol. 7, p. 8740.

100 *Daily Telegraph*, 24 January 1902, p. 8.

101 *ibid.*, 31 January 1902, p. 9.

102 Major-Gnl Sir J. Bruche Collection, 'Victorian Units and Staff of 2nd Battalion, 1st Commonwealth Contingent'.

103 A detailed nominal roll of the eighth battalion, held by the State Library of Tasmania, shows that only 60 recruits in a force of 500 men were veterans.

104 *Brisbane Courier*, 24 January 1902, p. 5; *Advertiser*, 7 January 1902, p. 5; *Daily Telegraph*, 6 January 1902, p. 5, and 25 January 1902, p. 5.

[105] *Daily Telegraph*, 18 February 1902, p. 6.
[106] *Brisbane Courier*, 27 January 1902, p. 4.
[107] *Advertiser*, 21 February 1902, p. 5.
[108] *Age*, 13 February 1902, p. 5.
[109] 24 August 1901, p. 6.
[110] 5 October 1901, p. 9.
[111] 21 October 1901, p. 5. In September, 447 adults and 1964 children died out of a total of 55 092 adults and 54 326 children held.
[112] 24 August 1901, p. 9.
[113] *Daily Telegraph*, 31 January 1902, p. 8.
[114] *ibid.*, 1 February 1902, p. 11. But the same body three days later carried by 39 votes to 25 a resolution seeking much the same things as the petition sought —*ibid.*, 4 February 1902, p. 8.
[115] *ibid.*, 5 April 1902, p. 9, and 16 April 1902, p. 7.
[116] Evatt, *Australian Labor Leader*, pp. 144-5.
[117] *C. of A.P.D.*, vol. 7, p. 8954.
[118] *Advertiser*, 24 January 1902, p. 4.
[119] *Age*, 12 April 1902, p. 11.
[120] *Daily Telegraph*, 10 March 1902, p. 5.
[121] *ibid.*, 18 March 1902, p. 5.
[122] *ibid.*, 11 February 1902, p. 7, 19 February 1902, p. 7, 21 February 1902, p. 5, and 22 February 1902, p. 10. The meetings were largely prompted by Continental criticism of Britain.
[123] *Cassell's History of the Boer War*, vol. 2, p. 182.
[124] Macdonald, 'A History of the Australian Contingents in the South African War', in Harding, *War in South Africa*, p. 649.
[125] Green, *The Story of the Bushmen*, p. 78. Another account noted that the Bushmen charged in 'the dare-devil manner peculiarly their own'—*Cassell's History of the Boer War*, vol. 2, p. 423.
[126] Green, *op. cit*, pp. 86-91.
[127] *W.A.P.D.*, vol. XVIII, p. 2085.
[128] *Selections from the Smuts Papers*, vol. 1, p. 586. Smuts compared the brash and confident attitude of the Australians before leaving Rustenburg with their crestfallen demeanour when they returned.
[129] *ibid.*, p. 588.
[130] *Sydney Morning Herald*, 9 October 1900, p. 3, and 23 October 1900, p. 5, Reports of James Green, Methodist Chaplain, who was with the Bushmen at Elands River.
[131] Boer War Diaries and Letters of F. V. Weir, Diary entry of 16 August 1900.
[132] *Selections from the Smuts Papers*, vol. 1, p. 593.
[133] This transcript of the poem was quoted by a Bushman diarist in Bufton, *Tasmanians in the Transvaal War*, p. 160.
[134] *Sydney Morning Herald*, 23 October 1900, p. 5.
[135] *Selections from the Smuts Papers*, vol. 1, p. 592; Green, 'The Siege of Eland's River Camp' in Barton, *The Story of South Africa*, pp. 483-4.
[136] *Argus*, 16 August 1900, p. 5.
[137] Conan Doyle, *The Great Boer War*, pp. 404-6.
[138] *ibid.*, pp. 431-3.
[139] Green, *op. cit.*, p. 212.
[140] Macdonald, 'A History of the Australian Contingents in the South African War', in Harding, *War in South Africa*, p. 684.
[141] Watkins Yardley, *With the Inniskilling Dragoons*, p. 240.
[142] *Sydney Morning Herald*, 16 January 1901, p. 7, letter from Sgt Tom Thomson.

Notes (Chapter 4)

[143] Extracts from Diary of Major Walter Blake Nisbet, entry of 3 November 1900.
[144] Lewis, *On the Veldt*, p. 123.
[145] Harington, *Plumer of Messines*, p. 49.
[146] Diary, entries of 29 June, 3 July and 6 July 1901.
[147] *ibid.*, 29 June 1901.
[148] *ibid.*, 3 July 1901.
[149] *ibid.*, 3-6 October 1901.
[150] *ibid.*, taken from various entries.
[151] *ibid.*, 7 October 1901. Another Australian noted that the native girls were not so friendly, for when men of the 2nd V.M.R. chased naked Swaziland maidens (supposedly to find out if they spoke English), the girls squatted on the ground and pushed sand between their thighs—Kelly, 'Personal Account', p. 15.
[152] Cox Papers, Package 1.
[153] *ibid.*, Packet 2.
[154] Watkins Yardley, *op. cit.*, p. 338.
[155] Conan Doyle, *op. cit.*, pp. 462-3; *Official History*, vol. IV, pp. 203-4.
[156] *Daily Telegraph*, 19 June 1901, p. 7.
[157] *ibid.*
[158] *ibid.*, 22 June 1901, p. 9.
[159] *Cassell's History*, vol. II, p. 744.
[160] Arthur, *Life of Lord Kitchener*, vol. 2, p. 36.
[161] Schikkerling, *Commando Courageous*, pp. 219-30.
[162] Kruger, *Good-bye Dolly Gray*, p. 436; Arthur, *op. cit.*, vol. 2, p. 36.
[163] p. 13.
[164] 30 September 1901, p. 5.
[165] 1 October 1901, p. 5.
[166] 3 October 1901, p. 377.
[167] 10 October 1901, p. 418.
[168] 29 October 1901, p. 4.
[169] *C. of A.P.D.*, vol. 4, pp. 5405-7.
[170] *ibid.*, vol. 5. pp. 6642-3.
[171] Minute from Governor-General to Prime Minister of Australia, 7 November 1901, Commonwealth Archives MP 84/2. A claim was made that the men's release had been secured by a petition to the King by Australians in London—*Daily Telegraph*, 29 October 1901, p. 4. But Barton claimed that the release was due 'very largely' to the action of his government—*C. of A.P.D.*, vol. 5. p. 6643.
[172] *C. of A.P.D.*, vol. 7, p. 8771.
[173] Minute of 30 November 1901 to Governor-General, Commonwealth Archives, MP 84/2. Returns for the entire period of the war were actually supplied but only the return for the period 1 April 1902 to 30 June 1902 is held by Commonwealth Archives. The cover sheets for the remainder of the war are extant as tantalizing reminders of records that summarized the more serious disciplinary offences of Australians in the field.
[174] Major-General E. Tivey Collection, diary entry of 1 June 1902.
[175] *Conditions of Service of South African and Over-Sea Contingents Employed in the South African War, 1899-1902*, Report from Lord Tennyson, Governor-General, to Secretary of State for the Colonies, 3 August 1903.
[176] Green, 'The Campaigns of the Australian Commonwealth Horse', in Barton, *op. cit.*, pp. 596-607.
[177] Major-General Sir J. Bruche Collection.
[178] *ibid.*, Battle Orders of 30 June and 1 July 1902.

179 Commonwealth Archives, MP 84/2.
180 *C. of A.P.P.*, vol. 2, 'Report of the Royal Commission, S S. *Drayton Grange*', p. 17.
181 *ibid.*, p. 14. There were reports of expectoration on decks and walls, urination in the shower baths, and lack of body cleanliness.
182 *Elgin Commission*, vol. 41, pp. 446-7.
183 *Age*, 19 January 1900, p. 9.
184 Diary of Sergeant Robert Hodgson; *Age*, 2 February 1901, p. 10. Animosity towards the Scottish Horse squadrons was also evident among the men of the 5th V.M.R. with whom recruits travelled to South Africa. This resulted in frequent fights.
185 Kelly, 'Personal Account', pp. 36-7.
186 Hayes, *Hull Down*, p. 134.
187 *C. of A.P.D.*, vol. 3, p. 3391.
188 *N.S.W.P.D.*, Second Series, vol. I, pp. 452, 607. See considered that the scheme would take many young men away from the state permanently, for they were under no obligation to return when they finished their tour of duty with a South African regiment.
189 *Daily Telegraph*, 15 August 1901, p. 5.
190 *Elgin Commission*, vol. 41, pp. 447, 455.
191 *ibid.*, vol. 41, p. 447.
192 *Sydney Morning Herald*, 2 February 1901, p. 9.
193 *Daily Telegraph*, 15 August 1901, p. 5., and 21 August 1901, p. 7. Thomas returned to South Africa himself, and achieved some note as defence counsel at the court martial of Lieuts H. Morant and P. Handcock.
194 Hayes, *op. cit.*, p. 127.
195 *Daily Telegraph*, 27 September 1901, p. 5. I have found no references to the embarkation of further indulgence passengers.
196 *S.A.P.D.*, 1900, p. 125.
197 *Q.P.D.*, vol. LXXV, p. 1506.
198 *N.S.W.P.D.*, vol. CVI, p. 3395.
199 *ibid.*, vol. CVII, p. 4493.
200 *ibid.*, 1901, Second Series, vol. 1, p. 955.
201 *Scapegoats of the Empire.*
202 *Bushman and Buccaneer.*
203 *Breaker Morant.*
204 p. 26.
205 Letter A.M. 77/8, M.L.
206 Quoted in Bathurst *Western Advocate*, 2 March 1964, p. 3.
207 *Daily Telegraph*, 27 March 1902, p. 5.
208 *C. of A.P.D.*, vol. IX, pp. 11250-1.
209 *ibid.*, p. 11381.
210 29 March 1902, p. 9.
211 31 March 1902, p. 4.
212 10 April 1902, p. 5, and 12 April 1902, p. 9.
213 8 April 1902, p. 4. Morant was an adult migrant to Australia.
214 9 April 1902, p. 4.
215 12 April 1902, p. 3.
216 5 April 1902, Red page.
217 12 April 1902, p. 7. Handcock was a blacksmith; Morant had done some droving.
218 19 April 1902, Red page.
219 *Western Advocate*, 2 March 1964, p. 3.
220 Letter to the author, 15 July 1973.

221 Kelly, 'Personal Account', p. 4.
222 *Daily Telegraph*, 22 August 1901, p. 7.
223 *ibid.*, 2 June 1902, p. 9.
224 p. 2.
225 30 March 1901, p. 3.
226 Kelman, Diary, vol. 2, entry of 27 May 1901.
227 *Daily Telegraph*, 12 June 1901, p. 7.
228 *Royal Commission on Pay*, pp. 39, 48. A further Royal Commission sat in 1907 to rule on some claims not finalized by the first Commission.
229 *Daily Telegraph*, 20 February 1902, p. 5.
230 *ibid.*, 3 March 1902, p. 6. The speeches were understandably subdued in their praise of the contingents.
231 3 March 1902, p. 6.
232 28 May 1902, p. 6.
233 The Imperial Bushmen and the Commonwealth contingents, having been raised at the request of the Home government were regarded as entirely the responsibility of Imperial authorities.
234 *Argus*, 30 March 1900, p. 6. For details of Imperial pensions and Patriotic Fund benefits see *Argus*, 28 February 1900, p. 5.
235 See *S.A.P.D.*, 1900, p. 359; *Q.P.D.*, vol. LXXXV, p. 1564; *V.P.D.*, vol. 97, p. 293 and vol. 100, p. 396; and *N.S.W.P.D.*, Second Series, vol. 1, p. 1038.
236 *S.A.P.D.* 1900, p. 858; *N.S.W.P.D.* vol. CIV, p. 1432.
237 *Daily Telegraph*, 4 June 1902, p. 6.
238 *ibid.*, 9 June 1902, p. 6.
239 3 June 1902, p. 4.
240 2 June 1902, p. 5.
241 7 June 1902, p. 8.
242 3 June 1902, p. 4.

5 *Opinions of the Australian Soldier*

1 See *Sydney Morning Herald*, 17 February 1900, p. 9, Paterson's interview with Olive Schreiner; Schikkerling, *Commando Courageous*, p. 228; and Hales, *Campaign Pictures . . .* , p. 106.
2 Letter to author, 21 October 1969.
3 Vol. 40, p. 437.
4 *ibid.*, p. 79. Australians would not have been flattered by the comparison, and the history of the conflict does not support Roberts's favourable opinion of the IY
5 *ibid.*, p. 80.
6 *ibid.*, p. 43.
7 Vol. 41, p. 462.
8 *ibid.*, p. 584.
9 Vol. 40, p. 80.
10 Vol. 41, p. 451.
11 *ibid.*, pp. 313, 451.
12 Vol. 40, pp. 79-80.
13 Vol. 41, p. 451.
14 *ibid.*, p. 342.
15 *ibid.*, p. 342.
16 *ibid.*, p. 325.
17 See Conan Doyle, *The Great Boer War*, p. 188; Arthur, *Life of Lord Kitchener*, vol. 1, p. 290; Watkins Yardley, *With the Inniskilling Dragoons*,

p. 209; Bridges, *Alarms and Excursions*, p. 37; and *The Times History*, vol. V, p. 156.

[18] See Report of Captain R. R. Thompson, 26 April 1900; and *V.P.D.*, vol. 93, pp. 2945, 3023.

[19] *N.S.W.V. & P.*, 1900, vol. 4, 'Select Committee on the Administration of the Military Department'. The committee was vindictive and partisan for Sleath had an intense dislike for General G. A. French. It was not supported by the Lyne government, and its findings, for what they were worth, were put aside on the grounds that Commonwealth responsibility for defence was imminent.

[20] 'Oriel' in the *Catholic Press*, 20 January 1900, p. 22.

[21] See Wigmore and Harding, *They Dared Mightily*, pp. 14 ff.

[22] See *Brisbane Courier*, 15-19 August 1901. The *Evening Observer* had inquired whether C.B. in Ricardo's case meant Concealed from Boers, Caught Behind, Companion of the Boulder, etc.

[23] *The Five Nations*, p. 175. Kipling had in mind other overseas colonials as well.

[24] *Argus*, 24 March 1900, p. 4. 'Killed in Action'.

Appendices

[1] *Daily Telegraph*, 6 October 1899, p. 5.

[2] *ibid.*

[3] *The Times History*, vol. 5, Appendix I.

[4] Extracted from *Official History*, vol. 4, p. 697.

[5] Chamberlain, *To Shoot and Ride*, p. 70.

Bibliography

Manuscript Sources

National Library of Australia
Cox Papers, MS. 37.
Hutton Papers, MS. 1215.
Murray Papers, Series 2, MS. 2245.
Ricardo Papers, MS. 1928.

Australian War Memorial Library
Bruche, Major-General Sir J. Collected Papers.
Harnett, Trooper H.L. Letters and Diary.
Hodgson, Sgt Robert. Diary.
Kelly, Alured. 'Personal Account of Service with 2nd Victorian Contingent'.
Kelman, W.N. Diary.
Price, Lieut-Colonel Tom. 'Services of Victorian Troops in the Boer Campaign'.
Steel, Trooper W.A. Diary.
Techow, Private Otto. Diary.
Tivey, Major-General E. Collected Papers.
Reports of New South Wales officers in South Africa to the Military Commandant, File 565/5/2.

Mitchell Library
Antill, J.M. 'Record of N.S.W. Mounted Rifles'. A paper in the Macarthur Collection.
Barham, W.H. Diary, MS. B1680.
Holme, Charles B. Letters, Microfilm.
Nisbet, Major W.B. Extracts from Diary, MS, B1323.
Weir, F.V. Diaries and Letters, MS. 1024/1.
Uncatalogued MSS., Sets 30 and 267.

Other
Copy of the Diary of Q.M.S. Rauchle, 'A' Battery. Held by Captain I. Macinnis, R.A.A., Victoria Barracks, Sydney.
Collection of Papers on the South African War. Held by Captain I. Macinnis.

Parliamentary and Other Official Papers

Parliamentary Debates for all Australian Colonies, July 1899-June 1902.

Parliamentary Debates for the Commonwealth, 1901-02.

Report and Proceedings of the Select Committee on the Administration of the Military Department, *N.S.W.V. & P.*, 1900, vol. 4.

Report of the Royal Commission, S.S. *Drayton Grange, C.P.P.*, 1901-02, vol. 2.

Report of the Royal Commission of Inquiry into Claims of Members of New South Wales Contingents in South Africa together with Copy of Commission, Minutes of Proceedings, Evidence and Appendix. Sydney, 1906.

'Report of His Majesty's Commissioners Appointed to Inquire into the Military Preparations and Other Matters Connected with the War in South Africa', being vols 40-2 of *Reports from Commissioners, Inspectors and Others.* London, 1903.

Reports of Colonial Military Commandants, collected by colony in single volumes covering several years. Australian War Memorial Library.

Correspondence of Colonial Governors with Colonial Office, 1899. Microfilm, National Library of Australia.

New South Wales, C.O. 201/625

Victoria, C.O. 390/148

Queensland, C.O. 234/67-70.

A collection of reports, memorials, etc., of the New South Wales Government concerning the South African War, with a binder's title of 'N.S.W. Soudan and South Africa Contingents 1885-1907' but referred to throughout this book as 'New South Wales Government Papers'. Australian War Memorial Library.

Letters to Lord Beauchamp, 1899-1901. A3012, Mitchell Library.

New South Wales Governor—Miscellaneous Papers, 1899-1901. 2/8094, State Archives.

Miscellaneous Papers on the South African War. MP 84/2, Commonwealth Archives, Canberra.

Conditions of Service of South African and Over-Sea Contingents Employed in the South African War, 1899-1902. H.M.S.O., London, 1904.

South Australian Statistical Register, 1898. Adelaide, 1899.

Bibliography

Newspapers

Advertiser, Adelaide, January 1900-June 1902.
Age, Melbourne, May 1899-June 1902.
Argus, Melbourne, May 1899-June 1902.
Barrier Miner, Broken Hill, October-December 1899.
Brisbane Courier, July 1899-June 1902.
Bulletin, Sydney, July 1899-June 1902.
Catholic Press, Sydney, July 1899-September 1900.
Daily Telegraph, Sydney, July 1899-September 1902.
Grenfell Record, October 1899-June 1900.
Launceston Examiner, October-December 1899.
Manaro Mercury [sic], Cooma, July-December 1899.
Punch, Melbourne, 3 and 10 October 1901.
Singleton Argus, October-December 1899.
Sydney Morning Herald, June 1899-March 1901.
West Australian, Perth, October-December 1899.
Western Advocate, Bathurst, January-March 1964.
Western Argus, Kalgoorlie, September-December 1899.
Worker, Brisbane, July 1899-June 1902.
Press Cuttings, 1898-1919, Cox Papers, M.L.
Press Cuttings, 1893-1904, Hutton Papers, N.L.A.
Photostat copies of relevant sections of the *South African News*, 14
February and 30 March 1901.

Books and Articles in Periodicals

Abbott, J. H. M. *Plain and Veldt*, London, 1903.
   Tommy Cornstalk, London, 1902.
Amery, L. S. (ed.). *The Times History of the War in South Africa*,
   6 vols and Index, London, 1900-09.
Arthur, Sir George. *Life of Lord Kitchener*, 3 vols, London, 1920.
Atkinson, L. D. Australian Defence Policy, A Study of Empire
   and Nation (1897-1910), Ph.D. thesis, A.N.U., 1964.
Barton, G. B. and others. *The Story of South Africa*, Australasian
   Edition, Sydney, n.d.
Birch, James, H. Jnr. *History of the War in South Africa*, With an
   appendix on the Australasian Colonies in the War. Toronto,
   n.d.
Blackmore, E. G. *The Story of the South Australian Bushmen's
   Corps, 1900*, Adelaide, 1900.
Bridges, Sir Tom. *Alarms and Excursions*, London, 1938.
Bufton, John, *Tasmanians in the Transvaal War*, Hobart, 1905.
Cassell's History of the Boer War, 2 vols, London, 1903.

Chamberlain, W. M. *To Shoot and Ride,* Military Historical Society of Australia Publication, 1967.

Churchill, W. S. *My Early Life,* London, 1930.

Coghlan, T. A. *The Wealth and Progress of New South Wales, 1898-9,* Sydney, 1900.

Conan Doyle, Arthur. *The Great Boer War,* London, 1903.
The War in South Africa, Its Cause and Conduct, London, 1902.

Creswicke, Louis. *South Africa and the Transvaal War,* 6 vols, Edinburgh, 1900-01.

Cutlack, F. M. *Breaker Morant,* Sydney, 1962.

Davitt, Michael. *The Boer Fight for Freedom,* New York and London, 1902.

Dawson, W. H. *War Songs, 1899-1900,* Hobart, 1901.

De Wet, C. R. *Three Years War,* London, 1902.

Evatt, H. V. *Australian Labour Leader,* Sydney, 1940.

Forrest, Sir George. *The Life of Lord Roberts, K.G., V.C.,* London, 1914.

Gardner, Brian. *Mafeking, A Victorian Legend,* London, 1966.
Allenby, London, 1965.

Gibson, G. F. *The Story of the Imperial Light Horse in the South African War,* n.p.p., 1937.

Gilbert, Sharrad A. *Rhodesia — and After,* London, 1901.

Goldmann, C. S. *With General French and the Cavalry in South Africa,* London, 1902.

Gordon, Donald C. *The Dominion Partnership in Imperial Defense, 1870-1914,* Baltimore, 1965.

Green, James. *The Story of the Bushmen,* Sydney, 1903.

Hales, A. G. *Campaign Pictures of the War in South Africa (1899-1902): Letters from the Front,* London, 1900.

Hall, D. O. W. *The New Zealanders in South Africa, 1899-1902,* Wellington, 1949.

Hancock, W. K. and Van Der Poel, Jean (eds). *Selections from the Smuts Papers,* vol. 1, Cambridge, 1966.

Harding, William. *War in South Africa,* With a History of the Australian Contingents in the South African War, by Donald Macdonald, Melbourne, n.d.

Harington, Sir Charles. *Plumer of Messines,* London, 1935.

Haydon, A. P. 'South Australia's First War' in *Historical Studies of Australia and New Zealand,* vol. 11, no. 42.

Hayes, Sir Bertram. *Hull Down,* London, 1925.

Headlam, Cecil (ed.). *The Milner Papers,* 2 vols, London, 1931-33.

Hobson, J. A. *The War in South Africa,* London, 1900.

Hughes, Colin A. and Graham, B. D. *A Handbook of Australian Government and Politics, 1890-1964,* Canberra, 1968.

Hutchinson, Frank and Myers, Francis. *The Australian Contingent,* Sydney, 1885.

Jackson, Murray Cosby. *A Soldier's Diary, South Africa 1899-1901,* London, 1913.

James, David. *Lord Roberts,* London, 1954.

Kipling, Rudyard. *The Five Nations,* London, 1903.

Kruger, Rayne. *Good-bye Dolly Gray,* London, 1959.

Lewis, Major R. C. *On the Veldt,* Hobart, 1902.

McLean, Major A. A. *Letters, South Africa 1899-1902,* Sydney, 1931.

Magnus, Philip. *Kitchener, Portrait of an Imperialist,* London, 1958.

Maurice, Sir Frederick (ed.). *History of the War in South Africa, 1899-1902,* 4 vols with companion vols of maps, London, 1906-10. (Referred to throughout this book as the *Official History.*)

Meintjes, Johannes. *De La Rey, Lion of the West,* Johannesburg, 1966.

Murray, P. L. (ed.). *Official Records of the Australian Military Contingents to the War in South Africa,* Melbourne, 1911.

'Oriel' (John Sandes). *Ballads of Battle,* Melbourne, n.d.

Paterson, A. B. *Happy Dispatches,* Sydney, 1935.

Rio Grande and Other Verses, Sydney, 1933.

Pearse, Henry, H. S. *The History of Lumsden's Horse,* London, 1903.

Penny, Barbara. 'Australia's Reactions to the Boer War—a Study in Colonial Imperialism' in *Journal of British Studies,* vol. VII, no. 1.

'The Australian Debate on the Boer War', in *Historical Studies,* vol. 14, no. 56.

Pilcher, Colonel T. D. *Some Lessons from the Boer War,* London, 1903.

Reay, W. T. *Australians in War: With the Australian Regiment from Melbourne to Bloemfontein,* Melbourne, 1900.

'Renar, Frank' (Frank Fox). *Bushman and Buccaneer,* Sydney, 1902.

Satchwell, A. E. *On Active Service,* Camperdown, n.d.

Schikkerling, R. H. *Commando Courageous,* Johannesburg, 1964.

Scot Skirving, R. 'Our Army in South Africa', National Library Pamphlets, vol. 185, no. 3589.

Semmler, Clement. *The Banjo of the Bush,* Melbourne, 1966.

Simpson, Lieut-Colonel R. J. S. *The Medical History of the War in South Africa,* London, 1911.

Spurgin, Karl B. *On Active Service with the Northumberland and Durham Yeomanry,* London, n.d.

Stacey, Colonel C. P. 'Canada and the South African War', in *Canadian Army Journal,* vol. 4, nos 2-4.

Stirling, John. *The Colonials in South Africa 1899-1902,* Edinburgh, 1907.

Tremearne, A. J. N. *Some Austral-African Notes and Anecdotes,* London, 1913.

Twistleton, Corporal F *With the New Zealanders at the Front,* Skipton, n.d.

Vernon, P. V. (ed.). *The Royal New South Wales Lancers, 1885-1960,* Sydney, 1961.

Watkins Yardley, J. *With the Inniskilling Dragoons,* London, 1904.

Wigmore, Lionel in collaboration with Harding, Bruce. *They Dared Mightily,* Australian War Memorial Publication, 1963.

Wilkinson, Frank. *Australian Cavalry: The New South Wales Lancers and the First Australian Horse,* Sydney, 1901.
Australia at the Front: A Colonial View of the Boer War, London, 1901.

Wilson, H. W. *With the Flag to Pretoria,* 2 vols, London, 1900.

Witton, George R. *Scapegoats of the Empire,* Melbourne, 1907.

Index

Index

Imperial Federation, 2-3
Imperial South African Association, 7
Imperial Yeomanry, 128, 182, 183, 224n., 230n.
indulgence passengers, 167-8, 169, 229n.
invalids, 125, 128, 177, 186
Isaacs, Isaac, 173

Jones, Private Victor, 86

Kilpatrick, Corporal — , 92
Kimberley, relief of, 99-100
Kingston, Charles, 16-17, 26, 49
Kipling, Rudyard, 87, 186
Kitchener, General Lord: directs war against civilian population, 2, 121, 144; takes command of South African Field Force, 120; requests Australian reinforcements, 140, 142, 144; raises siege of Elands River, 154; reacts to Wilmansrust defeat, 161; involved in court martial and execution of Handcock and Morant, 170-4 *passim*
Knight, Lieut-Colonel G. C., 66
Kruger, President Paul, 1, 10, 18, 105, 113, 120

Labor parties: in debates on first contingent, 25-32; in debates on second contingent, 59-60; influence on Barton's attitude to further involvement in the Transvaal, 146, 147; in debate on federal contingent, 147; attitude to petition of Anti-War League, 150; dissension within N.S.W. party, 212n.
Lambie, W. J., 94-5
Lansdowne, Lord, 22
Lawson, Henry, 33-4, 68, 217n.
Lee-Enfield rifle, 43, 214n.
Lee-Metford rifle, 43, 214n.
Legge, Captain J. G., 89
Lenehan, Major R. W., 170, 171
lice, 116, 222n.
looting, 117, 222n.
Lyne, William: becomes premier, 18, 210n.; reluctance to commit troops without parliamentary sanction, 18, 20, 23-4, 35-6; in debate on first contingent, 30-1; determines composition of first contingent, 35-6; in public parades for troops, 48,

71, 72, 125, 127, 135; plans a second contingent, 57-63, 64-5; criticized, 60, 67; knighted, 63; approves more troops, 130, 131, 141, 224n.; on demobilization in South Africa, 169; as acting federal minister for defence, 177

McCulloch, W., 19, 20, 21, 75, 82, 126-7, 140, 142, 144, 145
McEachern, M., 143, 167
McGowen, James, 32
Mackay, Lieut-Colonel K., 6, 37
McKnight, Major W., 160, 164
McLean, A., 59, 61, 135-6
McLeod, D., 133-4
Madden, Sir John, 126
Mafeking, siege of, 82; Australians at relief of, 152
Mafeking Day, 124, 126, 223n.
Majuba, 19, 103
Martini-Enfield rifle, 43
Martini-Henry rifle, 43
Mauser rifle, 42, 79
Meintjes, Johannes, 180-1
Methuen, General Lord, 82
militia: desire for war, 3, 5, 10, 12, 14; training with British regiments, 4; pre-war strength, 5-6
Milner, Lord, 88, 104, 123, 143
Moor, Captain — , 95
Moran, Cardinal, 45, 46, 68
Morant, Lieutenant H., 170-4, 229n.
Morayshire, 175
Murdoch, Walter, 187
Murray, Captain Hubert, 122
Murray, John, 28, 59-60, 73-4, 216n., 226n.

nationalism, 2, 3, 4, 34, 43, 50-1, 68, 89, 96-7, 104, 125, 128, 135, 213n., 217n.
New South Wales Army Medical Corps, 35, 37, 65, 83, 86, 100, 102-3, 108-9, 121
New South Wales Lancers, 4, 11, 23, 24, 35, 65, 83-4, 91-2, 99-100, 110-11, 112-13, 114, 118, 208n., 217n.; Aldershot detachment incident, 53-7
New South Wales Mounted Rifles, 36, 65, 83, 87, 100-2, 106, 110, 112, 113, 115, 117, 118-19, 121, 159-60, 175
New Zealand troops: offered, 23, 25,

234